EDUCATION RIGHTS OF CHILDREN WITH DISABILITIES: A REVISED & UPDATED PRIMER FOR ADVOCATES

Also available from the Center for Law and Education:

ENSURING ACCESS, EQUITY AND QUALITY FOR STUDENTS WITH DISABILITIES IN SCHOOL-TO-WORK SYSTEMS: A GUIDE TO FEDERAL LAW AND POLICIES

LINKING OUTSIDE THE BOX: USING TITLE I RESOURCES FOR HIGH SCHOOL REFORM

PARENT GUIDE TO HIGH SCHOOL ACADEMIES

URGENT MESSAGE: FAMILIES CRUCIAL TO SCHOOL REFORM

A full catalogue of these and other Center for Law and Education publications, including ordering information, is available on-line at the Center's web site, <www.cleweb.org>.

EDUCATION RIGHTS OF CHILDREN WITH DISABILITIES: A REVISED & UPDATED PRIMER FOR ADVOCATES

BY EILEEN L. ORDOVER
ATTORNEY AT LAW

Center for Law and Education
Boston, Massachusetts and Washington, D.C.

The Advocado Press

Education Rights of Children with Disabilities: A Revised & Updated Primer for Advocates is intended to assist advocates in understanding the complex area of the education rights of children and youth with disabilities in preschool, elementary and secondary education. It focuses on the broad legal provisions relevant to this topic; it is not intended to provide legal assistance for individual cases, and cannot substitute for the independent judgment of a competent attorney. Readers interested in getting help with a particular problem should contact an attorney.

Visit the Center for Law and Eduction online at <http://www.cleweb.org> for more information about the rights of all students to quality education, legal updates and supplements to this book.

Center for Law and Education
1875 Connecticut Ave. N.W., Suite 510
Washington, DC 20009
202-986-3000 (phone)
202-986-6648 (fax)
www.cleweb.org

Published by The Advocado Press, P.O. Box 145, Louisville, KY 40201

Library of Congress Cataloging-in-Publication Data

Ordover, Eileen L.,
    Education rights of children with disabilities : a revised & updated primer for advocates / by Eileen L. Ordover.
       p. cm.
    Includes index.
    ISBN 0-912585-22-6
    1. Handicapped children—Education—Law and legislation—United States.   I. Title.
    KF4210 .O73 2001
    344.73'0791--dc21
                          2001005337

CONTENTS

ABOUT THIS BOOK

Education Rights of Children with Disabilities: A Revised & Updated Primer for Advocates analyzes rights to high quality public preschool, elementary and secondary education. It focusses primarily on two federal statutes: the Individuals with Disabilities Education Act, originally enacted in 1975 as Public Law 94-142 and known as both the Education for All Handicapped Children Act and the Education of the Handicapped Act before being renamed in 1990, and Section 504 of the Rehabilitation Act of 1973.

These laws were enacted in the 1970s to combat pervasive discrimination against people with disabilities, and created an affirmative set of obligations for states, schools and school districts. Unfortunately, they have yet to end discrimination in public education. For example, students with disabilities continue to drop out of school in greater numbers than their peers without disabilities, and to graduate from high school with a diploma in lower numbers. In amending the Individuals with Disabilities Education Act ("IDEA") in 1997, Congress explicitly found that "the implementation of this Act has been impeded by low expectations, and an insufficient focus on applying...proven methods of teaching and learning for children with disabilities." Congress also found that "education for children with disabilities can be made more effective by having high expectations...and ensuring their access in the general curriculum to the maximum extent possible."*

This book is about having and enforcing high expectations. It is intended to assist advocates in using the law to ensure that all children and youth with disabilities receive a high quality public education: one that affords meaningful, effective opportunities to learn the body of knowledge and range of skills that all children are expected to master, while addressing each student's unique disability-related needs.

IDEA, §504 and their respective implementing regulations afford comprehensive and detailed education rights to children with disabilities. They are not, however, the only sources of students' rights and protections. The education rights of children with disabilities are also shaped by

* See 20 U.S.C. §1400(c)(4), (5)(A).

their constitutional rights to equal protection of the laws and due process, as well as civil rights statutes prohibiting discrimination on the basis of race and sex, and federal laws addressing equal educational opportunity for students with limited English proficiency, the rights of homeless students, and quality in vocational education programs and compensatory education programs for educationally disadvantaged students. These laws are briefly introduced in Chapter 1.

This book must also be read together with your state's constitution, statutes, regulations and judicial decisions regarding the educational rights of children who have disabilities. IDEA and §504 establish both entitlements and prohibitions against certain kinds of state and local practices. State law, however, may provide students with disabilities additional rights and protections. At a minimum, state law provides the details for IDEA and §504 implementation and compliance. If state law undermines, contradicts or violates IDEA or §504 mandates, it is, of course, invalid.

Legal research for this book was completed in early 2001, and it went to press in July, 2001. The administrative materials and judicial decisions cited for various points are intended, by and large, to be illustrative rather than comprehensive. Advocates should be aware of the need to research further the law in their respective jurisdictions, in addition to updating our research, as needed. Readers may also wish to visit the Center for Law and Education's site online at <http://www.cleweb.org> for information about legal updates and supplements to this book, as well as analyses of legal issues not addressed here.

Attorneys and legal workers will be familiar with the legal notations, symbols and citations used, particularly in the endnotes. Others may find their meaning less than obvious. Appendix A explains the general format for citing cases, statutes and regulations and includes an explanation of the various symbols, notations and abbreviations used in this book. Appendix B is a Table of Cases listing the judicial decisions and U.S. Department of Education documents cited in this book.

CHAPTER 1

THE BASIC LEGAL FRAMEWORK: IDEA, SECTION 504, THE ADA AND RELATED LAWS

A. THE INDIVIDUALS WITH DISABILITIES EDUCATION ACT, OR IDEA

Congress enacted Public Law 94-142, the Education for All Handicapped Children Act, in 1975 in response to the widespread failure of public school systems to provide appropriate — or in many cases, any — education to children with disabilities. The Act, which was renamed the Individuals With Disabilities Education Act ("IDEA") in 1990, provides states with funds to assist in providing specialized educational services for students with disabilities. In return, a state accepting these funds — as well as local school systems and other public agencies in the state involved in educating children — must comply with the Act's substantive and procedural requirements. These include providing all eligible children with a free appropriate public education ("FAPE") — comprising, among other things, specialized instruction and related services — in the least restrictive environment. IDEA was last substantially amended in 1997.[1]

The Office of Special Education Programs or "OSEP," a part of the Office of Special Education and Rehabilitative Services ("OSERS") within the U.S. Department of Education, administers IDEA. OSEP is also responsible for ensuring compliance with the Act including, when necessary, taking enforcement action against states that are out of compliance. In addition, state departments of education are responsible for ensuring that local school districts (as well as other public, and in certain instances, private, agencies in the state that provide educational services) comply with IDEA. IDEA is also enforced through administrative complaints, due process hearings and lawsuits initiated by parents and students whose IDEA rights have been violated.

1. Eligibility

Only a student who is a "child with a disability" within the meaning of IDEA is entitled to its protections. For purposes of IDEA,

> "[t]he term 'child with a disability' means a child with mental retardation, hearing impairments (including deafness), speech or language impairments, visual impairments (including blindness), serious emotional disturbance..., orthopedic impairments, autism, traumatic brain injury, other health impairments, or specific learning disabilities...*who by reason thereof needs special education and related services.*"[2]

The regulations implementing IDEA define each of these conditions in detail.[3] For example, the regulations explicitly include attention deficit disorder and attention deficit hyperactivity disorder as examples of conditions that may trigger IDEA eligibility under the category of "other health impairment."[4]

At the discretion of a state and the local school system involved, the term "child with a disability" may also include 3 through 9 year olds who are "(i) experiencing developmental delays, as defined by the State and as measured by appropriate diagnostic instruments and procedures, in...physical development, cognitive development, communication development, social or emotional development, or adaptive development; and (ii) who, by reason thereof need special education and related services."[5] Note that a local school system may not adopt developmental delay as a basis for IDEA eligibility unless the state, too, has done so.[6]

Any child who falls within the IDEA definition of a "child with a disability" is protected by IDEA and eligible for the education it guarantees, *even if he or she is advancing from grade to grade.*[7] Similarly, all "children with disabilities" are entitled to education and services regardless of the severity of their disabilities.[8] IDEA does not allow for the possibility that some children are too severely disabled to be served; states and school systems may not refuse to provide educational services on the ground that a child is too severely disabled to benefit from them.[9] Finally, an otherwise-eligible child may not be denied services under IDEA on account of his or her immigration status.[10]

2. Age Ranges

IDEA compels states to serve all children with disabilities aged 3 through 21 years unless, with respect to 3 through 5 year olds and 18 through 21 year olds, this requirement would be inconsistent with a state law or practice or a court order.[11] Once a state, school district or other public agency undertakes to serve 3 through 5 or 18 through 21 year olds, however, all of IDEA's substantive and procedural requirements apply.[12]

A 1997 amendment to IDEA allows states to pass laws denying IDEA services to some 18 through 21 year-olds who are incarcerated in adult correctional facilities. Such state laws may exclude these youth from services if, in their last educational placement before being incarcerated, they were not identified as a "child with a disability" under IDEA, and did not have an IDEA "individualized education program."[13] These youth may be denied IDEA services *only* if the state actually has passed a law excluding them.[14]

3. End of Eligibility

A student's eligibility for services under IDEA may end in one of three ways. First, eligibility may end if a proper evaluation determines that he or she no longer meets the definition of a "child with a disability" — either because the student no longer has one of the listed disabilities, or because even though he or she still has one of them, the student no longer needs special education and related services as a result. Secondly, eligibility ends when a youth reaches the maximum age of entitlement under federal and state law (see above).

Finally, eligibility also ends — even before a youth reaches the maximum age for education and services under IDEA — once a student has *graduated* with a *regular* high school diploma.[15] Thus "graduation" *without* a regular diploma, for example, with a certificate of completion or attendance, or with a "special education" diploma, does *not* end a student's right to services. Nor does receipt of a General Equivalency Diploma ("G.E.D") end a student's eligibility, as a G.E.D. does not signify that a student has completed the curriculum and otherwise attained the standards required for a regular high school diploma in the student's state or local school system. Further, receipt of a G.E.D. does not signify, or entail, graduation from high school.

A student whose eligibility has ended may nonetheless be entitled to additional educational services to compensate for past violations of his or her IDEA rights.[*]

---

[*] For a discussion of compensatory education as a remedy for IDEA violations, see Chapter 8.

B. SECTION 504 OF THE REHABILITATION ACT OF 1973

Section 504 of the Rehabilitation Act of 1973 ("§504") is a civil rights statute designed to prohibit discrimination on the basis of disability. Modeled after Title VI of the Civil Rights Act of 1964 and Title IX of the Education Amendments of 1972 — which address racial or national origin and sex discrimination, respectively — it applies to recipients of federal funds. Section 504 as amended[16] provides in relevant part that:

> "No otherwise qualified individual with a disability in the United States...shall, solely by reason of her or his disability, be excluded from the participation in, be denied the benefits of, or be subjected to discrimination under any program or activity receiving federal financial assistance..."[17]

Because virtually all local schools and school districts receive federal funds of some sort, §504 provides an additional tool for ensuring that school-age children with disabilities receive the education to which they are entitled. Section 504 is enforced through administrative complaints and compliance reviews by the U.S. Department of Education's Office for Civil Rights or "OCR," and also through litigation by individuals who allege deprivation of their §504 rights.

1. Individuals Protected

For purposes of §504, an "individual with a disability" is one who "...(i) has a physical or mental impairment which substantially limits one or more of such person's major life activities, (ii) has a record of such an impairment, or (iii) is regarded as having such an impairment."[18]

"Major life activities" means activities such as caring for one's self, performing manual tasks, walking, seeing, hearing, speaking, breathing, learning and working.[19] These examples of "major life activities" are listed in the §504 regulations. Courts have found other activities to be "major life activities" for §504 purposes as well. Examples include handling stressful situations, interacting with others, engaging in typical social relationships, reproduction, sleeping and engaging in leisure pastimes.[20]

Virtually all children eligible for special education and related services under IDEA fall within the above-described definition of an "individual with a disability," and so are protected by §504 as well. Because the §504 definition of an "individual with a disability," however, is broader than the IDEA definition of a "child with a disability," §504 protects many children who are *not* IDEA-eligible. For example, a child who has an "other health impairment," such as epilepsy or AIDS, but who does not need specialized instruction, is not a "child with a disability" within the IDEA definition. Such a child is, nonetheless, protected against discrimination by §504 and its implementing regulations if the condition "substantially limits" a "major life activity." Similarly, a child who does not have any of the kinds of disabilities required for IDEA eligibility might nonetheless have an impairment that substantially limits a major life activity, or have a history of such an impairment, or be regarded as having such an impairment — and so be covered by §504.[21]

In order to be protected from discrimination by §504, an "individual with a disability" must be "otherwise qualified." For purposes of public preschool, elementary or secondary school services and activities, a child or student is "otherwise qualified" if he or she is:

- of an age during which individuals who do not have a disability are provided with such services, or
- of any age during which it is mandatory under state law to provide such services to individuals with disabilities, or
- is someone IDEA requires the state to provide with a free appropriate public education.[22]

2. Operation and Reach of §504

Regulations promulgated by the U.S. Department of Education interpret and implement §504's broad ban on discrimination as it applies to recipients of Department of Education funds.[23] In regard to preschool, elementary and secondary education, these regulations operate in two basic ways: first, by generally prohibiting certain practices as illegal discrimination and, second, by compelling school systems to take certain affirmative steps to ensure that all students with disabilities receive a free appropriate public education.

Free Appropriate Public Education Like IDEA, the regulations implementing §504 require public school systems to provide a free appropriate public education in the least restrictive environment regardless of the nature or severity of a student's disability.[24] A free appropriate public education under §504 may include either "regular" or "special" education, along with any needed related aids and services.[25] Many specific §504 requirements concerning issues such as the evaluation and placement of pupils with disabilities, the components of a free appropriate public education, the circumstances under which a student with disabilities may be removed from the regular education setting, and procedural safeguards mirror or complement IDEA mandates.*

Prohibited Discriminatory Practices In addition to establishing specific requirements for preschool, elementary and secondary school programs, the U.S. Department of Education's §504 regulations bar all recipients of federal Department of Education funds from engaging in certain discriminatory practices. The §504 regulations of all other federal agencies contain comparable provisions. Key illegal practices include:

- denying a qualified individual with a disability the opportunity to participate in or benefit from an aid, benefit or service;[26]

- affording a qualified individual with a disability an opportunity to participate in or benefit from an aid, benefit or service that is not equal to that afforded others;[27]

- providing a qualified individual with a disability with an aid, benefit or service that is not as effective as that provided to others;[28]

- providing different or separate aid, benefits or services to individuals with disabilities or to any class of individuals with disabilities — unless necessary to provide them with aid, benefits, or services that are as effective as those provided to others;[29]

- denying a qualified individual with a disability the benefits of any program or activity, excluding him or her from participation, or otherwise subjecting him or her to discrimination because a recipient's facilities are inaccessible to or unusable by people with disabilities;[30]

- otherwise limiting a qualified individual with a disability in the enjoyment of any right, privilege, advantage, or opportunity enjoyed by others receiving an aid, benefit or service;[31]

- using policies or practices that have the effect of subjecting children with disabilities to discrimination, or of defeating or substantially impairing the objectives of the education program for students with disabilities.[32]

These broad prohibitions have been used successfully to challenge a wide variety of school practices not specifically addressed by other §504

---

* Section 504 also protects students who attend private day care, preschool, elementary and secondary schools that receive federal funds, or that are used as placements by public school systems, from disability-based discrimination. The §504 rights of these students vary depending upon the kinds of programs and services offered and the circumstances under which a particular student has come to attend.

regulations or by IDEA. Examples include, among others, shortened school days due to transportation schedules; failure to offer particular courses required for receipt of a high school diploma; withholding complete information about field trips from parents of children with disabilities; refusing to enroll students with disabilities in a particular vocational education program; failure to utilize adaptive equipment in order to make driver's education course accessible to mobility impaired students; and offering only limited electives in a segregated school for emotionally disturbed students in comparison to the range of electives available to other students.[33] Although the following chapters focus chiefly on specific, affirmative requirements under §504 and IDEA, parents, students and their advocates should keep these general prohibitions in mind as well in asserting and defending education rights.

C. THE AMERICANS WITH DISABILITIES ACT, OR ADA

The Americans with Disabilities Act ("ADA") was passed by Congress in 1990. The ADA is divided into five parts or "Titles." Most relevant to quality public education for students with disabilities is Title II, which prohibits discrimination by public entities — such as public schools, school systems, state departments of education, etc. — *regardless* of whether they receive federal funds.[34] In the context of public education, the ADA is enforced by the U.S. Department of Education's Office for Civil Rights, as well as through lawsuits filed by students whose rights have been violated.

1. Individuals Protected

Like §504, Title II of the ADA protects only "qualified" individuals from discrimination, stating that

> "no qualified individual with a disability shall, by reason of
> such disability, be excluded from participation in or be denied
> the benefits of the services, programs, or activities of a public
> entity, or be subjected to discrimination by any such entity."[35]

The ADA definition of an "individual with a disability" parallels the §504 definition, discussed above.[36]

A "qualified" individual with a disability under Title II of the ADA is someone who,

> "*with or without* reasonable modifications to rules, policies, or
> practices, the removal of architectural, communication, or trans-

portation barriers, or the provision of auxiliary aids and services, meets the *essential* eligibility requirements for the receipt of services or the participation in programs or activities provided by a public entity."[37]

Public entities such as schools must make "reasonable modifications," remove "barriers," and provide "auxiliary aids and services" as needed to enable an individual to meet "essential eligibility requirements," and thus be a "qualified" individual with a disability.

2. Operation and Reach

As is the case with §504, the ADA statute is implemented by regulations that provide further detail about what constitutes unlawful discrimination. The Title II ADA regulations were modeled on the §504 regulations, and prohibit all of the discriminatory practices made illegal under §504.[38] The ADA regulations also make explicit some obligations that are implicit in the older §504 regulations. For example, the ADA regulations state that public entities, including schools, must make reasonable changes in their policies, practices and procedures when necessary to avoid disability discrimination (unless the changes would "fundamentally alter" the nature of the program in question), and may not use eligibility criteria that screen out or tend to screen out an individual with a disability, or individuals with a particular kind of disability, from full and equal participation in programs, unless the criteria are necessary to the program.[39]

D. RELATED LAWS

While IDEA, §504 and, to a lesser extent, the ADA are the focus of this book, they are not the only laws relevant to the right of students with disabilities to a quality public education. Other laws of which parents and advocates should be aware include the following:

State "special education" laws Virtually all states have enacted their own special education statutes and regulations. These state laws supplement IDEA, and often fill in many details not addressed by federal law. State law may not be used to diminish IDEA or other federal rights. State statutes or regulations that give students and parents *greater* protection than does IDEA are permissible; statutes or regulations that undermine IDEA protections are not.

Title VI of the Civil Rights Act of 1964 Title VI prohibits recipients of federal funds from discriminating on the basis of race, ethnicity or national origin.[40] This includes discrimination on the basis of a child's limited English proficiency.[41]

Equal Educational Opportunities Act of 1974 The Equal Educational Opportunities Act[42] deals primarily with illegal racial segregation in school assignment, and legal remedies to address it. Another important provision requires states and local school districts to take "appropriate action to overcome language barriers that impede equal participation by...students in...instructional programs,"[43] augmenting Title VI as a source of rights for children who have limited English proficiency.

Title IX of the Education Amendments of 1972 Title IX prohibits recipients of federal education funds from discriminating on the basis of sex.[44] This includes discrimination against teens who are pregnant or parenting.[45]

Stewart B. McKinney Homeless Assistance Act The McKinney Act includes provisions protecting the education rights of homeless children and youth in states that accept funds under the Act. In addition to addressing issues such as residency requirements and other barriers to school enrollment, attendance and success, it requires that homeless students be given meaningful opportunities to meet the same challenging student performance standards set for all children in the state, and that students with disabilities who are homeless be provided services comparable to those provided other students with disabilities.[46]

Title I of the Elementary and Secondary Education Act Title I[47] is the largest federal spending program for elementary and secondary education, channeling funds to areas with high concentrations of low-income students to promote school reform. The Title I law contains numerous program requirements for participating schools, all of which focus on assisting students to attain the challenging academic standards set by the state for all students. Title I explicitly identifies students with disabilities as intended beneficiaries of its reforms.[48]

Carl D. Perkins Vocational and Technical Education Act The Carl D. Perkins Vocational and Technical Education Act[49] governs about a billion dollars in federal vocational education appropriations annually. The overwhelming majority of school districts receive Perkins Act funds, and are

subject to its requirements. These include mandates, added to the law in
1990 and strengthened in 1998, for programs of high quality that prepare
students to meet the challenging state academic standards set for all students and to enter high-wage careers and postsecondary education; teach
them all aspects of the industry they are studying (rather than narrow
skills) and integrate academic and vocational learning. Perkins also
includes strong equity mandates, requiring states and schools to plan for
successful participation by students with disabilities (and other members
of what Perkins calls "special populations," including students who have
limited English proficiency, or whose families are economically disadvantaged) in these high quality programs.[50]

State education reform laws Many states have enacted comprehensive
school reform laws that address such issues as standards for what all students should know and be able to do, testing and assessment of students
and promotion and graduation requirements. These laws have a profound
impact on the education and education rights of children with disabilities,
regardless of whether the laws explicitly address their participation.

Family Educational Rights and Privacy Act The Family Educational
Rights and Privacy Act ("FERPA")[51] addresses student records, and
applies to all educational institutions that receive funds from the U.S.
Department of Education — and so to virtually all public schools (and
many private ones as well). FERPA protects the right of parents to inspect
and review their child's education records, and the right of students aged
18 and over to inspect and review their own records. FERPA also protects
the confidentiality of education records, and provides parents and students with opportunities for correcting inaccurate records.

NOTES

1. *See* Public Law 105-17, 111 Stat. 37 (June 4, 1997), codified at 20 U.S.C. §1400 *et seq.*.

2. 20 U.S.C. §1401(3)(A) (emphasis added).

3. *See* 34 C.F.R. §§300.7(c), 300.541.

4. *See* 34 C.F.R. §300.7(c)(9).

5. 20 U.S.C. §1401(3)(B); 34 C.F.R. §300.7(b).

6. *See* 34 C.F.R. §300.313(4).

7. 34 C.F.R. §300.121(e)(1).

8. 20 U.S.C. §1412(a)(3)(A).

9. *Id. See also, e.g., Timothy W. v. Rochester School District*, 875 F.2d 954 (1st Cir.), *cert. denied*, 493 U.S. 983, 110 S. Ct. 519 (1989).

10. *See Inquiry of Breecher*, 18 IDELR 261 (OSEP 6/29/91); *Inquiry of Gould* , 26 IDELR 24 (OSEP 2/5/97). *See also Plyler v. Doe*, 457 U.S. 202, 102 S.Ct. 2382 (1982) (exclusion from public education in general).

11. 20 U.S.C. §1412(a)(1)(B). The U.S. Department of Education regulations implementing IDEA further explain this requirement. *See* 34 C.F.R. §300.300.

12. 34 C.F.R. §300.300(b)(4).

13. 20 U.S.C. §1412(a)(1)(B)(ii); 34 C.F.R. 300.122(a)(2).

14. 34 C.F.R. §300.122(b)(2).

15. 34 C.F.R. §300.122(a)(3).

16. 29 U.S.C. §794.

17. 29 U.S.C. §794(a).

18. 29 U.S.C. §705(20)(B). The term "physical or mental impairment" means any physiological disorder or condition, cosmetic disfigurement, or anatomical loss affecting one or more of the following body systems: neurological, musculoskeletal, sense organs, respiratory (including speech organs), cardiovascular, reproductive, digestive, genito-urinary, hemic and lymphatic, skin or endocrine systems, as well as any mental or psychological disorder, such as mental retardation, organic brain syndrome, emotional or mental illness, and specific learning disabilities. 34 C.F.R. §104.3(j)(2)(i).

19. 34 C.F.R. §104.3(j)(2)(ii).

20. *Bragdon v. Abbott*, 524 U.S. 624, 118 S.Ct. 2196 (1998) (reproduction); *McAlindin v. County of San Diego*, 192 F.3d. 1226 (9th Cir. 1999), as amended by 201 F.3d 1211, *cert. denied*, 120 S.Ct. 2689 (2000) (sleeping, interacting with others, engaging in sexual relations); *Doe v. New York University*, 666 F.2d 761, 775 (2nd Cir. 1981) (psychiatric impairment limited medical student's major life activity of handling stressful situations such as those encountered in medical training; court noted her prior academic achievements, and lack of learning difficulties); *Doe v. District of Columbia*, 796 F. Supp. 559 (D.D.C. 1992) (plaintiff who has HIV-positive was limited in the major life activities of "procreation, sexual contact and normal [sic] social relationships"); *Perez v. Philadelphia Housing Authority*, 677 F. Supp. 357 (E.D. Penn. 1987), *aff'd. without opinion*, 841 F.2d 1120 (3rd Cir. 1988) (back pain affected major life activities of walking, sitting, standing, driving, caring for home and child, and engaging in leisure pastimes). Note that *Brangdon* and *McAlindin* interpreted the term "major life activity" as used in the Americans with Disabilities Act ("ADA"). However, as the ADA definition of "individual with a disability" was drawn almost verbatim from the Rehabilitation Act definition, "major life activity" should have the same meaning under both laws. *See Brangdon*, 524 U.S. at 631-32, 118 S.Ct. At 2202.

21. For example, a student who has been erroneously classified as having mental retardation or who has a record of "incorrigible" behavior might be "regarded as having...an impairment" or have "a record of...an impairment" for purposes of §504. In addition, a child who does not have any of the disabilities listed in IDEA might nonetheless have an actual, current "impairment" for §504 purposes. A child who is

HIV positive but asymptomatic — and so not "other health impaired" as defined by IDEA — would fall within this category. *See Bragdon v. Abbott, supra.*

22. 34 C.F.R. §104.3(k)(2).

23. The Department's §504 regulations are codified at 34 C.F.R. part 104.

24. 34 C.F.R. §§104.33(a), 104.34(a).

25. 34 C.F.R. §104.33(b).

26. 34 C.F.R. §104.4(b)(1)(i).

27. 34 C.F.R. §104.4(b)(1)(ii).

28. 34 C.F.R. §104.4(b)(1)(iii).

29. 34 C.F.R. §104.4(b)(1)(iv).

30. 34 C.F.R. §104.21. This provision should be read along with 34 C.F.R. §§104.22, 104.23, which delineate the circumstances under which recipients need or need not remove architectural barriers in order to meet this requirement.

31. 34 C.F.R. §104.4(b)(1)(vii).

32. 34 C.F.R. §104.4(b)(4).

33. *See*, respectively, *Orange County (FL) School District*, 28 IDELR 492 (OCR 11/18/97) (shortened school day due to transportation schedule); *Muscogee (GA) County School District*, EHLR 257:540 (OCR 6/30/84)(failure to offer biology to in separate program for students labeled "mildly mentally handicapped" or learning disabled, where biology was a diploma requirement); *Mt. Gilead (OH) Exempted Village School District*, 20 IDELR 765 (OCR 8/13/93) (withholding complete information about field trips from parents of children with disabilities); *Nashville-Davidson County (TN) Schools*, 16 EHLR 379 (OCR 12/21/89) (refusing to enroll students with disabilities in particular vocational education program); *Tucson (AZ) Unified School District No. 1*, EHLR 352:47 (OCR 2/16/84) (failure to utilize adaptive equipment in order to make driver's education course accessible to mobility impaired students); *Carbon- Lehigh (PA) Intermediate School District #21*, EHLR 352:108 (OCR 9/20/85) (offering only limited electives in segregated school for emotionally disturbed students in comparison to range of electives available to regular education students). *See also Pocantico Hills (NY) Central School District*, 20 IDELR 265 (OCR 5/3/93) (exclusion of child with learning disabilities and behavioral manifestations from summer camp program); *Garaway (OH) Local School District*, 17 EHLR 237 (OCR 9/13/90) (carrying mobility impaired student on and off school bus rather than providing accessible transportation); *Sumter County (SC) School District #17*, 17 EHLR 193 (OCR 9/28/90) (disabled student disciplined more harshly than others); *Duchesne County (UT) School District*, 17 EHLR 240 (OCR 9/13/90) (providing special education students with shorter school day and longer bus rides than regular education students); *Fayette County (KY) School District*, EHLR 353:279 (OCR 3/1/89) (admission to after school program); *Jefferson County (KY) School District*, EHLR 353:176 (OCR 9/19/88) (admission to summer enrichment program); *New Carlisle-Bethel Local School District*, EHLR 257:477 (OCR 1/30/84) (inaccessible classrooms prevented mobility impaired student from taking certain classes).

34. The other Titles of the ADA address employment (Title I), public accommodations and services operated by private entities (Title III), telecommunications (Title IV) and miscellaneous other issues (Title V).

35. 42 U.S.C. §12132.

36. See 42 U.S.C. §12102(2).

37. 42 U.S.C. §12131(2) (emphasis added).

38. *See* 28 C.F.R. §35.130(b).

39. 28 C.F.R. §35.130(b)(7), (8).

40. 42 U.S.C. §2000d; *see also* 34 C.F.R. part 100 (U.S. Department of Education/Office for Civil Rights regulations).

41. *See Lau v. Nichols*, 414 U.S. 563, 94 S.Ct. 786 (1974).

42. 20 U.S.C. §1701 *et seq.*

43. 20 U.S.C. §1703(f).

44. 20 U.S.C. §1681; *see also* 34 C.F.R. part 106 (U.S. Department of Education/Office for Civil Rights regulations).

45. For the Title IX regulations explicitly addressing discrimination based upon pregnancy, parenting or family status, see 34 C.F.R. §§106.21(c), 106.40.

46. *See generally* 42 U.S.C. §§11431 - 11434.

47. 20 U.S.C. §6301 *et seq.*

48. *See, e.g.,* 20 U.S.C. §§6301(b)(3); 6311(b)(3)(F)(i), (ii); 6312(b)(4)(B); 6314(b)(2)(v); 6315(b)(2)(A)(i). For a discussion of Title I, as amended by the Improving America's Schools Act of 1994, see Margot Rogers, *Planning for Title I Programs* (1995), available from the Center for Law and Education, 1875 Connecticut Ave., N.W., Suite 510, Washington, D.C. 20009 (phone: 202/986-3000; fax: 202/986-6648). As this book went to press in July, 2001, Congress was in the process of reauthorizing and amending Title I. Advocates should check for the current law.

49. 20 U.S.C. §2301 *et seq.*, as amended by Carl D. Perkins Vocational and Applied Technology Education Amendments of 1998, Pub. L. No. 105-332, 112 Stat. 3076 (October 31, 1998).

50. *See* Carl D. Perkins Vocational and Applied Technology Education Amendments of 1998, Pub. L. No. 105-332, 112 Stat. 3076 (October 31, 1998), sec. 1, §§122(c)(7), (8) and 134(b)(7) (8), 112 Stat. at 3104, 3115 (to be codified at 20 U.S.C. §§2342(c)(7), (8) and 2354(b)(7), (8). For a full discussion of this topic, see Eileen L. Ordover and Leslie T. Annexstein, *Ensuring Access, Equity, and Quality for Students in School-to-Work Systems* (1999), available from the Center for Law and Education, 1875 Connecticut Ave., N.W., Suite 510, Washington, D.C. 20009 (phone: 202/986-3000; fax: 202/986-6648).

51. 20 U.S.C. §1232g. See also the FERPA regulations, which may be found at 34 C.F.R. part 99.

CHAPTER 2

THE BASIC ENTITLEMENT: A FREE APPROPRIATE PUBLIC EDUCATION WITH MAXIMUM APPROPRIATE INTEGRATION

IDEA requires school systems to provide eligible children with a "free appropriate public education" consisting of "special education" and "related services" and including an appropriate preschool, elementary or secondary education in the state involved.[1] For purposes of §504, a "free appropriate public education" may consist of either "special" education or "regular education" and "related aids and services."[2] The concept of "education" under these laws is broad, encompassing traditional academics together with social, health, vocational, emotional, communicative, physical, self-help and functional skill needs.[3] Both laws also call for children with disabilities to be educated in regular education settings with non-disabled peers to the maximum extent appropriate in view of their individual needs.[4] This latter requirement is often referred to as "least restrictive environment."

Another component of the "free appropriate public education" mandated by IDEA is the Individualized Education Program ("IEP") that is designed at least annually for each child. Under IDEA, a school system is *not* providing a free appropriate public education if it is not following a properly developed IEP.[5] School systems have an affirmative obligation to keep abreast of promising new methods and strategies for meeting the educational needs of children with disabilities, and to employ them as appropriate in designing and implementing IEPs.[6] An IEP must, among other things, set forth annual goals and benchmarks or short-term objectives for the student, describe the special education and related services the child is to receive, and justify the extent, if any, to which he or she will not fully participate in regular education settings with non-disabled peers and/or in the general curriculum adopted for all students.[7] IDEA and its regulations set forth extensive requirements governing the content of IEPs and the process for developing them.[*] Section 504 does not require the development of an IEP. However, the §504 regulations provide that implementation of an IEP developed pursuant to IDEA is one means of providing an "appropriate" education under §504.[8]

A. THE MEANING OF "APPROPRIATE": EDUCATIONAL QUALITY, STATE STANDARDS, PROCEDURAL COMPLIANCE, AND THE CONCEPT OF "BENEFIT"

1. IDEA

IDEA defines "free appropriate public education" ("FAPE") by describing its components: special education and related services meeting state and IDEA standards provided at public expense, with no cost to parent or child, under public supervision, in conformity with the child's IEP.[9] By definition, a "free appropriate public education" must "...meet the standards of the State educational agency...[and] include an appropriate preschool, elementary or secondary education in the State involved..."[10] These latter two requirements make it clear that the right to FAPE includes the right to full opportunity to participate in, and meaningful opportunities to learn, same curriculum as nondisabled children, known as the "general" curriculum[11] — and to meet the standards of learning set by the state for *all* students.[12] The IDEA Amendments of 1997 underscore this pre-existing right. As discussed in detail in chapter 3, which focuses on the right to learn in the general curriculum, numerous provisions added to the law in 1997 — including those addressing evaluations, IEP content, IEP teams, and participation in assessments — emphasize that children with disabilities are to be given meaningful opportunities to learn in the general curriculum, *regardless* of the setting (placement) in which they are receiving their education.[13]

The U.S. Supreme Court addressed the meaning and parameters of FAPE in the 1982 case of *Board of Education of the Hendrick Hudson Central School District v. Rowley*.[14] In *Rowley*, the court ruled that, *assuming a child is receiving an appropriate preschool, elementary or secondary education in the state involved AND that the education meets the standards of the state education agency,* the special education and related services offered a child with disabilities must meet two additional criteria in order to constitute FAPE, or be "appropriate":

---

[*] These requirements are discussed in Chapter 6. Requirements governing the educational evaluations upon which IEPs must be based are discussed in Chapter 5.

(1) the IEP must be developed in accordance with the procedures set forth in IDEA, including those governing resolution of disputes between parents and school systems

AND

(2) the IEP must be "reasonably calculated to enable the child to receive educational benefits."[15]

The requirement that an IEP enable a student to receive educational benefits in order to be deemed "appropriate" does not mean that *any* degree of benefit is enough to satisfy IDEA standards. The IEP must be one "under which educational 'progress,'" "significant learning," and "meaningful benefit" are likely, in light of a child's individual abilities and potential.[16] And, as the IDEA Amendments of 1997 make clear (and as further discussed in chapter 3), this includes meaningful, significant progress in learning what all other students are expected to know and be able to do, as reflected in the general curriculum.[17] It is also important to remember that the student in *Rowley* was performing above average work in a regular class — and so, in essence, was attaining the standards set for all children, in the general curriculum.[18]

Rowley also held that IDEA does not require states and school systems to provide education designed to maximize a child's potential.[19] Advocates, however, should pay close attention to their *state's* law concerning the quality of education to which children with disabilities are entitled. As interpreted in *Rowley*, IDEA sets a "basic floor" for education quality. It does not prohibit states from setting higher quality and benefit standards,[20] and a state may do so by statute, regulation, judicial decision, or state constitutional provision. Because special education and related services under IDEA must meet the standards of the state educational agency,[21] where a higher state quality standard exists, it is automatically "incorporated" into, and then mandated by, IDEA.[22] In such a state, an education meeting the higher state quality standard is an IDEA right, and IDEA compliance may thus require IEPs designed to maximize potential or otherwise exceed the *Rowley* benefit standard.

2. §504

The §504 regulations provide two measures for determining whether the education provided to a child with a disability is "appropriate" and otherwise of proper quality, as follows.

Appropriateness   First, for purposes of §504, "appropriate education" means regular *or* special education *and* related aids and services "designed to meet the individual educational needs of" students with disabilities "as adequately as the needs of" nondisabled students are met.[23] Implementation of an IEP developed in the manner set forth in IDEA is one way of meeting this requirement.[24] In order to be "appropriate" within the meaning of §504 education must also be based upon adherence to §504 requirements governing placement in the least restrictive environment, evaluations and procedural safeguards for students and parents (including notice and hearing rights and access to student records).[25] Least restrictive environment is discussed elsewhere in this chapter. Evaluations and procedural safeguards are discussed in chapters 5 and 8, respectively.

Comparable Benefits and Services   Section 504 also requires school systems to provide students with disabilities with benefits and services comparable to those provided to non-disabled students. This requirement flows from regulations prohibiting the following, among others, as "discriminatory practices":

- affording a disabled student an opportunity to participate in or benefit from an aid, a benefit or a service that is not equal to that afforded others; and

- providing a disabled student with an aid, benefit or service that is not as effective as that provided to others.[26]

In order to be equally effective (as required by these regulations), aids, benefits or services must afford students with disabilities an equal opportunity to obtain the same result, gain the same benefit, or reach the same level of achievement as nondisabled students.[27]

The regulations implementing Title II of the ADA include virtually identical provisions.[28] Advocates may use these §504 and ADA regulations to challenge a wide variety of discriminatory practices. These regulations form a basis, for example, of the right to equal opportunity to participate and meaningful opportunities to learn in the general curriculum.[29] They also make it illegal, for example, to provide children with disabilities with a shorter school day than that provided non-disabled students, except when a shorter day is "demonstrably required by the individual educational needs" of a particular child.[30]

In addition, the regulations expressly provide that any facility that is identifiable as being for students with disabilities must be comparable, in terms of both the facility itself and the services and activities conducted in it, to other facilities.[31]

B. THE MEANING OF "SPECIAL EDUCATION": SPECIAL EDUCATION IS NOT A PLACE

As used in IDEA, "special education" does not refer to any particular classroom, school or other setting in which children with disabilities are educated. "Special education" merely means *"specially designed instruction...*to meet the unique needs of a child with a disability."[32] "Specially designed instruction," in turn, means "adapting...the content, methodology, or delivery of instruction...[t]o address the unique needs of the child that result from...disability...and...[t]o ensure access...to the general curriculum, so that he or she can meet the educational standards...that apply to all children."[33]

Under these definitions, "special education" is a kind of instruction, not a place. Once instruction for an individual child has been tailored to address his or her needs it may, depending upon those needs, be provided in a variety of settings including a regular education classroom. Thus a school district cannot fulfill its obligation to provide special education by, for example, automatically placing a child with a particular disability in a particular classroom or program designated to serve that group.[34] In addition to illegally circumventing IDEA requirements, such conduct constitutes illegal discrimination under §504.[35] Any automatic placement also violates the least restrictive environment/maximum appropriate integration mandates of both laws, discussed below.

C. THE MEANING AND SCOPE OF "RELATED SERVICES"

The related services mandated by IDEA consist of "[t]ransportation and such developmental, corrective and other supportive services...as may be required to assist a child with a disability to benefit from special education."[36] The §504 regulations do not define the "related aids and services" required for §504 compliance. However, as is the case with the "special education" component of a free appropriate public education, related services developed and delivered in accordance with IDEA requirements will ordinarily satisfy the §504 requirement as well.[37]

Under both IDEA and §504, the particular related services a child is to receive must be based upon an individualized determination of his or her unique needs — not upon the category of his or her disability.[38] Thus, for example, a blanket rule or policy that allowed only children with severe emotional disturbance to receive counseling as a related service would violate both laws. In addition, as discussed in Chapter 6, schools must provide *all* necessary related services, not simply those readily available within the school system.

1. Transportation

Where needed to accommodate the needs of a child receiving special education under IDEA, transportation includes:

- travel to and from school and between schools where a student's educational program is provided at more than one site;
- travel in and around school buildings; and
- specialized equipment such as special or adapted buses, lifts and ramps.[39]

2. Developmental, Corrective and Supportive Services

IDEA and its regulations list the following as *examples* of developmental, corrective and supportive services falling within the category of "related services":

- speech-language pathology and audiology services;
- psychological services;
- physical therapy;
- occupational therapy;
- medical services for diagnostic or evaluation purposes only, provided by a licensed physician to determine a child's medically related disability resulting in the child's need for special education and related services;
- orientation and mobility services for children with visual impairments;
- recreation, including assessment of leisure function, therapeutic recreation services, leisure education and recreation programs in schools and community agencies;
- counseling services provided by qualified social workers, psychologists, guidance counselors or other qualified personnel;
- parent training and counseling aimed at assisting parents in understanding the needs of their child, providing parents with information about child development, and helping them acquire skills to

allow them to support implementation of their child's IEP;

- rehabilitation counseling services;
- early identification and assessment of disabilities in children;
- school health services provided by a qualified school nurse or other qualified personnel; and
- social work services in school, including group and individual counseling with the child and family, working with problems in a child's home, school or community that affect his or her adjustment in school, and mobilizing school and community resources to enable the child to receive maximum benefit from his or her educational program.[40]

These services are not the only ones that qualify as "related services" under IDEA: if a child needs a particular service in order to benefit from special education and the service is a developmental, supportive or corrective one, it is also a "related" one and must be provided regardless of whether it is expressly listed in IDEA or its regulations.[41] For some children, for example, a part or full time aide might constitute a required related service, as might certain equipment or assistive technology, such as a computer or tape recorder.[42]

3. The "Medical Exclusion" and Assistance with Health-Related Needs In School

As noted above, the IDEA definition of "related services" includes "medical services...for diagnostic and evaluation purposes only."[43] "Medical services," in turn, are defined in the IDEA regulations as "services provided by a licensed physician to determine a child's medically related disability that results in the child's need for special education and related services."[44] All other physician services are excluded from the range of related services that school systems must provide. This is known as the "medical exclusion." On the other hand, if a service can be provided by a non-physician, under these rules, it does *not* fall under the medical exclusion, and must be provided if it otherwise meets the definition of a related service.

Nonetheless, schools reluctant to assist students with health-related needs during the school day have in the past attempted to label such assistance "medical services" and beyond their responsibilities under IDEA, even though the assistance did not require a physician. This has been the case particularly where schools perceive a child's needs as too complex, too intensive or too costly to meet. Two U.S. Supreme Court decisions decided fifteen years apart make it clear that schools *must* provide necessary in-school assistance with health-related needs, so long as they can be provided by a non-physician.

The first decision, in the 1984 case of *Irving Independent School District v. Tatro*,[45] required a school system to provide clean intermittent catheterization to a student needing it every three to four hours during the school day. The Court held that if a student cannot attend school unless provided with certain health-related assistance during the school day, such help is a "supportive service" necessary to assist him or her to benefit from special education, and that if it can be provided by a school nurse, trained layperson or other non-physician, it is *not* an excludable medical service; rather, it is a "school health service" as defined by the IDEA regulations — and so a required related service under IDEA.[46]

The second case, *Cedar Rapids Community School District v. Garret F.*,[47] was decided in 1999. The student in *Garret F.* needed a range of assistance with physical needs during the school day, including suctioning of his tracheotomy tube and other tasks related to his use of a ventilator. The school system characterized these as "continuous nursing services" and claimed that they were not required related services but, rather, fell under the medical exclusion because of their intensity and cost. The Supreme Court rejected the school system's position, holding that the 15 year-old rule of *Tatro* was sound and applicable. Therefore, the school system had to provide the services Garret F. needed, even if they were "continuous," and even if they required a nurse. In explaining its decision, the Court stated, "[t]his case is about whether meaningful access to public schools will be assured....It is undisputed that the services at issue must be provided if Garret is to remain in school. Under the statute, our precedent, and the purposes of the IDEA, the District must fund such 'related services' in order to help guarantee that students like Garret are integrated into the public schools."[48]

D. ASSISTIVE TECHNOLOGY

1. IDEA

Assistive technology devices or services can be an important component of education for some students. Depending upon individual needs, IDEA may require schools to provide assistive technology as part of a child's "special education" (meaning specially designed instruction), as a "related service" necessary to assist a child to benefit from special education, or as a supplementary aid or service necessary to allow a child to learn in the regular education classroom (see discussion below).[49]

When needed, IDEA requires both assistive technology "devices" and assistive technology "services."[50] Like all other entitlements under IDEA, assistive technology devices and services must be provided at no cost to parent or child. An "assistive technology device" is any item, piece of equipment, or product system that is used to increase, maintain, or improve a child's functional capabilities.[51] An "assistive technology service" is any service that directly helps a child with a disability to choose, acquire or use an assistive technology device. Such services include

- evaluating a child's assistive technology needs,
- buying, leasing or otherwise obtaining an assistive technology device,
- choosing, designing, fitting, customizing, adapting, applying, maintaining, repairing or replacing an assistive technology device,
- coordinating and using other therapies, interventions or services with assistive technology,
- training or technical assistance for a child and, if appropriate, the child's family, and
- training or technical assistance for professionals, employers or others who are substantially involved in the child's major life functions.[52]

IEP teams must consider whether a child needs assistive technology devices and services when developing the IEP, and, if so, include them in the IEP and provide them.[53] Like all decisions regarding a child's IEP, decisions regarding the use and provision of assistive technology devices and services must be based upon appropriate evaluation data and made by the IEP team.[54] If a child needs to use a particular assistive technology device at home or in other non-school settings in order to receive a free appropriate public education, the IEP team must include this in the IEP and make arrangements for the child to be able to do so.[55]

Depending upon the particular circumstances, schools also may be required to utilize assistive technology to meet other IDEA requirements (discussed elsewhere in this book), for example, the requirements that tests used to evaluate children with sensory, manual or speaking impairments be selected and administered so as to best ensure that results accurately reflect whatever the test is intended to measure, rather than simply reflecting back the child's impairment; that evaluation materials be provided in a child's native language "or other mode of communication," unless it is clearly not feasible to do so; that students with disabilities have equal opportunities for full participation in the full range of educational programs, nonacademic programs and services, and extra curricular activities offered; and that students with disabilities participate in general state- and district-wide assessments, with appropriate accommodations when necessary.[56]

2. Section 504

Assistive technology may be required as a §504 matter, too. Assistive technology devices and services, like other forms of "special education" or "related services," must be provided as necessary to meet the obligation under the §504 regulations to provide a free appropriate public education designed to meet individual student needs as well as the needs of students without disabilities are met.[57] Assistive technology may also be required to make real students' rights to receive their education in regular education classrooms with supplementary aids and services to the maximum extent feasible,[58] to nondiscriminatory evaluations,[59] and to equal opportunity to participate in nonacademic and extracurricular services and activities.[60]

Public school systems also may be required to provide assistive technology devices and services to accommodate a student's disability if necessary to enable the student to attend school,[61] or to comply with the prohibition against affording a qualified student with a disability opportunities that are not equal to those afforded others, or providing aids, benefits or services that do not afford a student with a disability an equal opportunity to obtain the same result, gain the same benefit or reach the same level of achievement as other students.[62] The ADA regulations contain similar prohibitions on unequal, or less effective, opportunities and services,[63] and specifically call for the provision of "auxiliary aids and services" when needed to avoid discrimination.[64]

E. "FREE" MEANS "FREE": USE OF SOCIAL SECURITY, SSI BENEFITS AND INSURANCE

Whether due under IDEA or §504, all special education, related services, assistive technology and required evaluations must be provided at public expense, without cost to child, parent or guardian.[65] Parents cannot be required to use their child's Social Security or SSI benefits to fund services owed them under these laws.[66]

Schools may not require a parent to use *private* health insurance to pay for or defray the cost of any services necessary to provide a child with a free appropriate public education under IDEA; schools may access private insurance only with the parent's informed consent.[67] *Each time* a school would like to use a family's private insurance, it must obtain informed consent and explain to the child's parents that they may refuse to allow their insurance to be used, and that any such refusal will not relieve the school of its duty to ensure that the child receives all necessary services at no cost to the family.[68]

The rules under IDEA regarding the use of insurance are different for children who have public insurance, such as Medicaid. They do not expressly require schools to obtain informed consent from a parent before tapping a child's Medicaid or other public insurance.[69] However, with a few exceptions not relevant here, both IDEA and the Family Educational Rights and Privacy Act ("FERPA")[70] require schools to obtain parental consent before disclosing information from a child's education records to outside parties such as a Medicaid agency or other public health insurance agency.[71] Therefore, while the school may not need consent to tap into a child's public insurance benefits, it *will* need informed parental consent before it can pass along the *information* it must provide to Medicaid (or any other public health insurance program) in order to do so.

Under IDEA, "consent" means (1) that the parent has been fully informed of all relevant information, in his or her native language or other mode of communication; (2) that the parent understands and agrees in writing; (3) that the consent describes what the school system seeks to do, and lists the records that will be released and to whom; and (4) that the parent understands that giving consent is voluntary, and that he or she can revoke it at any time.[72] By virtue of these requirements, parents should always have advance notice of the school's efforts to use a child's public health insurance to pay for special education services, and an opportunity to prevent any related disclosure of information from the child's education records.[73]

In addition, before tapping a child's Medicaid or other public health insurance, the school system must make sure that tapping the child's public health insurance will *not*

- decrease available lifetime coverage or any other benefit,
- result in the family paying for services that the child needs outside of school, and that otherwise would be covered by the public insurance program,
- increase premiums or lead to discontinuation of the insurance, or
- risk loss of eligibility for home and community-based waivers, based on total health-related expenditures.[74]

School personnel acting without the participation of the child's parent would lack the information necessary to ensure that none of these bad consequences will ensue. Thus, to comply with these provisions, it would seem that before tapping public insurance, school officials, at a minimum, must inform the parent of the school's interest in utilizing public insurance benefits; explain exactly what it is that they propose to do, as well as the above-listed constraints on their freedom to do so; seek from the parent (and other relevant sources) the information necessary to make the required determinations; solicit any parental concerns; and give parents a meaningful opportunity to express any such concerns.

School officials may not require parents to sign up for Medicaid or other public insurance as a condition for their child receiving services under IDEA.[75] Nor may they require parents whose children *are* enrolled in public insurance programs to incur any out-of-pocket expenses, such as paying a deductible or co-payment.[76]

Whether insurance is public or private, parents and students who suffer financial loss when insurance is used to pay for what should have been part of a *free* appropriate public education may recover their losses from the responsible school system.[77] Parents and advocates should also note that while the above specific provisions regarding public and private insurance use come from the IDEA regulations, the U.S. Department of Education/Office for Civil Rights has long held that schools may not require parents to use health insurance to help pay for services due under §504 if doing so would pose a risk of financial loss to parent or child.[78]

F. INTEGRATION TO THE MAXIMUM EXTENT APPROPRIATE

1. Inclusion in and exclusion from regular education settings

IDEA requires that a student's IEP be implemented in a setting that allows him or her to be integrated into the regular education setting to the maximum extent consistent with his or her needs. Each state and school system must ensure that:

> "to the maximum extent appropriate, children with disabilities, including children in public or private institutions or other care facilities, are educated with children who are not disabled, and that special classes, separate schooling, or other removal of children with disabilities from the regular education environment occurs only when the nature or severity of the disability is such that education in regular classes with the use of supplementary aids and services cannot be achieved satisfactorily."[79]

This language creates what courts have variously called a legal "presumption" of, or a statutory "preference" for, education in regular education classrooms with non-disabled peers.[80]

The §504 regulations similarly provide that students with disabilities shall be educated with non-disabled persons "to the maximum extent appropriate" and shall be placed in the regular program *unless it is demonstrated by the recipient* that the education of the person in the regular environment with the use of supplementary aids and services cannot be achieved satisfactorily."[81]   Both laws also require school systems to ensure that each child with a disability participates in mainstream non-academic and extra-curricular activities, including meals and recess periods, "to the maximum extent appropriate to the needs of" that child.[82] The §504 regulations additionally state that school systems "shall provide non-academic and extracurricular services and activities in such manner as is necessary to afford handicapped [sic] students an equal opportunity for participation in such services and activities."[83] IDEA regulations include the same requirement.[84]

As the above-emphasized language in the §504 regulation indicates, a school district proposing to remove a child from the regular education classroom has the burden of proving that such removal — whether partial or total — is necessary because education there cannot reasonably be accomplished with the use of supplementary aids and services and/or modification of the regular education curriculum. Courts have held that school districts bear this burden of proof as an IDEA matter as well.[85] In addition, the 1997 Amendments to IDEA recognize and underscore that the burden of proof rests with the school district: effective July 1, 1998, all Individualized Educational Programs were required to contain "an explanation of the extent, if any, to which the child will not participate with nondisabled children in the regular class...."[86] In contrast, prior law required "a statement of...the extent to which such child will be able to participate in regular education programs."[87]

IDEA presumes that the first placement option considered for each child by his or her placement team is the regular education classroom in the school the child would attend if he or she did not have a disability, with appropriate supplementary aids and services.[88] The statute "does not permit states to make mere token gestures to accommodate handicapped [sic] students [in regular education classrooms]; its requirement for modifying and supplementing regular education is broad."[89]

As courts have recognized, "the decision as to whether any particular child should be educated in a regular classroom setting...is necessarily an inquiry into the needs and abilities of one child, and does not extend to a group or category of handicapped [sic] children..."[90] Further, "before the school district may conclude that a handicapped [sic] child should be educated outside the regular classroom, it must consider...the whole range of supplemental aids and services...for which it is obligated under [IDEA] and the regulations promulgated thereunder to make provision."[91] Only when the child's education cannot be achieved satisfactorily in the regular education classroom, with one or more of such supplementary aids and services, may he or she be placed in another setting; consideration of these issues must occur "prior to and during the development of the IEP."[92]

School districts thus have a very strong legal duty to assess the extent to which, given appropriate supports, a child may be educated in the regular education setting before attempting a more restrictive placement.[93] Such supports might include, but are not limited to, assistance of an itinerant teacher with special education training, a classroom aide, use of computers or other assistive technology devices, modification of the regular education curriculum, consultation between the regular education teacher and special education personnel, provision of some special education and related services within the regular education classroom, etc.[94]

IDEA prohibits a school district from excluding a child with disabilities from the regular education setting simply because it disagrees philosophically with integration or inclusion as an educational method,[95] and from excluding a child simply because he or she cannot learn or perform at the same level as his or her prospective regular education classmates.[96] Indeed, an express provision added to the IDEA regulations in 1999 stresses that a child with a disability may not be excluded from an age-appropriate regular education classroom simply because he or she needs modifications in the curriculum.[97] Further, the mandate for maximum appropriate placement in the regular education classroom may not be avoided by a mere showing that a separate placement may be academically superior to placement in an unmodified regular classroom; rather, the school must demonstrate that it has considered "whether supplemental aids and services would permit satisfactory education in the regular classroom."[98]

2. The relevance of behavior

The federal courts have held that one relevant factor for determining whether a child's education may be "achieved satisfactorily" — the language used in both IDEA and the §504 regulation — in the regular classroom is "what effect the presence of the...child [with a disability] in a regular classroom would have on the education of other children in that classroom."[99] Courts applying this factor have examined two ways in which the "effect" of a child's "presence" has been claimed (by schools) to weigh against inclusion, both of which are often cited when efforts are made to exclude children with behavioral manifestations from regular education classrooms: (1) the child requires a disproportionate amount of teacher attention and/or (2) the child's behavior disrupts the class. Judicial decisions make it clear that such "effects" are relevant only where they persist *even with* the provision of appropriate services aimed at ameliorating them.

For example, in a decision considering the first kind of claimed effect, the U.S. Court of Appeals for the Eleventh Circuit rejected the notion that the mere fact that a child requires more teacher attention than his or her peers justifies exclusion, emphasizing the school's obligation to consider supplemental aids and services that accommodate the child's need for additional attention.[100] The 1997 amendments to IDEA make even more explicit this obligation, requiring IEPs to include "a statement of the program modifications or supports for school personnel that will be provided for the child...to be educated with...nondisabled children."[101]

The U.S. Court of Appeals for the Third Circuit has explicitly addressed the second often-claimed effect, i.e. that the child's behavior is too disruptive for regular education placement. The school district in this case had excluded the student from the regular education classroom because of, in the court's words, his "extremely disruptive behavior" in a prior inclusive kindergarten placement, and in other teaching environments. The district court had found, however, that "the behavioral problems Rafael experienced...were exacerbated and remained uncontained due to the inadequate level of services provided there, [and] that Rafael's behavioral problems were diminished in settings where an adequate level of supplementary aids and services were provided."[102] The lower court also found "nothing in the record to suggest that *at this point in time* Rafael would present similar behavior problems if provided with an adequate level of supplementary aids and services within the matrix of a regular education class."[103] All of this being the case, the Third Circuit held, "consideration of the possible negative effects of Rafael's presence on the regular classroom environment does not support the School District's decision to exclude him from the regular classroom."[104] In a similar vein, the U.S. Department of Education, in interpreting its regulations implementing IDEA, has since explained that "if the child can appropriately function in the regular classroom with appropriate behavioral supports, strategies or interventions, placement in a more restrictive environment would be inconsistent with the least restrictive environment provisions of the IDEA."[105]

3. Degrees of removal from regular education settings

In addition to protecting the right of children with disabilities to participate in regular education classes and activities, the requirement of maximum appropriate integration protects children whose needs cannot be met in regular education classes from overly restrictive and isolated placements. Thus, for example, IDEA and §504 integration requirements would be violated if a child who could be educated appropriately in a classroom located within a "regular" education elementary school and serving other children with disabilities, were nonetheless placed in a segregated school for children with disabilities.[106]

4. Removal from "base" or "home" schools

In addition to the statutory prohibition on unnecessary removal from regular education settings, the IDEA regulations require that each child's placement be "as close to home as possible," and, "unless the IEP requires some other arrangement," be in the same school he or she would attend if nondisabled.[107] The federal Courts of Appeals generally have not been receptive to the argument that these provisions entitle a child to attend his or her home or base school. Although one appellate court has stated that the regulations create a presumption in favor of placement in base schools,[108] four others have held to the contrary, characterizing the regulations as creating a preference or factor to be considered.[109] In a *Notice of Interpretation* published subsequent to these decisions, the U.S. Department has explained that "IDEA presumes that the first placement option considered for each disabled student by the student's placement team...is the school the child would attend if not disabled, with appropriate supplementary aids and services to facilitate such placement."[110]

In three of the cases in which courts ruled that the above-described IDEA regulations create something less than a presumption of base school placement,[111] the courts, *on the facts before them*, upheld a school system's decisions to (1) centralize a particular specialized program, service, or facility rather than replicate it in the student's base school, and (2) to place the individual student before it in the school housing that centralized program, service, etc., rather than in his or her base school. It is important to note that in each case, the court concluded that the student would receive an appropriate education and services and participate in regular education settings to the maximum extent appropriate in the non-base school. In addition, all of the non-base schools were schools for all students — none were segregated schools or centers exclusively for children with disabilities. Furthermore, the schools in which the students were placed were not, the courts seemed to suggest, significantly farther from their homes than were their base schools.[112] While these considerations do not make the results in these three cases any less discouraging, they do make it clear that, as an IDEA matter, whether a school system may exclude a student with disabilities from his or her base school must be determined on a case-by-case basis, in light of the particular facts. (In the fourth case,[113] the Court of Appeals addressed the abstract legal question of whether IDEA includes a presumption that the least restrictive environment is the neighborhood school, but, because the parents and school system had already reached agreement on a placement, did not analyze the facts of the case.)

NOTES

1. 20 U.S.C. §§1401(8), 1412(a); 34 C.F.R. §300.13.

2. 34 C.F.R. §104.33(b).

3. *See, e.g., Seattle School District No. 1 v. B.S.*, 82 F.3d 1493, 1500 (9th Cir. 1996) ("[e]veryone agrees that A.S. is exceptionally bright and thus able to test appropriately on standardized tests. This is not the sine qua non of 'educational benefit,' however. The term 'unique educational needs' [shall] be broadly construed to include...academic, social, health, emotional, communicative, physical and vocational needs"); *Babb v. Knox County School System*, 965 F.2d 104, 109 (6th Cir.), *cert. denied*, 506 U.S. 941, 113 S.Ct. 380 (1992) (education under IDEA encompasses "both academic instruction and a broad range of associated services traditionally grouped under the general rubric of 'treatment'"); *Timothy W. v. Rochester School District*, 875 F.2d 954, 962 (1st Cir.), *cert. denied*, 493 U.S. 983, 110 S.Ct. 519 (1989) ("the Act's concept of special education is broad, encompassing not only traditional cognitive skills, but basic functional skills as well"); *Kruelle v. New Castle County School District*, 642 F.2d 687, 693-94 (3rd Cir. 1981) ("the concept of education is necessarily broad...[w]here basic self-help...skills...are lacking, formal education begins at that point"); *Battle v. Commonwealth of Pennsylvania*, 629 F.2d 269, 275 (3rd Cir. 1980), *cert. denied*, 452 U.S. 968 (1981) (same). *Cf. Stacey G. v. Pasadena Independent School District*, 547 F. Supp. 61, 77 (S.D. Tex. 1982) ("...an essential element of an appropriate education for a child as handicapped as Stacey is an opportunity to develop skills that would allow Stacey to be as self-sufficient as possible and to function outside of an institution").

4. *See* 20 U.S.C. §1412(a)(5); 34 C.F.R. §§300.550 through 300.556; 34 C.F.R. §104.34.

5. 20 U.S.C. §1401(8)(D); *Board of Education of the Hendrick Hudson Central School District v. Rowley*, 458 U.S. 176, 206 n.27, 102 S.Ct. 3034, 3051 n.27 (1982).

6. *See Timothy W., supra,* 875 F.2d at 973 ("...educational methods...are not static, but are constantly evolving and improving. It is the school district's responsibility to avail itself of these new approaches in providing an education program geared to each child's individual needs"); *see also* 20 U.S.C. §§1412(a)(14), 1453(c)(3)(D)(vii) (state must have in effect system to acquire and disseminate to teachers, administrators, school board members and related services personnel significant knowledge derived from education research and other sources, and for adopting, where appropriate, promising practices, materials and technology); 20 U.S.C. §1413(a)(3) (local school systems shall ensure that personnel are appropriately prepared to carry out IDEA, consistent with §1453(c)(3)(D); 34 C.F.R. §300.382(g).

7. 20 U.S.C. §1412(d)(1); 34 C.F.R. §300.347.

8. 34 C.F.R. §104.33(b)(2).

9. 20 U.S.C. §1401(8).

10. *Id.*

11. *See* 34 C.F.R. §300.347(a)(2)(i) (defining "general curriculum").

12. Most states have set standards for what all students should know and be able to do at various points in their elementary and secondary years. Some states have done so acting under state education reform laws, under the federal Goals 2000: Educate America Act, or both. Regardless, these standards are "standards of the State educational agency," as well as components of "an appropriate...elementary or secondary education in the State involved," and so are part of the free appropriate public education to which all children with disabilities are entitled under IDEA.

13. *See, e.g.*, 20 U.S.C. §1414(b)(2)(A), (c)(1)(iv) and 34 C.F.R. §§300.532(b), 300.533(a)(2)(iv) (evaluations); 20 U.S.C. §§1414(d)(1)(A), (d)(4) and 34 C.F.R. §§300.343(c)(2)(i), 300.347, 300 (IEP content); 20 U.S.C. §1414(d)(1)(B) and 34 C.F.R. §§300.344(a)(2), (4)(ii) (IEP team composition); 20 U.S.C. §1412(17) and 34 C.F.R. §300.138 (participation in assessments).

14. 458 U.S. 176, 102 S.Ct. 3034 (1982).

15. 458 U.S. at 206-207, 102 S.Ct. at 3051.

16. *Ridgewood Bd. of Ed. v. N.E.*, 172 F.3d 238, 247-8 (3rd Cir. 1999); *Board of Education of East Windsor Regional School District v. Diamond*, 808 F.2d 987, 991 (3rd Cir. 1986). *See also San Diego v. California Special Education Hearing Office*, 93 F.3d 1458 (9th Cir. 1996) ("benefit" alone insufficient; progress towards IEP goals required); *Cordrey v. Euckert*, 917 F.2d 1460, 1473 (6th Cir. 1990), *cert. denied*, 499 U.S. 938, 111 S. Ct. 1391 (1991) (child must benefit meaningfully within his or her potential); *Doe v. Smith*, 879 F.2d 1340, 1341 (6th Cir. 1989), *cert. denied*, 493 U.S. 1025), 110 S. Ct. 730 (1990) (benefit must be more than *de minimis*); *Polk v. Susquehanna Intermediate Unit 16*, 853 F.2d 171, 184 (3rd Cir.), *cert. denied* 488 U.S. 1030,109 S.Ct. 838 (1988) (*de minimis* or trivial benefit insufficient; whether benefit is *de minimis* must be gauged in relation to child's potential); *Hall v. Vance County Board of Education*, 774 F. 2d 629, 636 (4th Cir. 1985) ("[c]learly, Congress did not intend that a school system could discharge its duty...by providing a program that produces some minimal academic advancement, no matter how trivial"); *Johnson v. Lancaster-Lebanon Intermediate Unit 13*, 757 F. Supp. 606, 618 (E.D. Penn. 1991) (educational program must be sufficient for student to make "meaningful educational progress"); *Chris D. v. Montgomery County Board of Education*, 743 F. Supp. 1524, 1531 (M.D. Ala. 1990)(rejecting implicit school board contention that "a benefit is conferred anytime a student is not left to vegetate").

17. *See* 20 U.S.C. §§1412(a)(16(A)(ii), 1412(17)(A), 1414(b)(2)(A), 1414(c)(1)(iii), 1414(d)(A)(i)(I), 1414(d)(1)(A)(ii)(I), 1414(d)(1)(A)(iii)(II). *See also Carter v. Florence County School District No. 4*, 950 F.2d 156, 160 (4th Cir. 1991), *aff'd. on other grounds*, 510 U.S. 7,114 S.Ct. 361 (1993) (goal of four months' progress per year in reading and mathematics was inadequate for high school student in question, allowing her to continue to fall behind classmates at alarming rate).

18. *See* 458 U.S. at 202 - 03, 102 S.Ct. at 3049.

19. 458 U.S. at 200, 102 S.Ct. at 3048.

20. *Town of Burlington v. Department of Education*, 736 F.2d 773, 788 (1st Cir. 1984), *aff'd.*, 471 U.S. 359, 105 S.Ct. 1996 (1985).

21. 20 U.S.C. §1401(8)(B); 34 C.F.R. §300.13(b).

22. *See, e.g., Town of Burlington, supra*, 736 F.2d at 789; *Seattle School District No. 1, supra*, 82 F.3d at 1499 n.2; *Johnson v. Independent School District No. 4*, 921 F.2d 1022, 1029 (10th Cir. 1990), *cert. denied*, 500 U.S. 905, 111 S. Ct. 1685 (1991); *Thomas v. Cincinnati Board of Education*, 918 F.2d 618, 620 (6th Cir. 1990); *Geis v. Board of Education of Persippany-Troy Hills*, 774 F.2d 575, 581 (3rd Cir. 1985); *Students of California School for the Blind v. Honig*, 736 F.2d 538, 544-545 (9th Cir. 1984), *vacated as moot*, 471 U.S. 148, 105 S.Ct. 1928; *LIH v. New York City Board*

of Education, 103 F. Supp. 2d 658, 668-9 (E.D.N.Y. 2000); *Pink v. Mt. Diablo Unified School District,* 738 F. Supp. 345, 346-347 (N.D. Cal. 1990); *Barwacz v. Michigan Department of Education,* 674 F. Supp. 1296, 1303-1304 (W.D. Mich. 1987).

23. 34 C.F.R. §104.33(b)(1)(i).

24. 34 C.F.R. §104.33(b)(2).

25. 34 C.F.R. §104.33(b)(1)(ii).

26. 34 C.F.R. §104.4(b)(ii), (iii).

27. 34 C.F.R. §104.4(b)(2).

28. *See* 28 C.F.R. §35.130(b)(ii), (iii).

29. For a full discussion of the right to learn in the general curriculum under §504, the ADA and IDEA, see chapter 3.

30. *See, e.g., South Central (IN) Area Special Education Cooperative,* 17 EHLR 248, 250 (OCR 9/25/90). *See also Orange County (FL) School District,* 28 IDELR 492 (OCR 11/18/97); *Duchesne County (UT) School District,* 17 EHLR 240 (OCR 9/13/90); *East Baton Rouge (LA) Parish School System,* EHLR 353:252, :255 (OCR 6/14/89); *Tippecanoe (IN) School Corporation,* EHLR 353:217 (OCR 6/14/88).

31. 34 C.F.R. §104.34(c).

32. 20 U.S.C. §1401(25) (emphasis added); *see also* 34 C.F.R. §300.26 (1999). The term special education "includes instruction conducted in the classroom, in the home, in hospitals and institutions, and in other settings," 20 U.S.C. §1401(25)(A), as well as "instruction in physical education." 20 U.S.C. §1401(25)(B).

33. 34 C.F.R. §300.26(b)(3).

34. *See, e.g., Corey H. v. Board of Education of Education of the City of Chicago,* 995 F. Supp. 900 (N.D. Ill. 1998) (placement of children in segregated settings based upon the category of their disabilities violated IDEA's individualization and least restrictive environment mandates); *Board of Education of the County of Cabell v. Dienelt,* 1986-87 EHLR DEC. 558:305, :308 (S.D. W.Va. 1987) (school board failed to provide free appropriate public education when it attempted to place student with learning disabilities in its "generalized special education program without reference to the child's individualized needs"), *aff'd. per curiam,* 843 F.2d 813 (4th Cir. 1988). *See also* Judith E. Heumann and Thomas Hehir, U.S. Department of Education/Office of Special Education Programs Memorandum 95-5, November 23, 1994 (hereinafter "OSEP Memorandum 95-5"), *reprinted at* 21 IDELR 1152 (educational decisions under IDEA may not be based solely on category or severity of disability, administrative convenience or the configuration of the delivery system); *Inquiry of Siegel,* 16 EHLR 797 (OSEP 4/22/90) ("[i]t is impermissible...for public agencies to make placements on the basis of the category of a child's handicapping [sic] condition....").

35. *See* 34 C.F.R. §§104.34-104.35 (requiring individualized decisions regarding placement and services, based upon individualized evaluations). *See also* 34 C.F.R. §104.4(b)(1)(iv), which prohibits recipients of federal funds from providing different or separate services to people with disabilities or any category of people with dis-

abilities unless such treatment is necessary to provide them services as effective as those provided to non-disabled people.

36. 20 U.S.C. §1401(22).

37. 34 C.F.R. §104.33(b)(2).

38. *See, e.g., Inquiry of Rainforth*, 17 EHLR 222 (OSEP 10/24/90) (regarding IDEA); *Prescott (AZ) Unified School District No. 1*, EHLR 352:540 (OCR 5/22/87) (regarding §504). *See also* OSEP Memorandum 95-5, *supra* (IDEA).

39. 34 C.F.R. §300.24(b)(15).

40. 20 U.S.C. §1401(22) and 34 C.F.R. §300.24. Each of these services is further defined in 34 C.F.R. §300.24(b).

41. 34 C.F.R. part 300, App. A, question 34.

42. Depending upon a student's particular circumstances, a school system might be required to provide a computer or other assistive technology as "special education," as a "related service" or as a "supplementary aid or service" to facilitate his or her education in the regular education setting pursuant to IDEA's least restrictive environment requirements. 34 C.F.R. §300.308. *See also Inquiry of Goodman*, 16 EHLR 1317 (OSEP 8/10/90).

43. 20 U.S.C. §1401(22).

44. 34 C.F.R. §300.24(b)(4).

45. 468 U.S. 883, 890, 104 S.Ct. 3371, 3376 (1984).

46. *Id.*, 468 U.S. at 892-893, 104 S.Ct. at 3377-3378.

47. 526 U.S. 66, 119 S.Ct. 992 (1999).

48. 526 U.S. at 79, 119 S. Ct. at 1000.

49. 34 C.F.R. §300.308(a).

50. *Id.*

51. 20 U.S.C. §1401(1); 34 C.F.R. §300.5.

52. 20 U.S.C. §1401(2); 34 C.F.R. §300.6.

53. 20 U.S.C. §1414(d)(3)(B)(v); 34 C.F.R. §300.346(a)(v), (c).

54. For a discussion of evaluation and IEP development requirements, see chapters 5 and 6, respectively.

55. 34 C.F.R. §300.308(b).

56. *See*, respectively, 34 C.F.R. §300.532(e); 20 U.S.C. §1414(b)(3)(A)(ii) and 34 C.F.R. §300.532(a)(ii); 34 C.F.R. §§300.304 - 300.306; 20 U.S.C. §1412(a)(17).

57. *See, e.g., Harrison County (WV) School District*, EHLR 353:120 (OCR 6/29/88) (school district's delay in obtaining communication device for student who could not speak and refusal to allow her to use it in regular education classes violated obligation to provide related aids and services under 34 C.F.R. §104.33).

58. See 34 C.F.R. §104.34(a) and discussion below.

59. 34 C.F.R. §104.35(b)(3).

60. 34 C.F.R. §104.37.

61. *Cf. Tatro v. State of Texas*, 625 F.2d 557, 564-65 (5th Cir. 1980), *aff'd on other grounds sub nom., Irving Independent School District v. Tatro*, 468 U.S. 883, 104 S.Ct. 3371 (1984) (school district's refusal to provide child with clean intermittent catheterization during school day violated §504, as she needed such service in order to participate in district's preschool program).

62. 34 C.F.R. §104.4(b)(1)(ii) - (iii), (b)(2).

63. *See* 28 C.F.R. §35.130(b)(1)(ii), (iii).

64. *See* 28 C.F.R. §§35.130(f), 130.135. "Auxiliary aids and services" include "(1) [q]ualified interpreters, note takers, transcription services, written materials, telephone handset amplifiers, assistive listening devices, assistive listening systems, telephones compatible with hearing aids, closed caption decoders, open and closed captioning, telecommunications devices for deaf persons (TDDs), videotext displays, or other effective methods of making aurally delivered materials available to individuals with hearing impairments; (2) [q]ualified readers, taped texts, audio recordings, Brailled materials, large print materials, or other effective methods of making visually delivered materials available to individuals with visual impairments; (3) [a]cquisition or modification of equipment or devices; and (4) [o]ther similar services and actions." 28 C.F.R. §35.104.

65. 20 U.S.C. §§1401(8)(A), (25); 34 C.F.R. §300.13(a); 34 C.F.R. §104.33(c).

66. *McLain v. Smith*, 16 EHLR 6 (E.D. Tenn. 1989).

67. 34 C.F.R. §300.142(f).

68. *Id.* See also 34 C.F.R. §300.500(b)(1), regarding consent in general.

69. 34 C.F.R. §300.142(e).

70. 20 U.S.C. §1232g.

71. 34 C.F.R. §300.571; 34 C.F.R. §99.30 (FERPA regulations). *See also Inquiry of Wisconsin Department of Public Instruction*, 28 IDELR 497 (Family Policy Compliance Office 1997). The Family Policy Compliance Office, part of the U.S. Department of Education, enforces compliance with FERPA.

72. 34 C.F.R. §300.500(b)(1).

73. In many states, the Medicaid (or other public insurance) agency requires parents to sign a broad consent form allowing it to obtain from other agencies, including schools, the information it needs in order to administer the public insurance program. The Family Policy Compliance Office, which enforces FERPA, has stated that, depending upon the details, these consent forms may satisfy the requirement of prior parental consent for disclosure of information from education records. *See Inquiry of Wisconsin Department of Public Instruction, supra.* However, a broad consent form provided by the public insurance agency as a part of the application process, and before the school even decided that it would like to tap the public insurance (for which the child presumably has not yet even been found eligible), would not seem to meet the IDEA requirements for consent discussed above.

74. 34 C.F.R. §300.142(e)(2)(iii).

75. 34 C.F.R. §300.142(e)(2)(i).

76. 34 C.F.R. §300.142(e)(2)(ii).

77. *See Shook v. Gaston County Board of Education*, 882 F.2d 119 (4th Cir. 1989), *cert. denied*, 493 U.S. 1093, 110 S. Ct. 1166 (1990); *Seals v. Loftis*, 614 F. Supp. 302 (E.D.Tenn. 1985).

Financial loss from the use of insurance might occur in a variety of ways, including, e.g., a decrease in available lifetime coverage under the policy; a decrease in available annual coverage or any other benefit under the policy; payment of a deductible amount for a particular service; an increase in premiums; discontinuation of the policy; or decreased future insurability with a different insurance company if the educational services for which insurance is used are deemed treatment for a pre-existing medical condition. It also includes the kinds of losses, listed above, that preclude a school from tapping Medicaid or other public insurance benefits.

78. *See Trans Allied-Medical Services, Inc.*, 16 EHLR 963(OCR 5/30/90).

79. 20 U.S.C. §1412(a)(5) (emphasis added); *see also* 34 C.F.R. §300.550.

80. *Hartmann v. Loudon Co. Bd. of Ed.*, 118 F.3d 996, 1001 (4th Cir. 1997), *cert. denied*, 522 U.S. 1046, 118 S.Ct. 688 (1998) ("mainstreaming provision establishes a presumption"); *Bd. of Ed. Sacramento City Unified School District v. Holland*, 14 F.3d 1398, 1403 (9th Cir.), *cert. denied*, 512 U.S. 1207, 114 S.Ct. 2679 (1994) (provision sets forth Congress's preference for educating children with disabilities in regular classrooms with their peers"), *affirming* 786 F. Supp. 874, 878 ("strong preference for mainstreaming which rises to the level of a rebuttable presumption"); *Oberti v. Bd. of Ed. of Borough of Clementon School District*, 995 F.2d 1204, 1214 (3rd Cir. 1993) ("presumption in favor of mainstreaming"); *Greer v. Rome City School District*, 950 F.2d 688, 695 (11th Cir. 1991), *opinion withdrawn and remanded on other grounds*, 956 F.2d 1025 (11th Cir. 1992), *previous opinion reinstated by rehearing en banc*, 967 F.2d 470 (11th Cir. 1992) ("[w]ith this directive...Congress created a statutory preference for educating handicapped children with nonhandicapped children"); *Daniel R.R. v. State Bd. of Ed.*, 874 F.2d 1036, 1045 (5th Cir. 1989) ("presumption in favor of mainstreaming"); *Lachman v. Illinois Bd. of Ed.*, 852 F.2d 290, 295 (7th Cir.), *cert. denied*, 488 U.S. 925, 109 S.Ct. 308) (1988) ("strong preference"); *A.W. v. Northwest R-1 School. Dist.*, 813 F.2d 158, 162 (8th Cir.), *cert. denied*, 484 U.S. 847, 108 S.Ct. 144 (1987) ("strong congressional preference"); *Roncker v. Walter*, 700 F.2d 1058, 1063 (6th Cir.), *cert. denied*, 464 U.S. 864, 104 S.Ct. 196 (1983) ("very strong Congressional preference").

81. 34 C.F.R. §104.34(a) (emphasis added). Section 504 also prohibits the provision of different or separate educational services to students with disabilities or to any class of students with disabilities unless those services are necessary to provide students with disabilities with services that are as effective as those provided to others. 34 C.F.R. §104.4(b)(iv).

82. 34 C.F.R. §300.553; 34 C.F.R. §104.34(b).

83. 34 C.F.R. §104.37(a)(1).

84. 34 C.F.R. §300.306(a).

85. *E.g., Oberti, supra*, 995 F.2d at 1219; *Daniel R.R., supra*, 874 F.2d at 1044- 45 (5th Cir. 1985) (preference for mainstreaming rises to the level of a rebuttable presumption); *Tokarcik v. Forest Hills School District*, 665 F.2d 443, 458 (3rd Cir. 1981), *cert. denied*, 458 U.S. 1121, 102 S.Ct. 3508 (1982); *Holland, supra*, 786 F. Supp. at 880 n.7, 882; *Davis v. District of Columbia Board of Education*, 530 F. Supp. 1209, 1211-1212 (D.D.C. 1982). *But see Hudson v. Bloomfield Hills Public Schools*, 910 F. Supp. 1291 (E.D. Mich. 1995), *affirmed and opinion adopted*, 108 F.3d 112 (6th Cir.), *cert. denied*, 522 U.S. 822, 118 S.Ct. 78 (1997). As virtually all public schools receive federal funds and therefore must comply with 34 C.F.R. §104.34(a), the school will always bear the burden of proof as a §504 matter, regardless of judicial interpretations of the burden of proof under IDEA.

86. 20 U.S.C. §1414(d)(1)(A)(iv) as amended.

87. See former 20 U.S.C. §1401(a)(20).

88. 34 C.F.R. part 300, Appendix A, question 1.

89. *Daniel R.R., supra*, 874 F.2d at 1048; *see also Oberti, supra*.

90. *Holland, supra*, 786 F. Supp. at 878. *See also Daniel R.R., supra*, at 1048 (LRE analysis is "an individualized, fact-specific inquiry that requires us to examine carefully the nature and severity of the child's handicapping condition, his needs and abilities, and the school's response to the child's needs").

91. *Greer, supra*, 950 F.2d at 696. *See also* 34 C.F.R. part 300, Appendix A, question 1 ("before a disabled child can be placed outside of the regular education environment, the full range of supplementary aids and services that if provided would facilitate the student's placement in the regular classroom must be considered").

92. *Greer, supra*, 950 F.2d at 692.

93. *Daniel R.R., supra*, 874 F.2d at 1048. *See also* 34 C.F.R. Part 300, Appendix A, question 1.

94. OSEP Memorandum 95-5, *supra. See also Oberti, supra*, 995 F.2d at 1216 (supplemental aids and services include resource rooms, itinerant instruction, special education training for the regular teacher, behavior modification, "or any other available aids or services appropriate to the child's particular disabilities"); *Daniel R.R., supra; Inquiry of Goodman*, 16 EHLR 1317 (OSEP 8/10/90) (assistive technology). *See also* 34 C.F.R. §300.551(b)(2).

95. *Roncker, supra*, 700 F.2d at 1063, citing *Campbell v. Talladega City Board of Education*, 518 F. Supp. 47, 55 (N.D. Ala. 1981).

96. *Daniel R.R., supra*, 874 F.2d at 1047.

97. 34 C.F.R. §300.552(e).

98. *Greer, supra*, 950 F.2d at 696.

99. *Greer, supra*, 950 F.2d at 697; *see also Hartmann, supra*, 118 F.3d at 1004-5; *Oberti, supra*, 995 F.2d at 1217; *Daniel R.R., supra*, 874 F.2d at 1049; *Roncker, supra*, 700 F.2d at 1063. In so holding, courts have relied upon a U.S. Department of Education comment to 34 C.F.R. 300.552 since deleted from the IDEA regulations. The comment stated,

"[W]here a handicapped child is so disruptive in a regular classroom that the education of other students is significantly impaired, the needs of the handicapped child cannot be met in that environment. Therefore regular placement would not be appropriate to his or her needs."

Comment to 34 C.F.R. §300.552 (1998), citing 34 C.F.R. part 104, Appendix A, ¶24 (emphasis added). This comment was deleted from the comprehensive IDEA regulations promulgated in March, 1999. *See* 34 C.F.R. §300.552(1999). In a Notice of Interpretation issued with the 1999 regulations, the Department explained,

"The determination of appropriate placement for a child whose behavior is interfering with the education of others requires careful consideration of whether the child can appropriately function in the regular classroom if provided appropriate behavioral supports, strategies and interventions. If the child can appropriately function in the regular classroom with appropriate behavioral supports, strategies or interventions, placement in a more restrictive environment would be inconsistent with the least restrictive environment provisions of the IDEA. If the child's behavior in the regular classroom, even with the provision of appropriate behavioral supports, strategies or interventions, would significantly impair the learning of others, that placement would not meet his or her needs and would not be appropriate for that child."

34 C.F.R. part 300, Appendix. A, question 39. *See also* OSEP Memorandum 95-5, *supra*, 21 IDELR at 1155 (explaining, under prior §300.553, the relevant factor as being "the degree of disruption of the education of other students, resulting in the inability to meet the unique needs of the disabled student").

100. *Greer, supra*, 950 F.2d at 697. *See also Oberti, supra*, 995 F.2d at 1217.

101. 20 U.S.C. §1414(d)(1)(A)(iii)(III) as amended.

102. *Oberti, supra*, 995 F.2d at 1222-23 (internal quotation marks omitted).

103. *Id.* at 1222 (emphasis in original) (internal quotation marks omitted).

104. *Id.* at 1223.

105. 34 C.F.R. part 300, Appendix A, question 39.

106. *See, e.g., Roncker, supra*.

107. 34 C.F.R. §300.552(b)(3), (c). On a related note, the §504 regulations provide that "whenever a recipient places a person in a setting other than the regular education environment…it shall take into account the proximity of the alternate setting to the person's home." 34 C.F.R. §104.34(a).

108. *Oberti, supra*, 995 F.2d at 1224, n.31.

109. *Flour Bluff Independent School District v. Katherine M.*, 91 F.3d 689, 693- 4 (5th Cir. 1996) ("proximity preference or factor is not a presumption that a disabled student attend his or her neighborhood school"); *Murray v. Montrose County School District*, 51 F.3d 921, 929 (10th Cir.), *cert. denied*, 516 U.S. 909, 116 S. Ct. 278 (1995) ("there is at most a preference for education in the neighborhood school"). *See also Schuldt v. Mankato Independent School District No. 77*, 937 F.2d 1357, 1361 (8th Cir. 1991), *cert. denied*, 502 U.S. 1059, 112 S.Ct. 937 (1992) ("[w]e interpret section 300.552 as directing the school district to locate Erika at a school

where her teachers can fully implement her program…'as close to home as possible' is not a mandate that the school district place Erika at [her neighborhood school]…."); *Barnett v. Fairfax Co. Schl. Bd.*, 927 F.2d 146, 153 (4th Cir.), *cert. denied*, 502 U.S. 859, 112 S.Ct. 175 (1991) ("we do not interpret this section as imposing upon a school board an absolute obligation to place a child in his base school…this section requires only that a school board take into account, as one factor, the geographical proximity of the placement in making these decisions").

110. 34 C.F.R. part 300, App. A, question 1.

111. *Barnett, supra; Flour Bluff, supra; Schuldt, supra. See also Kevin G. v. Cranston School Committee,* 965 F. Supp. 261 (D.R.I. 1997), *aff'd per curiam,* 130 F.3d 481 (3rd Cir. 1997), *cert. denied*, 524 U.S. 956, 118 S.Ct. 2377 (1998).

112. *See Barnett, supra*, 929 F.2d at 149, 153 (difference of five miles); *Flour Bluff, supra*, 91 F.3d at 695 (difference of seven miles); *Schuldt, supra,* 937 F.2d at 1359 (5 blocks versus four miles to nearest fully accessible school). *See also Kevin G., supra*, 965 F. Supp. at 262 (same street versus three miles).

113. *Murray, supra.*

CHAPTER 3

A CLOSER LOOK AT FAPE: THE RIGHT TO PARTICIPATE IN THE GENERAL CURRICULUM AND THE RELEVANCE OF STATE STANDARDS

All too often, and contrary to IDEA and §504, receiving special education services has meant being excluded from the "regular," or "general," curriculum, and so from opportunities to learn what all other children are expected to learn. In recent years, as a central part of education reform initiatives, most states have adopted content and student performance standards for what all children should know and be able to do at various points in their schooling. The general curriculum reflects these standards.

IDEA, §504 and Title II of the Americans with Disabilities Act give students with disabilities clear legal rights to participate in the general curriculum — *regardless* of the kind of classroom or setting in which they are receiving their education — and to have meaningful opportunities to learn what state standards say all children should know and be able to do. This includes the right to specially designed instruction and support services geared to attainment of the standards and successful learning in the general curriculum. This chapter discusses these participation rights.

A. THE RIGHT TO BE TAUGHT WHAT OTHER CHILDREN ARE EXPECTED TO LEARN AS A COMPONENT OF FAPE UNDER IDEA

1. The Definition of FAPE and the Relevance of State Standards

As discussed in chapter 2, IDEA defines a "free appropriate public education" as special education and related services that

- are provided at public expense, under public supervision, at no charge to parents;

- are provided in conformity with a properly developed IEP;
- include an appropriate preschool, elementary or secondary education in the state involved; and
- meet the standards of the state education agency.[1]

The latter two criteria are central to the right of students with disabilities to meaningful opportunities to learn what other children are expected to learn. They establish that the goals and content of a child's special education (specially designed instruction) and related services are not to be designed in a vacuum but, rather, by reference to the meaning and content of education for *all* students in that state.[2]

In addition, the general curriculum and any state (or local) content and student performance standards define (in part) "an appropriate elementary or secondary education in the State involved." State-adopted content and performance standards also comprise "standards of the state educational agency." To afford FAPE, then, special education and related services must include, among other things, specialized instruction and support services aligned with the general curriculum and the standards set for all students.[3] Put another way, students with disabilities must be given meaningful opportunities to learn the body of knowledge and range of skills that all students are expected to master, through specialized instruction and services designed to address their unique disability-related needs *and* to enable them to succeed in the general curriculum.

2. Other IDEA Provisions Regarding Participation in the General Curriculum

Amendments made to IDEA in 1997 reinforce and make more explicit this mandate from prior law. Critical provisions include the following:

Evaluations Evaluations must gather information about strategies and interventions that the child needs to participate and progress in the general curriculum.[4]

Definition of Specially Designed Instruction The "specially designed instruction" that makes up "special education" includes adapting the content, methodology or delivery of instruction to ensure a child's access to the general curriculum, so that he or she can meet the educational standards that apply to all children.[5]

Individualized Education Programs IEPs must describe how the child's disability affects participation and progress in the general curriculum. They must also contain goals and objectives geared towards enabling him or her to do so. IEPs are to include special education, related services, supplementary aids and services and supports for school personnel that will allow the student to progress in the general education curriculum. IEPs must be reviewed periodically and revised to address any lack of expected progress in the general curriculum.[6]

IEP Teams IEP teams must include someone knowledgeable about the general education curriculum, as well as at least one of the child's regular education teachers if the child is or may be participating in the regular education environment.[7]

Promising Practices As did prior law, IDEA as amended in 1997 requires states and school systems to keep abreast of research-based promising practices for teaching students with disabilities the general curriculum, and to incorporate these practices as appropriate into IEPs.[8]

Assessment Children with disabilities must be included in general state- and district-wide assessments, with appropriate accommodations or alternate assessments where necessary.[9]

Performance Goals States must set goals for the performance of students with disabilities. These goals must be consistent with any goals and standards the state has set for students in general.[10]

Accountability The new law requires states and school districts to gather and make public information that parents can use to hold schools accountable for how well their children do in school. First, states must set "performance indicators" they will use to assess how well the state is doing in educating children with disabilities, including at least performance on assessments, drop-out rates and graduation rates. The state must report to the public on how well it is doing on these indicators every two years. In addition, the state must make public statistics showing how children with disabilities fare on the general assessments given to all students, including how many are participating and how they achieve.[11] It must do the same regarding children who take alternate assessments.[12]

B. THE RIGHT TO EQUALLY EFFECTIVE EDUCATIONAL PROGRAMMING UNDER §504 AND THE ADA

Apart from any IDEA requirements, the §504 and ADA regulations require schools to provide the vast majority of students with disabilities with the instruction and supports necessary to allow them to learn what the general curriculum teaches, including the knowledge and skills called for by any standards the state has adopted for all students. These regulations may also require schools to change practices that hinder effective access to the general curriculum, or other instruction tied to the standards set for all students.

1. Comparable Benefits

The §504 regulations require public school systems to provide all children with disabilities a "free appropriate public education" consisting of "regular or special education and related aids and services that…are designed to meet individual educational needs…as adequately as the needs of nonhandicapped [sic] persons are met…."[13] The regulations also prohibit schools from affording qualified students with disabilities "an opportunity to participate in or benefit from…[an] aid, benefit or service that is not equal to that afforded others," providing "an aid, benefit, or service that is not as effective as that provided to others," or providing "different or separate aid, benefits, or services unless…necessary to provide…aid, benefits, or services that are as effective as those provided to others."[14] The ADA regulations applicable to state and local governmental services contain the same prohibitions.[15]

In order to be "equally effective" under these regulations, aids benefits and services "must afford…equal opportunity to obtain the same result, to gain the same benefit, or to reach the same level of achievement in the most integrated setting appropriate to the [student's] needs."[16] The opportunity to learn the general curriculum and to meet content and performance standards, define the inputs and outcomes, respectively, of a quality education — and so the "aid, benefit or service" that is public education. If students capable of participating, with or without appropriate services, are denied educational opportunities designed to allow them to learn in the general curriculum and attain the standards set for all students, they are provided instead an "aid, benefit or service that is not equal to that afforded others," that "is not as effective as that provided to others," and that is unnecessarily "different or separate," in violation of the §504 and ADA regulations.[17]

2. "Criteria and methods of administration" that Discriminate

The §504 regulations also make it illegal for school systems running programs to "utilize criteria or methods of administration (i) that have the effect of subjecting qualified handicapped [sic] persons to discrimination on the basis of handicap [sic],[or] (ii) that have the...effect of defeating or substantially impairing accomplishment of the objectives of the...program with respect to handicapped [sic] persons...."[18] The ADA regulations contain a similar ban.[19] "Criteria" are written policies; "methods of administration" are a school system's actual practices.

In public school systems, learning what is included in the standards and the general curriculum is one of the key "objectives of the program or activity."[20] "Criteria or methods of administration" that limit the opportunities for students with disabilities to receive the educational programming necessary for them to do so "have the...effect of defeating or substantially impairing the accomplishment of"[21] this objective, and constitute prohibited discrimination.

Avoiding such discrimination requires school systems to identify and examine policies and practices that may have the effect of limiting access to the kind of instruction necessary to attain the standards or otherwise achieve in the general curriculum. Depending upon the circumstances, any number of policies and practices might have this effect. Examples include lack of coordination (in terms of both scheduling and content) between pull-out programs like resource rooms and the mainstream academic curriculum; providing a diluted curriculum in programs and classes labeled as serving students with behavioral (or any other) disabilities;[22] inappropriate reliance upon punitive discipline, including disciplinary exclusion; and the failure to provide for the appropriate integration of special education supports and related services, including behavioral supports, into what are conceived of as regular education classes.[23]

NOTES

1. *See* 20 U.S.C. §1401(8).

2. The principle that the content of the education provided all students is an important part of the framework for designing special education services reflects Congress' purpose in enacting IDEA: Congress acted not only to end the complete exclusion of many children with disabilities from public education, but also in response to its finding that "more than half of the children with disabilities in the United States do not receive *appropriate* educational services which would enable them to have *full equali-*

ty of opportunity."20 U.S.C. §1400(c)(2)(B), formerly 20 U.S.C. §1400(b)(3) (emphasis added). Accordingly, IDEA and its implementing regulations require states and local school systems to adopt and implement a goal of providing "full educational opportunity" to all children with disabilities. *See* 20 U.S.C. §§1412(a)(2), 1413(a)(1); 34 C.F.R. §300.304.

3. *See Board of Education of the Hendrick Hudson Central School District v. Rowley*, 458 U.S. 176, 188-89, 102 S.Ct. 3034, 3042 (1982) ("[a]lmost as a checklist for adequacy under the Act, the definition [of FAPE] requires that such [specially designed] instruction and services be provided at public expense and under public supervision, *meet the State's educational standards*, approximate the grade levels *used in the State's regular education*, and comport with the child's IEP…Thus if personalized instruction is being provided with sufficient support services to permit the child to benefit from the instruction, *and the other items on the definitional checklist are satisfied*, the child is receiving a 'free appropriate public education' as defined by the Act") (emphasis added). *See also Carter v. Florence County School District No. 4*, 950 F.2d 156, 159- 60. (4th Cir. 1991), *affirmed*, 510 U.S. 7, 114 S.Ct. 361 (1993) ((agreeing with district court's conclusion that "the IEP's goals of a mere four months progress [per school year] in mathematics and reading allowed Shannon to 'continue to fall behind her classmates at an alarming rate' and therefore 'ensured the program's inadequacy from its inception'").

4. 20 U.S.C. §1414(b)(2)(A), (c)(1)(iv); 34 C.F.R. §§300.532(b), 300.533(a)(2)(iv).

5. 34 C.F.R. §300.26(b)(3).

6. 20 U.S.C. §1414(d)(1)(A), (d)(4); 34 C.F.R. §300.347.

7. 20 U.S.C. §§1414(d)(1)(B); 34 C.F.R. §300.344(a)(2), (4)(ii).

8. 20 U.S.C. §1412(a)(14) as amended, incorporating by reference 20 U.S.C. §1453(c)(3)(D)(vii); 20 U.S.C. §1413(a)(3)(A), incorporating by reference 20 U.S.C. § 1453(c)(3)(D)); 34 C.F.R. §300.382(g). *See also Timothy W. v. Rochester School District*, 875 F.2d 954, 966-67, 973 (1st Cir.), *cert. denied*, 493 U.S. 983, 110 S. Ct. 519 (1989) ("Congress clearly saw education for the handicapped as a dynamic process, in which new methodologies would be continually perfected, tried, and either adopted or discarded, so that the state's educational response to each…child's particular needs could be better met"; "…educational methodologies are not static, but are constantly evolving and improving. It is the school district's responsibility to avail itself of these new approaches in providing an education program geared to each child's individual needs.").

9. 20 U.S.C. §1412(a)(17)(A); 34 C.F.R. §300.138. For the small number of children who cannot participate even with accommodations, states and school districts must create alternate assessments. *Id.* .

10. 20 U.S.C. §1412(16); 34 C.F.R. §300.137. This means that the state cannot set separate, weaker standards for students with disabilities. Rather, the state must supplement the goals and standards it uses for all students with any additional ones required by the unique needs of children with disabilities.

11. This requirement applies only if doing so would be statistically valid and would not result in the disclosure of performance results identifiable to individual children. 20 U.S.C. §1412(a)(17)(B)(iii)(I); 34 C.F.R. §300.139(a)(2).

12. 20 U.S.C. §§1412(16), (17); 34 C.F.R. §300.139.

13. 34 C.F.R. §104.33(a), (b)(1).

14. 34 C.F.R. §§104.4(b)(1)(ii) - (iv).

15. *See* 28 C.F.R. §35.130(b)(1)(ii) - (iv).

16. 34 C.F.R. §104.4(b)(2); 28 C.F.R. §35.130(b)(1)(iii).

17. See, e.g., *Muscogee (GA) County School District*, EHLR 257:540 (OCR 6/30/84), where the U.S. Department of Education/Office for Civil Rights ("OCR") investigated a complaint involving the curriculum provided students in a separate program for high school students with cognitive impairments and learning disabilities. Students in the program were not taught biology, a subject required by state standards for receipt of a regular high school diploma. OCR found that the failure to offer biology violated the above-quoted regulations.

18. 34 C.F.R. §104.4(b)(4). OCR has defined "criteria" as written or formal policies, and "methods of administration" as a state or school system's actual practices and procedures. *Illinois State Bd. of Ed.*, 20 IDELR 687 (OCR 12/3/93).

19. *See* 28 C.F.R. §35.130(b)(3). *See also* 28 C.F.R. §35.130(b)(7) (public entity must make reasonable modifications in policies, practices or procedures when necessary to avoid discrimination on basis of disability, unless entity can demonstrate that modifications would fundamentally alter the nature of its program, service or activity); 28 C.F.R. §35.130(b)(8) (public entity may not impose or apply eligibility criteria that screen out or tend to screen out individuals with disabilities *or any class of individuals with disabilities* from fully and equally enjoying any service, program or activity unless such criteria can be shown to be necessary for provision of the service, program or activity being offered) (emphasis added).

20. 34 C.F.R. §104.4(b)(4)(ii).

21. 34 C.F.R. §104.4(b)(4)(ii).

22. *See also* 34 C.F.R. §104.34(c) (services provided in facilities identifiable as being for individuals with disabilities be comparable in quality to those provided to nondisabled individuals).

23. *Cf.* Judith E. Heumann and Thomas Hehir, U.S. Department of Education/Office of Special Education Programs Memorandum 95-5, November 23, 1994, *reprinted at* 21 IDELR 1152 (educational decisions under IDEA may not be based solely on administrative convenience or the configuration of the delivery system); *Response to Inquiry of Latshaw*, EHLR 213:124 (OSEP 3/1/88).

CHAPTER 4

A Closer Look at FAPE: Behavior as an Education Issue

IDEA entitles all eligible children with disabilities to a free appropriate public education ("FAPE") consisting of an appropriate elementary or secondary education along with necessary special education and related services in the least restrictive environment consistent with their individual needs. For students whose disabilities involve behavioral consequences, this right includes the right to the educational and related services necessary to effectively address the behavior and the problems underlying it.

In fact, securing appropriate education and services for children whose disabilities involve behavioral manifestations was a key reason for enactment of IDEA. When considering Public Law 94-142 (the law that later become known as IDEA) in 1975, Congress had before it statistics showing that 82% of those children classified as emotionally disturbed were unserved, and that many of those who were served were receiving inappropriate services.[1] At hearings concerning the proposed law, many people spoke of the lack of educational services that prevented students with behavioral manifestations from participating in and benefitting from education programs. These services included specialized diagnostic evaluations, individualized tutoring, behavioral support programs, psychological counseling, and self-help and self-care skills training programs.[2] Thus, an important part of the history of IDEA is the recognition that for children with behavioral manifestations, access to school must be accompanied by a right to programming that takes into account behavioral needs.

A. THE RIGHT TO EFFECTIVE BEHAVIOR SERVICES AND SUPPORTS AS A COMPONENT OF FAPE: THE BROAD MEANING OF EDUCATION UNDER IDEA

Despite this history, many schools still fail to address appropriately the behavioral consequences of disability. Some ignore this duty altogether. Others provide what may be called behavioral programming, but in reality focuses exclusively on controlling the child in school. Rather than addressing behavior and its roots as part and parcel of the child's educational and developmental needs, behavior often is viewed narrowly as something to be "managed" or "controlled" so as not to disrupt classroom activities. Behavioral needs are treated as "add ons" to education — often in the form of "behavior management plans" — rather than as educational needs in their own right, to be addressed by specially designed instruction and support services. Similarly, behavioral manifestations are often viewed as relevant areas of educational concern (apart from discipline) only to the extent that they prevent a child from making sufficient *academic* progress, or deriving sufficient "benefit" from the education already being provided.

These approaches violate the duty to provide FAPE. IDEA embraces the broad understanding of education reflected in the hearings discussed above. The broad concept of education under IDEA encompasses, among other things, a child's unique social and emotional needs as well as his or her academic ones.[3] For children whose disabilities entail behavioral consequences, FAPE thus requires "special education" (meaning, as discussed in Chapter 2, specially designed instruction) aimed at behavioral issues, as well as any necessary behaviorally-related "related services."

Depending upon the circumstances, the duty to address the behavioral manifestations of disability as a component of FAPE may extend to behavior exhibited outside of school. Thus in one case, a court held that the school system's proposed placement did not provide a free appropriate public education because, although the child did relatively well in the familiar and contained environment of the school, in less familiar settings, or where relatively unsupervised, he had significant problems with self-control in his interactions with others.[4] Similarly, in another case, a court rejected as insufficient and a denial of FAPE a school's attempt at behavior management, noting that to the extent that the child at times behaved appropriately in class, "it is only because a teacher or other adult is literally standing over him," and that "[c]learly such a dependency building approach does nothing and in fact may make it more difficult to enable Cory to behave in a regular classroom or in the real world."[5]

The IDEA Amendments of 1997 underscore one aspect of schools' duty to address behavior. As amended by the 1997 legislation, the Act provides that as a "special factor," "in the case of a child whose behavior impedes his or her learning or that of others," the IEP team shall "consider, when appropriate, strategies, including positive behavioral interventions, strategies, and supports to address that behavior."[6] This provision makes explicit in the statute the long- standing IDEA requirement, derived from the statutory definitions of "FAPE," "special education," and "related services," that schools provide the behavioral supports necessary to sustain in-school learning. It does not limit or diminish other aspects of the duty to address behavior similarly derived from these definitions, including those discussed above.

B. THE RIGHT TO EFFECTIVE BEHAVIOR SERVICES AND SUPPORTS AS A COMPONENT OF LRE RIGHTS

IDEA's mandate that all children receive their education in the least restrictive environment ("LRE") is a second, independent source of schools' legal duty to address behavior. The LRE-based duty to address behavior has two aspects: (1) the provision of services necessary to alleviate barriers to regular education classroom learning, and (2) the provision of services that recognize behavioral issues as a subject of education in their own right. Failure to provide either type of service may violate LRE rights.

As discussed in Chapter 2, IDEA requires states and school systems to ensure that children with disabilities receive their education in regular education settings alongside peers without disabilities to the maximum extent appropriate. Exclusion from regular education settings is allowed only when the nature or severity of a child's disability prevents his or her education from being "achieved satisfactorily" in that setting even with the use of supplementary aids and services.[7] Most courts that have considered the issue have ruled that, in determining whether a child's education can be "achieved satisfactorily" in the regular education classroom, schools may take into account the extent to which a child's behavior would be disruptive there.[8] At the same time, however, courts have also recognized that the failure to provide appropriate behavioral supports, interventions and services *within* the regular education classroom may cause the objected-to "disruption," thereby setting a child up for failure and/or creating the alleged justification for exclusion.[9] Such failure by schools violates LRE rights.[10] As discussed in Chapter 2, as an integral part of the IEP development process, schools must consider the whole range of behaviorally oriented services that might make regular classroom placement work.[11]

Failure to address behavioral manifestations with appropriate services may also violate the LRE rights of children properly placed, for the time being, in separate, more restrictive settings. The right to be educated in the LRE encompasses the right to services that will enable a child to move into less restrictive educational settings. Where children are denied the behaviorally oriented services they need in order to reach the point where their education can be achieved satisfactorily in regular education classes, this aspect of LRE rights is violated.[12]

It is also important to remember that the right to education in regular education settings embraces the right to effective opportunities to learn in the regular curriculum as well as physical presence in the regular classroom.[13] Furthermore, as discussed in Chapter 3, independent provisions of IDEA and the §504 regulations protect the right of children with disabilities to full opportunity for equal participation and meaningful learning in the regular, or general curriculum. When behavioral manifestations affect a child's ability to learn and progress in the general curriculum, schools must provide appropriate services to address them, and to allow opportunities for the equal participation and meaningful learning that IDEA and §504 require.[*] All too frequently, however, children's behavioral needs are not appropriately addressed, and they are unlawfully placed in separate settings that offer an inferior, diluted curriculum. Parents and advocates should be alert to these issues, and work to ensure that behavioral issues do not result in *either* inappropriate exclusion from the regular classroom *or* exclusion from the general curriculum.

C. State of the Art Practices

IDEA expressly requires states to acquire and disseminate significant knowledge derived from educational research and other sources to teach-

---

[*] As discussed in Chapter 2, the §504 regulations require schools to provide regular or special education and related aids and services to children who need them. Thus a child with a disability that involves behavioral manifestations may be entitled under §504 to related aids and services to address behavior even if he or she does not need (or is not eligible for) special education.

ers, administrators, school board members, and related services personnel, and to adopt, when appropriate, promising practices, materials, and technology.[14] Local school districts must do the same.[15] As one court has explained,

> "[t]he law explicitly recognizes…that educational methodologies are not static, but are constantly evolving and improving. It is the school district's responsibility to avail itself of these new approaches in providing an education program geared to each child's individual needs."[16]

Implementation and enforcement of these obligations is critical if schools are to abandon outmoded, limited and ineffective practices that focus on control and punishment, in favor of approaches that do in fact provide a free appropriate public education in the least restrictive environment.

NOTES

1. H.R. Rep. No. 332, 94th Cong., 1st Sess., at n.12 (1975); S. Rep. No. 168, 94th Cong., 1st. Sess., at 5-8 (1975), *reprinted in* 1976 U.S.C.C.A.N. 1425.

2. *Education for All Handicapped Children Act, 1973-74: Hearings on S.6 Before the Subcommittee on the Handicapped of the Senate Committee on Labor and Public Welfare*, 93d Cong., 1st Sess. (1973-74) at 45, 87, 797, 809, 813, 790, 833.

3. *County of San Diego v. California Special Education Hearing Office*, 93 F.3d 1458, 1467 (9th Cir. 1996) (ìeducational benefit is not limited to academic needs, but includes the social and emotional needs that affect academic progress, school behavior, and socializationî); *Seattle School District No. 1 v. B.S.*, 82 F.3d 1493, 1500 (9th Cir. 1996) ("[e]veryone agrees that A.S. is exceptionally bright and thus able to test appropriately on standardized tests. This is not the sine qua non of `educational benefit,' however. The term 'unique educational needs' [shall] be broadly construed to include…academic, social, health, emotional, communicative, physical and vocational needs"). *See also, e.g., Babb v. Knox County School System*, 965 F.2d 104, 109 (6th Cir.), *cert. denied*, 506 U.S. 941, 113 S.Ct. 380 (1992) (education under IDEA encompasses "both academic instruction and a broad range of associated services traditionally grouped under the general rubric of `treatment'"). For examples of other cases stressing the broad meaning of education under IDEA, see *Timothy W. v. Rochester School District*, 875 F.2d 954, 962 (1st Cir.), *cert. denied*, 493 U.S. 983, 110 S.Ct. 519 (1989) ("the Act's concept of special education is broad, encompassing not only traditional cognitive skills, but basic functional skills as well"); *Kruelle v. New Castle County School District*, 642 F.2d 687, 693-94 (3rd Cir. 1981) ("the concept of education is necessarily broad…[w]here basic self-help…skills…are lacking, formal education begins at that point"); *Battle v. Commonwealth of Pennsylvania*, 629 F.2d 269, 275 (3rd Cir. 1980), *cert. denied*, 452 U.S. 968 (1981) (same); *Mohawk Trail Regional School District v. Shaun D.*, 35 F. Supp. 2d 34, 42-44 (D. Mass. 1999)

(discussing and rejecting school systemís contention that it need not provide services to address sexually inappropriate behavior of a student diagnosed with post traumatic stress disorder, mental retardation, pedophilia and other intertwined emotional, social and behavioral conditions). *Cf. Stacey G. v. Pasadena Independent School District*, 547 F. Supp. 61, 77 (S.D. Tex. 1982) ("...an essential element of an appropriate education for a child as handicapped as Stacey is an opportunity to develop skills that would allow Stacey to be as self-sufficient as possible and to function outside of an institution").

4. *David D. v. Dartmouth School Committee*, 775 F.2d 411, 423 (1st Cir. 1985), *cert. denied*, 475 U.S. 1140, 106 S.Ct. 1790 (1986). *But see Devine v. Indian River Co. School Board*, 249 F.3d 1289 (11th Cir. 2001).

5. *Chris D. and Cory M. v. Montgomery County Bd. of Ed.*, 753 F. Supp. 922 , 933 (M.D. Ala. 1990).

6. 20 U.S.C. §1414(d)(3)(B). *See also* 20 U.S.C. §1415(k)(1)(B) (requiring functional behavior assessment and implementation/revision of behavioral intervention plan after disciplinary actions); 20 U.S.C. §1415(k)(3) (requiring that the "interim alternative educational setting" into which children may be placed following certain incidents involving dangerous weapons or drugs, or upon a finding by a hearing officer that maintaining a child in his or her current placement is substantially likely to result in injury to the child or others, include services to address the behavior that triggered the placement change).

7. 20 U.S.C. §1412(a)(5)(A). The U.S. Department of Education regulations implementing Section 504 of the Rehabilitation Act of 1973, 29 U.S.C. §794, contain the same requirement. *See* 34 C.F.R. §104.34(a). *See also* 28 C.F.R. §35.130(d) (implementing Title II of the Americans with Disabilities Act, 42 U.S.C. §12132 *et seq.*) (public entities "shall administer services, programs, and activities in the most integrated setting appropriate to the needs of qualified individuals with disabilities"); 28 C.F.R. §35.130(b)(2) ("[a] public entity may not deny a qualified individual with a disability the opportunity to participate in services, programs, or activities that are not separate or different, despite the existence of permissibly separate or different programs or activities").

8. *Hartmann v. Loudon Co. Bd. of Ed.*, 118 F.3d 996 (4th Cir. 1997), *cert. denied*, 522 U.S. 1046, 118 S.Ct. 688 (1998); *Bd. of Ed. Sacramento City Unified School District v. Holland*, 14 F.3d 1398 (9th Cir. 1994), *affirming* 786 F. Supp. 874 (E.D. Cal. 1992), *cert. denied*, 512 U.S. 1207, 114 S.Ct. 2679 (1994); *Oberti v. Bd. of Ed. of Borough of Clementon School District*, 995 F.2d 1204 (3rd Cir. 1993); *Daniel R.R. v. State Bd. of Ed.*, 874 F.2d 1036 (5th Cir. 1989).

9. *Oberti, supra*; *Mavis v. Sobol*, 839 F. Supp. 968 (N.D.N.Y. 1994). *Cf. Morgan v. Chris L.*, 25 IDELR 227, 230 (6th Cir. 1997), *affirming* 927 F. Supp. 267 (E.D. Tenn. 1994), *cert. denied*, 520 U.S. 1271, 117 S.Ct. 2448 (1997) ("[w]hen school systems fail to accommodate a disabled student's behavioral problems, these problems may be attributed to the school system's failure to comply with the requirements of the IDEA"); *Stuart v. Nappi*, 443 F. Supp. 1235, 1241 (D. Conn. 1978) (school's "handling of the plaintiff may have contributed to her disruptive behavior"); *Howard S. v. Friendswood School District*, 454 F. Supp. 634, 640 (S.D. Tex. 1978)(finding that plaintiff, whom school officials sought to expel following a suicide attempt and hospitalization, "was not afforded a free, appropriate public education during the period

from the time he enrolled in high school until December of 1976, [which] was...a contributing and proximate cause of his emotional difficulties and emotional disturbance"); *Frederick L. v. Thomas*, 408 F. Supp. 832, 835 (E.D. Penn. 1976) (recognizing that an inappropriate educational placement can cause antisocial behavior).

10. *Oberti, supra*; *Mavis, supra*.

11. *Oberti, supra*, 995 F.2d at 1216 ("the school must consider the whole range of supplementary aids and services, including...special education training for the regular teacher, behavior modification programs, or any other available aids or services appropriate to the child's particular disabilities"); *Greer v. Rome City School District*, 950 F.2d 688, 696 (11th Cir. 1991), *opinion withdrawn and remanded on other grounds*, 956 F.2d 1025 (11th Cir. 1992), *previous opinion reinstated by rehearing en banc*, 967 F.2d 470 (11th Cir. 1992) ("prior to and during the development of the IEP" a school "must consider...the whole range of supplemental aids and services...for which it is obligated under [IDEA] and the regulations promulgated thereunder to make provision").

12. *Chris D. and Cory M., supra.*

13. *See Board of Education of the Hendrick Hudson Central School District v. Rowley*, 458 U.S. 176, 202-203, 102 S.Ct. 3034, 3049 (1982) ("[w]hen that `mainstreaming' preference...has been met and a child is being educated in the regular classrooms of a public school system...the system itself monitors the educational progress of the child. Regular examinations are administered, grades are awarded, and yearly advancements to higher grade levels are permitted for those children who attain an adequate knowledge of the course material. The grading and advancement system thus constitutes an important factor in determining educational benefit."). *See also* Judith E. Heumann and Thomas Hehir, U.S. Department of Education/Office of Special Education Programs, Memorandum 95-5, November 23, 1994, *reprinted at* 21 IDELR 1152 (individualized determination must be made for each child as to "the extent that the student will be able to participate in regular education programs").

14. 20 U.S.C. §1412(a)(14), incorporating by reference 20 U.S.C. §1453(c)(3)(D)(vii). *See also* 34 C.F.R. §300.382(g) (1999).

15. 20 U.S.C. §1413(a)(3)(A) (local educational agencies must ensure that all personnel necessary to carry out this part are appropriately and adequately prepared, consistent with the requirements of section 1453(c)(3)(D)).

16. *Timothy W., supra*, 875 F.2d at 973. See also 875 F. 2d at 966-967, discussing the history of amendments to IDEA, noting the "thesis present in the original Act, that it is the state's responsibility to experiment, refine, and improve upon the educational services it provides," and observing that "Congress clearly saw education for the handicapped as a dynamic process, in which new methodologies would be continually perfected, tried, and either adopted or discarded, so that the state's educational response to each handicapped child's particular needs could be better met."

CHAPTER 5

EDUCATIONAL EVALUATIONS: PURPOSE, SCOPE, RIGHTS AND SAFEGUARDS

Educational evaluations are the cornerstone of quality education for students with disabilities. Beyond determining whether a child is eligible for services and protections under IDEA and §504, proper evaluations assess the consequences of a child's disability, identify all of a child's areas of educational need and provide the information necessary to develop services and strategies for meeting those needs. Good evaluations are key to success in the general curriculum, to success in the least restrictive environment and to success in addressing all other educational needs arising from a student's disability.

IDEA and the §504 regulations address many aspects of educational evaluations. As discussed below, the law speaks to such issues as a school's duty to evaluate, the scope and content of evaluations, evaluation criteria, discrimination in the evaluation process, evaluation of children whose first language is other than English, and procedural rights and safeguards. Many details, however — such as the particular tests or other assessment tools that should be used to evaluate a child for a particular disability or the kind of expertise those conducting particular evaluations should have — are largely left to each state to regulate. Parents and advocates should therefore review their own state's regulations and standards.

A. THE DUTY TO EVALUATE

Both IDEA and §504 require states and school systems to take affirmative steps to identify, locate and evaluate all children in the state or system who have disabilities and need special education and related services.[1] Under IDEA, this obligation is known as the "child find" requirement. It extends to *all* children aged birth through 21, including highly mobile children (such as migrant and homeless children) and children who are advancing from grade to grade, but may have a disability and need services nonetheless.[2] Both laws also require school systems to conduct a comprehensive, individual evaluation meeting certain criteria *before* providing special education services for the first time.[3]

The school system's legal duty to identify and evaluate students who need, or may need, special education or related services lasts for as long as the student remains of school age. IDEA requires that a child be reevaluated whenever conditions so warrant, or if the child's parent or teacher requests a re-evaluation; at a minimum, a re-evaluation must be conducted at least once every three years.[4] In addition, a school system must conduct a re-evaluation before determining that a child is no longer a child with a disability under IDEA, meaning that he or she no longer needs special education and related services as a result of having one of the disabilities listed in the Act.[5] The §504 regulations require "periodic re-evaluation of students who have been provided special education and related services," as well as evaluations prior to any "significant change in placement."[6]

Various developments over the course of a child's school career may trigger the need for an initial or re-evaluation. For example, a sudden change in academic performance or behavior may suggest the need for an evaluation, whether or not the child has previously been identified as having a disability and/or needing special education or related services.[7] Similarly, psychiatric hospitalization should trigger an evaluation of a student's need for services under IDEA, or for special or regular education and related services under §504.[8]

B. NATURE AND SCOPE OF EDUCATIONAL EVALUATIONS

The evaluation has three purposes: (1) to determine whether a child has a disability; (2) to gather information about his or her educational needs; and (3) to help determine effective strategies for meeting those needs.[9] This includes gathering the information needed for designing the services and supports the child will need to learn in the general curriculum, and in regular education classes.[10]

The evaluation must be comprehensive, and must assess the child in all areas related to his or her disability(ies) (or suspected disability(ies)) including, where appropriate, health, vision, hearing, social and emotional status, general intelligence, academic performance, communicative status, and motor abilities.[11] The evaluation must be comprehensive enough to identify *all* of the child's special education and related services needs, *regardless of whether or not they are commonly linked to his or her particular disability category.*[12]

Decisions about whether a child has a disability, or about the kind of educational services he or she needs, cannot be based upon a single test or other procedure. On the contrary, evaluations must use a variety of assessment tools tailored to assess specific areas of educational need, not just general "IQ."[13]

C. PROTECTIONS IN THE EVALUATION PROCESS

1. Notice and Consent

Notice Under IDEA, a school system must give a parent prior written notice any time it proposes to conduct an evaluation.[14] Written notice is also required if the system refuses a parent's request for an evaluation.[15] These IDEA notice requirements apply to an initial evaluation designed to determine for the first time whether a child needs special education services, as well as to subsequent evaluations and re-evaluations.[16] The §504 regulations, too, require prior notice of evaluations.[17]

IDEA requires that notice be written in language understandable to the general public and given to the parent in his or her native language (unless this is clearly not feasible).[18] If the parent's native language (or other mode of communication) is not a written one, the school must have the notice translated orally, or by some other means, to the parent in his or her native language (or other mode of communication); ensure that the parent understands the notice; and ensure that there is written evidence that the school system has met these requirements.[19]

IDEA and the regulations also spell out detailed requirements governing the content of the notice.[20] These content requirements also apply to a number of other situations in which schools must give prior written notice, and are discussed in Chapter 8.

Consent IDEA requires schools to obtain *informed* parental *consent* before conducting any evaluation or re-evaluation.[21] In the case of re-evaluations, however, the school can proceed without consent if it has taken reasonable measures to obtain consent, but the parent has not responded.[22]

The term "informed" was added to IDEA in 1997, and is not defined in the law. However, its addition suggests that the standard of consent required has been heightened, strengthening the duty of school personnel to fully explain all relevant information and considerations to parents (including discussing risks and benefits, as well as potential consequences of giving or withholding consent) so that they are fully informed; to ensure that parents understand; and to ensure that any consent given is truly voluntary.[23]

If parents refuse to consent to an evaluation or re-evaluation, the school system may seek to pursue an evaluation by using the mediation or due process procedures generally available under IDEA to resolve disputes between parents and schools (see Chapter 8), unless doing so would be inconsistent with state law regarding parental consent.[24]

2. Criteria and Safeguards

Under IDEA, tests and other evaluation materials must be chosen and administered so as not to be racially or culturally discriminatory.[25] IDEA evaluation standards also:

- require school systems to assess a child in all areas related to the suspected disability, including, where appropriate, health, vision, hearing, social and emotional status, general intelligence, academic performance, communicative status and motor abilities;[26]

- require schools to use assessment tools and strategies that provide information that will directly assist professionals and parents to determine the child's educational needs;[27]

- require schools to provide and administer tests and other evaluation materials in the child's native language or other primary way in which the child communicates, unless this is clearly not feasible;[28]

- require schools, when evaluating children with limited English proficiency, to choose and administer evaluation tools in a way that ensures that they measure the child's disability (if any) and special education needs, rather than his or her English language skills;[29]

- require schools to use a variety of assessment tools and strategies to gather information about the child (including information from parents) needed to determine whether the child has a disability and needs special education, to enable the child to be involved and progress in the general curriculum, and to design an IEP;[30]

- prohibit school systems from using a single test or other procedure as the sole basis for deciding that a child is a child with a disability, or for designing an appropriate educational program for the child;[31] and

- require that if for some reason an assessment is not conducted under standard conditions, the evaluation report describe how it differed from standard conditions.[32]

In addition, both IDEA and §504 require school systems to ensure that:

- standardized tests and other evaluation materials have been proven valid for the specific purpose for which they are being used;

- tests and other evaluation materials are administered by trained and knowledgeable people following the instructions provided by the producer;

- the tests and other evaluation materials they use include methods designed to assess specific areas of educational need and not just IQ; and

- test results of children with impaired hearing or vision or manual or speaking skills actually reflect the child's aptitude, achievement or other factor being measured, rather than simply reflecting the fact that his or her vision, hearing, speaking skills or manual skills are impaired, unless the purpose of the test is to measure vision, hearing, speaking or manual skills.[33]

D. PROCEDURES FOR EVALUATIONS UNDER IDEA

1. Procedures for all students

Review of existing evaluation data The IDEA Amendments of 1997 added new evaluation procedures to the law. Now, at the start of an initial evaluation "if appropriate," and of any re-evaluation, a group consisting of the child's parent, the rest of the child's IEP team, and "other qualified professionals" review existing evaluation data and other information about the child, including evaluations and information provided by the parent, current classroom-based assessments and observations, and the observations of teachers and related services providers.[34] On the basis of this group review, including input from the child's parents, the group then decides what additional information, "if any," is needed to determine:

- whether the child has or continues to have one of the disabilities that may trigger IDEA eligibility;

- whether he or she needs or continues to need special education and related services;

- the child's present levels of performance and educational needs;

- what additions or changes in the child's education services are needed to enable him or her to participate and progress in the general curriculum;

- and what additions or changes in services are needed to enable him or her to meet the annual goals set out in the IEP.[35]

The school system then must arrange for the assessments (or other procedures or tests) needed to obtain this additional information.[36]

As part of a re-evaluation, but *not* as part of an initial evaluation, the group may on rare occasions conclude that no new data are needed [37] — and, so, that no new assessments will be done.* When this occurs, the school system must notify the parents of this decision, and the reasons for it. Parents then have the right to nonetheless request, and obtain from the school system, a new assessment to determine whether the student continues to be a "child with a disability" *as defined by IDEA*.[38] As discussed in Chapter 1, the definition under IDEA of a "child with a disability" has two parts, so that a "child with a disability" is a child who: (1) has one of the disabilities listed in IDEA *and* (2) needs specialized instruction and related services as a result.[39] The assessment must address *both* of these prongs of the definition of "child with a disability." However, the school system need not conduct the assessment unless the parent so requests.[40]

Two points are particularly important to remember. First, when parents *do* make such a request, it is binding; the school system *must* conduct, or arrange for, the assessment. Second, the assessment must be designed to determine not simply whether the child continues to have a disability listed in IDEA, but also *whether he or she needs special education and related services as a result of that disability*. This is an individualized determination. In order to make this determination, it would appear that the assessment(s) at a minimum need to address (1) the actual, current impact of the disability on the child's learning, academic, communicative, behavioral, social and emotional status; (2) the child's current levels of educational performance, including how that performance compares to what is expected of all children in the general curriculum; (3) any non-academic educational needs related to the disability; and (4) what specialized instruction and related services the child needs in light of what is learned in (1) - (3).

---

* Given the breadth and depth of the determinations to be made as part of the review, the fact that re-evaluations often are performed only once every three years, the developmental and other changes children undergo over time, and IDEA's emphasis on achievement in the general curriculum, determinations that no additional information and no new assessments are needed should be quite rare. A parent who disagrees with a decision that no new information and assessments are needed has the right to file a complaint and have a due process hearing on the issue, as discussed in Chapter 8.

Group members It is also important to keep in mind that the group review-ing existing evaluation data in order to decide what additional informa-tion is necessary — and, so, what, if any, tests or other assessments will be done as part of the evaluation — must include "qualified profession-als" *in addition to* the members of the child's IEP team. While neither IDEA itself nor the regulations specify who these qualified professionals must be, the inclusion of this provision in the law reflects Congress' recognition that IEP teams (as their composition is defined by the statute) alone do not have the knowledge and skills needed to interpret existing evaluation data, identify gaps, and determine how to fill them. The "qual-ified professionals" who supplement the IEP team must bring this expert-ise to the group, of which they must be an integral part, and enable it to make the four determinations listed above *in regard to this particular child*. At a minimum, it would seem that in order to do so, these qualified professionals must include individuals with special expertise in the child's disability or disabilities (or suspected disability); the potential developmental and educational consequences of the particular disability (including, for example, behavior manifestations or language develop-ment issues); the variety of assessment options for gathering information about needs in the general curriculum as well as other disability-related needs; in interpreting (and understanding the limits of) existing evalua-tion data and other information about the child; and, where the child has limited English proficiency, in the identification, assessment and educa-tion of limited English proficient students.

Meetings As noted above, IDEA requires that the review of existing evalua-tion data, including decisions about what additional information is neces-sary, be done by the *group* (comprised of the IEP team, which includes par-ents, and the other qualified professionals described above). The IDEA reg-ulations, however, state that this group may conduct its review without actu-ally having a meeting.[41] It is difficult to imagine, though, how group mem-bers, including parents, can interact to review information, contribute to one another's deliberations their own particular individual expertise (required, by law, to inform the review), and come to group decisions on the five required issues without meeting. While some schools may offer creative alternatives such as telephone conference calls or other interactive "high tech" methods for conducting these group activities, it is far more likely that meetings will be required in the vast majority of cases. If schools do not arrange for them, parents and their advocates should request them.

2. Additional Procedures for Evaluating Students Suspected of Having Specific Learning Disabilities

The standards described above apply to all evaluations, regardless of the student's disability or suspected disability. Additional IDEA requirements apply when a school system evaluates a student it suspects has a specific learning disability.

First, the decision as to whether a child suspected of having a learning disability is a "child with a disability" under IDEA must be made by the child's parents and a team of qualified professionals.[42] This team must include the child's regular teacher and at least one person qualified to conduct individual diagnostic tests of children (such as a school psychologist, speech-language pathologist or remedial reading teacher).[43] If the child does not have a regular teacher, the team must include instead a regular classroom teacher qualified to teach a child of his or her age; and if he or she is younger than school age, an individual qualified to teach a child of that age must be on the team.[44]

As part of the evaluation, at least one member of the team other than the child's regular teacher must observe his or her academic performance in the regular classroom. If the child is not in school, whether because he or she is too young or for some other reason, a team member must observe him or her in a setting appropriate for the child's age.[45] The team may determine that a child has a specific learning disability if:

(1) when provided with learning experiences appropriate for his or her age and ability levels, the child does not achieve what would be expected for someone of his or her age and ability in

- oral expression,
- listening comprehension,
- written expression,
- basic reading skill,
- reading comprehension,
- mathematics calculation, or
- mathematics reasoning;

AND

(2) the team finds that there is a "severe discrepancy" between the child's intellectual ability and what he or she is actually achieving in one or more of these listed areas.[46]

Neither IDEA nor its regulations define "severe discrepancy"; whether a severe discrepancy exists is determined by state law and standards.[47]

The team may not label a child as having a specific learning disability if the "severe discrepancy" between intellectual ability and actual achievement primarily results from environmental, cultural or economic disadvantage; a visual, hearing, or motor impairment; mental retardation; or emotional disturbance.[48]

The team's conclusions must be presented in a written report that states and explains:

- whether the child has a specific learning disability;
- the basis for the determination that the child does or does not have a specific learning disability;
- the relevant behavior noted during the required observation of the child;
- the relationship between the behavior observed and the child's academic functioning;
- any educationally relevant medical findings;
- whether there is a "severe discrepancy" between achievement and ability that cannot be corrected unless the child is provided with special education and related services; and
- the team's determination concerning the effects of environmental, cultural or economic disadvantage.[49]

In addition, each team member must certify in writing whether or not the report reflects his or her conclusion; a team member who disagrees must submit a separate written statement presenting his or her own conclusions.[50]

E. INTERPRETATION AND USE OF EVALUATION RESULTS

Evaluation results will be used first to determine whether the child has a disability and meets IDEA and/or §504 eligibility criteria. Under IDEA, "a group of qualified professionals" *and the child's parent* determine whether the child is an eligible child with a disability.[51] The §504 regulations call for evaluation data to be considered by a group of people, including individuals knowledgeable about the child.[52] As an IDEA matter, the school system must document the eligibility determination in writing, and provide the parent with a copy of both the eligibility determination and the evaluation report.[53] The eligibility determination must be provided in the parent's native language or mode of communication, unless this is clearly not feasible.[54] Although IDEA does not explicitly address translation of evaluation reports, it would seem that in order to comply with requirements regarding parent participation in IEP and placement meetings and decisions (as discussed in detail in Chapter 6), informed consent and the right to challenge school decisions (as discussed in Chapter 8), as well as to make meaningful for all parents and children the parent participation at the core of IDEA, schools must translate these reports into parents' native language.[55] Title VI of the Civil Rights Act of 1964 and the regulations implementing it, [56] which prohibit discrimination on the basis of race and national origin, should also require translation.[57]

In addition to the eligibility determination and evaluation report required by IDEA, both IDEA and the §504 regulations, as well as the Family Educational Rights and Privacy Act, give parents (and their authorized representatives) the right to examine any of their child's other education records pertaining to the evaluation (or to anything else).[58] This right includes the right to have school personnel explain and interpret these records.[59] As discussed in further detail in Chapter 8, the right to review these and all other education records may also include the right to obtain copies.

If a child is found eligible under IDEA or §504, evaluation results will then be used to develop educational goals, along with corresponding objectives or benchmarks; design specialized instruction to allow the child to achieve in the general curriculum, and to meet other disability-related needs, including, for example, communication needs, behavioral needs and assistive technology needs; decide upon the educational settings in which the child will receive educational services; and determine what kind of related services, aids and supplementary services will be necessary.

School systems may not use any single test or other evaluation tool— such as an IQ test— as the sole basis for determining whether a child has a disability and needs special education, or for determining what will constitute an appropriate educational program for him or her.[60] In addition, a child may not be found eligible for services under IDEA if the "determinant factor" for finding him or her eligible is a lack of instruction in reading or math, or limited English proficiency.[61] However, a child who has been denied instruction in reading or math, or who has limited

English proficiency, and who meets the IDEA definition of an eligible "child with a disability" *independently* of these two factors *is* eligible and entitled to a free appropriate public education.

In interpreting and using evaluation results, school systems must:

- draw upon information from a variety of sources, including aptitude and achievement tests, parent input, teacher recommendations, physical condition, social or cultural background and adaptive behavior;*

- ensure that information obtained from all of these sources is carefully documented and considered; and

- ensure that people knowledgeable about the meaning of the evaluation data participate in decisions regarding the child's educational program.[62]

Many of the tests and other procedures used in educational evaluations have been criticized by educators, psychologists, researchers and others as invalid for the purposes they are intended to serve, as racially or culturally biased, or as inaccurate for other reasons. Tests or other evaluation tools appropriate for some children may be inappropriate — and produce misleading results — for others. A great deal has been written on this subject, and parents and advocates should be prepared to scrutinize this issue carefully, particularly if the parent's assessment of the child differs from that of the evaluation team and/or the child is a member of a racial, ethnic or language minority.[63]

F. Right to an Independent Educational Evaluation

1. Independent Evaluations at Private Expense

Parents who disagree with an evaluation conducted by (or for) a school system, or who simply want a second opinion, always have the right to obtain a second, "independent educational evaluation" — that is, a second evaluation performed by someone who is not employed by the school

---

* The required social and cultural information should include information concerning the influences associated with socioeconomic status (e.g. health, nutrition, housing, access to books, etc.); family, cultural and educational background; language; degree of familiarity with the cultural concepts on which test items are based; and opportunities to learn the kind of information and have the kinds of experiences that tests assume. See American Educational Research Assn., American Psychological Assn. and National Council on Measurement in Education, Standards for Educational and Psychological Testing (1999) at pages 82 (standard 7.5), 83 (standard 7.10), 117-18 (standard 11.20) and 149 (standard13.15).

system — at their own expense, or at the expense of an agreeable evaluator or other outside party. Ordinarily, school systems must consider the results of any such evaluation when making decisions about the child's education.[64]

2. Independent Evaluations at Public Expense

Under certain circumstances, parents also have a right to an independent evaluation at *public expense* — most commonly the school system's.[65] Parents who disagree with a school- conducted or school-initiated evaluation have a *right* under IDEA to obtain an independent one at public expense unless the school system requests a due process hearing (described in Chapter 8) and then demonstrates that its own evaluation was "appropriate."[66] The right to an independent evaluation is triggered *each time* the school system conducts an evaluation, regardless of whether it is an initial evaluation or a re-evaluation.[67] A school system may not set a timeline or deadline within which parents must request a re-evaluation.[68]

In addition to defending its own evaluation as "appropriate" at a hearing, a school may also challenge a parent's right to an independent evaluation at public expense by demonstrating at a hearing that the independent evaluation did not meet the school system's criteria for evaluations.[69] Often state regulations and/or individual school systems require an independent evaluation to meet certain criteria if the school system is to pay for it. *Parents and advocates should check these local and state requirements before obtaining an independent evaluation.* Parents and advocates should also check to see if their state statute or regulations provide more liberal access to publicly-funded independent evaluations than does IDEA.

When a parent requests an independent evaluation, the school must provide information about where independent evaluations may be obtained, and the criteria or conditions that may apply if the school system is to pay.[70] Some school systems keep lists of independent evaluators it deems qualified, and attempt to limit parents to evaluators on the list. Depending upon the circumstances, this practice runs the risk of unlawfully limiting the right to an independent evaluation. The U.S. Department of Education/Office of Special Education Programs (OSEP), which enforces IDEA, has stated that if the list does not include all of the qualified independent evaluators within the geographic area, or if the list does not include evaluators who can appropriately evaluate a specific child, parents cannot be limited to choosing from the list.[71]

In regard to qualifications and other conditions, a state or school system may not apply stricter criteria to independent evaluations than it applies to evaluations conducted or initiated by school systems.[72] The IDEA statute itself says nothing about the kind, if any, of restrictions states and local school systems may place on publicly-funded evaluations — or even their authority to do so. The IDEA regulations state only that:

> "If an independent evaluation is at public expense, the criteria under which the evaluation is obtained, including the location of the evaluation and the qualifications of the examiner, must be the same as the criteria which the public agency uses when it initiates an evaluation, to the extent those criteria are consistent with the parent's right to an independent evaluation."[73]

It is important to note that under this regulation, schools may not impose any conditions that undermine the statutory right to an independent evaluation. No matter what the condition — and regardless of whether it might be permissible in other cases — schools must waive it if a child's unique needs so require. For example, a rule requiring evaluations to be performed in-state would have to be waived for a child whose unique needs required expertise not available within the state.[74]

Beyond the examples of location and qualifications mentioned in the regulation, OSEP, however, has taken the position that states and school systems may also set a ceiling on the cost of independent evaluations, subject to two conditions. First, the maximum fee must allow parents to choose among the various evaluators in the area qualified to conduct the specific test or procedure in question, eliminating only "unreasonably excessive" fees; districts cannot simply calculate the average of fees charged by various evaluators in the area for a particular procedure and declare that the maximum.[75] Second, districts must waive the maximum fee and pay for a more expensive evaluation where a child's unique circumstances so require.[76]

Parents do *not* have to obtain school system approval before obtaining an independent evaluation, explain their reasons for disagreeing with the school's evaluation, or even notify the school system in advance.[77] However, parents obtaining an independent evaluation without a school system commitment to pay for it run the risk that the system will later request a hearing and attempt to prove that it need not pay for the already-completed independent evaluation because its own evaluation was "appropriate." In addition, parents proceeding without first conferring with the school system run the risk that the evaluation they obtain will not meet those criteria the school system may legitimately impose, and so, the risk that they will not be entitled to payment for that reason as well.

Parents without the resources to pay in advance for an independent evaluation will usually not be able to obtain one unless the school system agrees in advance to pay. If the school system does *not* agree to pay and does *not* seek the hearing necessary to excuse it from paying, the parent has a "right" to an evaluation, but no way to take advantage of that right. Under the IDEA regulations, a school system may not simply ignore, or even deny, a request for an independent evaluation. Rather, it must "without unnecessary delay" either (1) ensure that the evaluation is provided, or (2) initiate a due process hearing to demonstrate that its own evaluation was appropriate, or that the evaluation for which the parent seeks public payment does not meet legitimate agency criteria (as discussed above).[78]

A parent faced with this situation has a right to file a complaint and request a due process hearing in order to compel the school system to fund the evaluation. At the hearing, the school system will have the burden of proving that its evaluation was appropriate (or that the parent's requested evaluation does not meet legitimate agency criteria) and that it therefore does not have to pay for another one.[79] The same complaint and hearing rights apply if the independent evaluation has already been performed and the school system refuses to reimburse the parent for it. Complaint and hearing procedures for these and all other IDEA disputes are explained in Chapter 8.

Finally, parents and advocates should note that under IDEA, a hearing officer in a due process hearing involving the content of a child's education program may request an independent evaluation in order to assist him or her in making a decision.[80] Parents cannot be charged for an evaluation requested by a hearing officer as part of a hearing; the evaluation must be provided at public expense.[81] Advocates for parents unable to pay for an independent evaluation and unsuccessful in convincing the school district to do so might consider asking that the hearing officer request an evaluation. It is important to check any state regulations on this issue, as IDEA *allows* hearing officers to request independent evaluations but does not require them to do so.

NOTES

1. 20 U.S.C. §§1412(a)(3)(A), 1413(a)(1); 34 C.F.R. §§300.125; 34 C.F.R. §104.32.

2. 34 C.F.R. §300.125(a)(2).

3. 20 U.S.C. §1414(a)(1); 34 C.F.R. §300.531; 34 C.F.R. §104.35(a).

4. 20 U.S.C. §1414(a)(2)(A); 34 C.F.R. §300.536(b).

5. 20 U.S.C. §1414(c)(5); 34 C.F.R. §300.534(c)(1).

6. 34 C.F.R. §104.35(a), (d).

7. *See* 34 C.F.R. 300.536(b). *See also* 34 C.F.R. §104.35(a) as interpreted by OCR in *School Administrative Unit 19 (NH)*, 16 EHLR 86 (OCR 1/4/89)(poor academic performance should trigger evaluation); *Akron (OH) City School District*, 19 IDELR 542 (OCR 11/18/92) (academic and behavioral difficulties, and school's awareness of Attention Deficit Disorder diagnosis should have triggered evaluation); *Mineral County (NV) School District*, 16 EHLR 668 (OCR 3/16/90) (inappropriate and/or disruptive behavior should trigger evaluation).

8. *Community Unit School District #300 (IL)*, EHLR 353:296 (OCR 1989).

9. 20 U.S.C. §1414(b)(2)(A), (3)(D); 34 C.F.R. §300.532(b), (d).

10. 20 U.S.C. §1414(b)(2)(A), (c)(1)(B)(iv); 34 C.F.R. §§300.532(b), 300.533(a)(2)(iv).

11. 20 U.S.C. §1414(b)(2)(C), (3)(C); 34 C.F.R. §300.532(g). *See also* 34 C.F.R. §104.35(c) (regarding §504 requirements).

12. 34 C.F.R. §300.532(h).

13. 20 U.S.C. §1414(b)(2)(A), (B); 34 C.F.R. §300.532(e). *See also* 34 C.F.R. §104.35(b) (regarding §504).

14. 20 U.S.C. §§1414(b)(1), 1415(b)(3); 34 C.F.R. §300.503(a)(1).

15. 20 U.S.C. §1415(b)(3)(B); 34 C.F.R. §300.503(a)(1).

16. 20 U.S.C. §1415(b)(3)(B); 34 C.F.R. §300.503(a)(1).

17. 34 C.F.R. §104.36. The regulation is silent as to whether the notice must be written.

18. 20 U.S.C. §1415(b)(4); 34 C.F.R. §300.503(c).

19. 34 C.F.R. §300.503(c)(2).

20. *See* 20 U.S.C. §1415(c), (d); 34 C.F.R. §§300.503(b), 300.504.

21. 20 U.S.C. §1414(a)(1)(C), (c)(3); 34 C.F.R. §300.505(a).

22. 20 U.S.C. §1414(c)(3); 34 C.F.R. §300.505(c).

23. For the definition of "consent" contained in the IDEA regulations promulgated before the term "informed" consent was added to the statute, see 34 C.F.R. §300.500(a) (1998). The IDEA regulations promulgated March 12, 1999 retain that language, without accounting for the addition of the word "informed." *See* current 34 C.F.R. §300.500(b)(1).

24. 20 U.S.C. §1414(a)(1)(C)(ii); 34 C.F.R. §300.505(b).

25. 20 U.S.C. §1414(b)(3)(A)(i); 34 C.F.R. §300.532(a)(1)(i). Racially discriminatory testing and evaluation methods may also violate Title VI of the Civil Rights Act of 1964, 42 U.S.C. §2000d *et seq*, and the Title VI regulations. *See* 34 C.F.R. §100.3(b).

26. 20 U.S.C. §1414(b)(3)(C); 34 C.F.R. §300.532(g).

27. 20 U.S.C. §1414(b)(3)(D); 34 C.F.R. §300.532(j).

28. 20 U.S.C. §1414(b)(3)(A)(ii); 34 C.F.R. §§300.532(a)(1)(ii).

29. 34 C.F.R. §300.532(a)(2).

30. 20 U.S.C. §1414(b)(2)(A); 34 C.F.R. §300.532(b).

31. 20 U.S.C. §1414(b)(2)(B); 34 C.F.R. §300.532(f). *See also* 34 C.F.R. §104.35 (§504 evaluation requirements).

32. 34 C.F.R. §300.532(c)(2).

33. 20 U.S.C. §1414(b)(3)(B); 34 C.F.R. §§300.532(c), (d) and (e); 34 C.F.R. §104.35(b).

34. 20 U.S.C. §1414(c)(1)(A); 34 C.F.R. §300.533.

35. 20 U.S.C. §1414(c)(1)(B); 34 C.F.R. §300.533(a)(2).

36. 20 U.S.C. §1414(c)(2); 34 C.F.R. §300.533(c).

37. *See* 20 U.S.C. §1414(c)(4); 34 C.F.R. §300.533(d).

38. 20 U.S.C. §1414(c)(4); 34 C.F.R. §300.533(d).

39. *See* 20 U.S.C. §§1401(3) ("child with a disability" is one who has one of the listed disabilities and "who, by reason thereof, needs special education and related services"); 1414(c)(4); 34 C.F.R. §300.533(d).

40. 20 U.S.C. §1414(c)(4); 34 C.F.R. §300.533(d).

41. 34 C.F.R. §300.533(b).

42. 34 C.F.R. §300.540.

43. *Id.*.

44. *Id.*

45. 34 C.F.R. §300.542.

46. 34 C.F.R. §300.541(a).

47. *See Inquiry of Scovill*, EHLR 211:14 (Bureau of Education of the Handicapped [a predecessor of OSEP] 3/3/78). OCR has ruled that under §504, if the team believes that a student has a learning disability, its determination must prevail even if the student's test scores do not fall within the state formula for "severe discrepancy." *See Georgia Department of Education*, EHLR 352:05 (OCR 5/20/85).

48. 34 C.F.R. §300.541(b).

49. 34 C.F.R. §300.543(a).

50. 34 C.F.R. §300.543(b).

51. 20 U.S.C. §1414(b)(4)(A); 34 C.F.R. §300.534(a)(1).

52. 34 C.F.R. §104.35(c); 34 C.F.R. part 104, Appendix A, §25.

53. 20 U.S.C. §1414(b)(4)(B); 34 C.F.R. §300.534(a)(2).

54. 20 U.S.C. §1415(b)(3), (4); 34 C.F.R. §300.503(a)(1), (c).

55. *See, e.g.* 34 C.F.R. §300.345(e) ("[t]he public agency shall take whatever action is necessary to ensure that the parent understands the proceedings at the meeting...."); 34 C.F.R. §300.500(b)(1) (defining "consent"). *See also Rowley, supra,*458 U.S. at 205-06 ("...the importance Congress attached to these procedural safeguards cannot be gainsaid...Congress placed every bit as much emphasis upon compliance with procedures giving parents and guardians a large measure of participation at every stage of the administrative process...as it did upon the measurement of the resulting IEP against a substantive standard...[T]he congressional emphasis upon full participation of concerned parties throughout the development of the IEP...demonstrates the legislative conviction that adequate compliance with the procedures prescribed would in most cases assure much if not all of what Congress wished in the way of substantive content in an IEP.").

56. *See* 42 U.S.C. §2000d; 34 C.F.R. §100.3(b).

57. *Cf. San Luis Valley (CO) Board of Cooperative* Services, 21 IDELR 304 (OCR 3/4/94) (failure to notify parents of rights and procedural safeguards in language they can best understand violated Title VI, §504 and Title II of the ADA); *Ogden (UT) City School District*, 21 IDELR 387 (OCR 3/23/94) (forms and notices in general); *Dade County (FL) School District*, 20 IDELR 267 (OCR 5/11/93) (failure to translate procedural safeguards notice into Spanish for limited English proficient parents and to provide information and explanations regarding daughter's program violated Title VI, §504 and Title II).

58. *See* 20 U.S.C. §1415(b)(1); 34 C.F.R. §§300.501(a)(1), 300.562; 34 C.F.R. §104.36; 20 U.S.C. §1232g(a) (Family Educational Rights and Privacy Act); 34 C.F.R. §99.10 (same). Note that under FERPA, certain kinds of records are not considered "education records," and so are not available to parents for review. These include, for example, certain mental health treatment records concerning a student aged 18 or over. *See generally* 34 C.F.R. §99.3 (defining "education records").

59. 34 C.F.R. §300.562(b)(1) (IDEA); 99 C.F.R. §99.10(c) (Family Educational Rights and Privacy Act). Note that the Family Educational Rights and Privacy Act applies to all students attending schools that receive funds from the U.S. Department of Education, regardless of whether or not the student is covered by IDEA, or even has a disability.

60. 20 U.S.C. §1414(b)(2)(B); 34 C.F.R. §300.532 (f)); 34 C.F.R. §104.35.

61. 20 U.S.C. §1414(b)(5); 34 C.F.R. §300.534(b)(1).

62. 20 U.S.C. §1414(b)(4)(A); 34 C.F.R. §300.535(a); 34 C.F.R. §104.35(c).

63. *See also* 20 U.S.C. §1414(b)(5) ("a child shall not be determined to be a child with a disability if the determinate factor for such determination is...limited English proficiency").

64. *See* 34 C.F.R. §300.502(c)(1) (results of evaluation must be taken into consideration "if it meets agency criteria").

65. 20 U.S.C. §1415(b)(1);34 C.F.R. §300.502.

66. 34 C.F.R. §300.502(b).

67. 34 C.F.R. §300.502(b)(1); *Inquiry of Fisher*, 23 IDELR 565 (OSEP 12/4/95); *Inquiry of Wilson*, 16 EHLR 83 (OSEP 10/17/90); *Inquiry of Thorne*, 16 EHLR 606 (OSEP 2/15/90).

68. 34 C.F.R. §300.502(e)(2).

69. 34 C.F.R. §300.502(b)(2).

70. 34 C.F.R. §300.502(a)(2).

71. *Inquiry of Imber*, 19 IDELR 352 (OSEP 8/18/92).

72. 34 C.F.R. §300.503(e)(1); *Inquiry of Rambo*, 16 EHLR 1078 (OSEP 6/22/90).

73. 34 C.F.R. §300.503(e)(1) (emphasis added).

74. *Inquiry of Anonymous*, 20 IDELR 1219 (OSEP 12/13/93); *see also Inquiry of Rambo, supra.*

75. *See Inquiry of* Anonymous, 22 IDELR 637 (OSEP 2/2/95); Inquiry *of Wilson, supra; Inquiry of Thorne, supra; Inquiry of Fields, supra.*

76. *See Inquiry of Anonymous, supra; Inquiry of Wilson, supra; Inquiry of Thorne, supra; Inquiry of Fields, supra.*

77. 34 C.F.R. §300.502(b)(4); *Warren G. v. Cumberland County School District*, 190 F.3d 80, 87 (3rd Cir. 1999); *Board of Education of Murphysboro Community Unit School District No. 186 v. Illinois State Board of Education*, 41 F.3d 1162, 1169 (7th Cir. 1994); *Hudson v. Wilson*, 828 F.2d 1059, 1065 (4th Cir. 1987); *Mullen v. District of Columbia*, 16 EHLR 792 (D.D.C. 1990); *Hiller v. Board of Education of the Brunswick Central School District*, 687 F. Supp. 735 (N.D.N.Y. 1988).

78. 34 C.F.R. §300.502(b)(2).

79. *Id.*

80. 34 C.F.R. §300.503(d).

81. *Id.*

CHAPTER 6

IEPs, PLACEMENT DECISIONS AND PARENT AND STUDENT PARTICIPATION

Students eligible for services under IDEA must have an Individualized Education Program ("IEP") *before* special education and related services begin.[1] A meeting must be held to develop a child's first IEP within 30 days of a decision that he or she is eligible for services under IDEA.[2] Thereafter, an IEP must be in effect at the beginning of every school year.[3] As discussed below, the IEP is developed by a team of particular individuals, including the child's parents. In developing the IEP, the team must consider the child's strengths and the parents' concerns for enhancing his or her education; the results of the initial or most recent evaluation of the child; and the child's performance on any state- or district-wide assessments.[4]

Failure to develop an IEP — as well as failure to follow the specific procedures set out in IDEA and the regulations for doing so — is a failure to provide a free appropriate public education.[5] Because in the past, contrary to legal requirements, IEPs often were not used as tools for enabling children with disabilities to learn what *all* children are expected to know and be able to do, IDEA now explicitly stresses aligning the IEP with the general curriculum.

The IEP is more than a blueprint for the education a child is to receive. School districts *must* provide all services contained in the IEP, and violate IDEA if they fail to do so.[6] The §504 regulations do not require an IEP; however, provision of special education and related services under an IEP meeting IDEA requirements is one way of providing the appropriate education §504 requires.[7]

A. IEP Content

1. Requirements for All Students

An IEP must always include the following:

- A statement of the child's current level of educational performance, including how disability affects his or her progress in the general curriculum;
    - This statement should describe the effect of the child's disability on both academic and non-academic (e.g. activities of daily living, mobility, emotional, behavioral) aspects of his or her performance. It should be written in objective, measurable terms, drawing upon evaluation results.
- Measurable annual goals, with either benchmarks or short-term objectives, addressing progress in the general curriculum and all other areas of educational need resulting from the child's disability;
    - Annual goals describe what the student can reasonably be expected to accomplish over the year; short-term objectives are measurable, intermediate steps towards the corresponding annual goal; benchmarks describe the amount of progress the child is expected to have made by certain points in the year.[8] Goals, objectives and benchmarks provide a basis for determining how well a child is progressing, what he or she is learning, whether the IEP needs to be revised and whether he is receiving an appropriate education.[9] The development of specific, measurable, well- defined, meaningful goals and short-term objectives or benchmarks is crucial.
        - All areas of need revealed by the statement of present educational performance should have corresponding annual goals and benchmarks or short-term objectives.
- An explanation of how the child's progress towards the annual goals will be measured, and of how the parents will be regularly informed of his or her progress (including being informed of whether that progress is sufficient to achieve the goals by the end of the year);
- A statement of the special education, related services and supplementary aids and services to be provided to the child (or on behalf of the child), and the program modifications or supports for school personnel to be provided;
    - These are all to be designed so as to permit the child to attain

the annual goals, progress in the general curriculum, participate in extracurricular and other nonacademic activities, and
be educated and participate with other children with and
without disabilities.[10]

- An explanation of the extent, if any, to which the child will not be
  educated in regular education classes;
- A statement of any individual modifications the child will need in
  the administration of state- or district-wide assessments of student
  achievement;
  - If the IEP team determines that a child will not participate in a
    particular state- or district-wide assessment, or part of an
    assessment, the IEP must also include a statement explaining
    why the particular assessment is not appropriate for the student,
    and how he or she will be assessed instead. [11]
- The projected date for the beginning of the services, modifications,
  etc. described in the IEP, and the anticipated frequency, location
  and duration of each.[12]

*The IEP must contain a statement of all services needed by the child,
not just those which are available within the school system.*[13] The school
system then must arrange to provide all of the services included in the
IEP.[14]

"Special factors" Because of implementation problems in the past, the
IDEA Amendments of 1997 expressly require IEP teams to consider and
address the following five "special factors," going to particular areas of
potential educational need, when designing IEPs:

- If a child's behavior impedes his or her learning or the learning of
  others, the team must consider positive behavioral interventions,
  strategies and supports to address it.
- If a child has limited English proficiency, the team must consider
  the child's language needs as they relate to the IEP.
- If a child is visually impaired, the team must provide for instruction in Braille and use of Braille unless the team, based upon an
  evaluation of the child's skills and current and future needs, determines that this would not be appropriate.
- The IEP team must consider the communication needs of all children, and in the case of children with hearing impairments, take
  into account his or her opportunities for direct communication with
  peers and professionals in the child's language and communication

mode and academic level, including opportunities for direct instruction.

- For all children, the team must consider whether the child requires assistive technology devices and services.[15]

Extended School Year Services The IEP should also indicate whether the child needs "extended school year" ("ESY") services, meaning services beyond the usual length of the school year in the school system involved. ESY services must be provided if necessary in order for a child to receive FAPE.[16] For example, a child might need ESY services if he or she will make insufficient progress in the general curriculum or other areas of educational need (academic or non-academic) during the standard school year, or if he or she is likely to regress over school breaks and have difficulty recovering lost skills.[17] ESY services may also be required if, due to the nature and effect of the disability, a child is at a critical developmental phase for learning certain skills.[18]

Whether a student will receive ESY services must be based upon individualized consideration of his or her needs. Schools may not limit ESY services to children with only particular kinds of disabilities, nor may they place general limits on the type, amount or duration of services to be offered.[19]

2. Additional IEP Components for Older Students

Transition planning and services Planning to prepare youth for the transition to adult life begins by age 14. From this age on, the IEP must include a statement of the student's "transition service needs," focused on his or her course of study.[20] A student's planned course of study might include, for example, participation in advanced placement courses or a school-to-work or vocational education program.[21] By age 16, and earlier if appropriate in light of the student's needs, the IEP must include the full range of needed "transition services."[22] Under IDEA, "transition services" means a coordinated set of activities for a student that promotes movement from school to post-school activities, including:

- employment;
- post-secondary education;
- vocational training;
- continuing and adult education;
- adult services;

- independent living; or
- community participation.[23]

Transition services must be based upon the individual student's preferences, interests and needs, and include:

- instruction;
- related services;
- community experiences;
- development of employment and other post-school adult living objectives; and
- acquisition of daily living skills and functional vocational evaluation when appropriate.[24]

The school system is responsible for ensuring that each youth receives all needed transition services. However, as discussed below, particular services might be provided by other agencies, such as vocational rehabilitation agencies. The IEP must specify the role such outside entities will play.[25] If an outside agency fails to provide the transition services for which it is responsible in the IEP, the school system must reconvene the youth's IEP team and devise alternative ways to meet his or her transition objectives.[26]

Transition planning and transition services requirements do not apply to youth with disabilities who are convicted as adults under state law and incarcerated in an adult prison, if their eligibility for IDEA services will end, because of age, prior to their release from prison.[27]

Transfer of Rights As discussed in further detail in Chapter 8, changes made to IDEA in 1997 address the transfer of IDEA rights (regarding notice, consent, participation in educational planning, and dispute resolution) from parent to child when the child reaches the age of majority under state law. Beginning at least one year before the student reaches the age of majority, the IEP must include a statement that he or she has been informed of the IDEA rights that will transfer when he or she becomes an adult.[28]

3. Options for Three through Five Year Olds

Under certain circumstances, school systems may provide 3 through 5 year olds with an "Individualized Family Service Plan" ("IFSP") instead of an IEP.[29] Ordinarily, IFSPs are provided only for infants and toddlers (aged birth through 2) participating in early intervention services under Part C of IDEA.*

Substituting an IFSP for an IEP must be consistent with state policy, and must be agreed to by the parents.[30] A school system contemplating offering an IFSP instead of an IEP must give the parents a detailed explanation of the differences between an IFSP and an IEP, and obtain informed written consent.[31] For example, parents should be made aware that unlike an IEP, an IFSP need not include an early education component provided by a qualified teacher of preschool children. Parents should also be made aware of the possible adverse developmental and educational consequences, both short- and long-term, of foregoing this component.

In addition, IFSPs for 3 through 5 year olds must be developed using the same procedures required for developing IEPs (see discussion below), rather than via the IFSP procedures required for infants and toddlers.[32] IFSPs for these older children must meet the content requirements governing IFSPs under the IDEA early intervention program for infants and toddlers with disabilities, discussed in Chapter 10.[33]

B. IEP Development and Parent and Student Participation

1. Requirements for All Students

Under IDEA, the IEP must be developed at a meeting, by the IEP team.[34] The team is composed of the following people:

- the child's parents
- at least one of the child's regular education teachers (if the child is, or may be, participating in the regular education environment)
- at least one of the child's special education teachers or providers
- a representative of the school system who is knowledgeable about the general curriculum, is knowledgeable about the school system's resources, and is qualified to provide, or supervise the provision of, specially designed instruction to meet the needs of children with disabilities
  - The school system representative must have the authority to commit the school system to provide whatever services are included in the IEP, in order to ensure that the IEP will be

---

* Early intervention services are discussed in Chapter 10.

implemented, and not be "vetoed" by school administrators or other school officials.[35]

- an individual who is qualified to interpret the instructional implications of evaluation results
- other individuals who have knowledge or special expertise regarding the child, at the discretion of the parent or school system
  - The determination of whether an individual has "knowledge or special expertise regarding the child" is made by the party inviting him or her, i.e. the parent or school system.[36]
- whenever appropriate, the student.[37]

As the U.S. Supreme Court has repeatedly stressed,[38] parent participation in decisionmaking is critical to the education rights Congress sought to protect in enacting IDEA. Consistent with the central role afforded parents, it is impermissible for school personnel to present a completed IEP to parents for their approval at the meeting.[39] While school personnel may bring proposed recommendations to the meeting, as may parents, the IEP must be developed *at* the meeting, with parents afforded the opportunity to participate as full-fledged collaborators in designing their child's education.[40]

Further, school systems are responsible for initiating IEP meetings and ensuring that parents are given a meaningful opportunity to attend and participate.[41] Towards this end, school districts must schedule the meeting at a mutually convenient time and place; notify parents of the meeting far enough in advance to ensure that they will have an opportunity to attend; and include in the notice of the meeting the purpose, time and location and a list of those who will attend.[42] The notice must also inform parents of their right to bring to the meeting others with knowledge or special expertise about the child,[43] and be provided in the parent's native language or other mode of communication.[44]

If neither parent can attend, the school district must use other methods to ensure that parents participate in the development of the IEP, including individual or conference telephone calls.[45] A meeting can be held without a parent only if school personnel cannot convince the parents that they should attend.[46] Even then, the school system must first try to arrange a mutually agreeable time and place and must keep records of its efforts to secure the parents' attendance.[47] These include detailed records of telephone calls made or attempted, and the results; copies of correspondence sent to the parents, and of any responses received; and detailed records of visits made to the home or parent's workplace, and the results.[48]

To ensure meaningful participation by parents, schools must arrange for translators and sign language interpreters for parents who need them.[49] The U.S. Department of Education/Office of Special Education Programs has stated that IDEA allows states or school systems to have policies prohibiting or limiting tape recording, but that any such policy must include exceptions when necessary to ensure that the parent understands the IEP or IEP process, or to implement other parental rights guaranteed by IDEA.[50] In addition, in at least two cases courts have ruled that parents have the right to tape record IEP meetings.[51]

The IEP must be implemented as soon as possible after the IEP meeting.[52] It must be accessible to all teachers and services providers who are responsible for implementing it, including the child's regular education teachers.[53] In addition, school personnel must inform each teacher and service provider of their specific responsibilities for implementing the IEP, and of the modifications, accommodations and supports included in the IEP.[54] School staff may not unilaterally change an IEP. Rather, in order to revise an IEP or change a placement, schools must follow the meeting and team process described above (regarding IEPs) and below (regarding placement decisions). As discussed in Chapter 8, they must also give parents prior written notice of any IEP or placement change.

Parents must be given a copy of the IEP, at no cost.[55] Although IDEA does not explicitly address translation of IEPs, it would seem that in order to comply with requirements regarding parent participation in IEP and placement meetings and reviews, informed consent and the right to challenge school decisions, as well as to make meaningful for all parents and children the parent participation at the core of IDEA, schools must translate IEPs into parents' native language.[56] Title VI of the Civil Rights Act of 1964 and the regulations implementing it, [57] which prohibit discrimination on the basis of race and national origin, should also require translation of IEPs.[58]

2. Additional Requirements Regarding Transition Planning and Services

Recognizing the unique issues and concerns at stake in transition planning, IDEA requires additional measures whenever transition needs or services are to be discussed.

Parent notification Whenever transition needs or services are to be discussed, the written notice ordinarily provided parents prior to an IEP meeting must also explain that these issues are on the agenda.[59] The notice must also inform the parent that the school will invite the student to attend, and identify any other agency that will be invited to send a representative to the meeting.[60] Receipt of such notice gives parents an opportunity to think about future goals, plans and services for their child, discuss them with him, and ask that additional or alternate agencies be included in the meeting.

Student participation Schools *must* invite the student to attend any meeting at which transition services are to be discussed, and to participate in the discussion of his or her future goals and plans.[61] This mandate, reflecting the importance of self-determination and empowerment, is a strong one: if the student does not attend, the school must take other steps to ensure that the student's preferences and interests are considered.[62]

Agency participation In light of the broad scope of required transition services under IDEA, the Act anticipates that outside agencies sometimes will participate with schools in providing them.[63] Towards this end, the law requires that meetings to discuss transition include a representative of any other agency that is likely to be responsible for providing or paying for a transition service.[64] Such agencies might include those dealing with vocational rehabilitation; employment and training; housing; specialized services for youth and adults with developmental disabilities, mental health needs, or other disabilities; and other providers relevant to the individual needs and preferences of the student.

If an agency invited to send a representative does not do so, the school system must take other steps to obtain the participation of that agency in planning transition services.[65] Once such participation is secured, the student's IEP must reflect the responsibility of each participating agency for providing particular transition services, including the school's.[66] As noted above, if an outside participating agency fails to provide agreed upon services, the school must act as soon as possible to hold a new meeting and develop alternative strategies for meeting the student's transition needs.[67]

C. Placement Decisions
Once a child's needs have been identified and appropriate services and

goals developed through the IEP process, a placement capable of providing those services and achieving those goals can be selected. Placement decisions must be individualized for each child, based upon his or her unique needs and abilities. Placement decisions may *not* be based upon category of disability, severity of disability, availability of special education and related services, configuration of the service delivery system, availability of space, or administrative convenience.[68]

Placements must be determined at least annually, must be consistent with IDEA's presumption in favor of placement in regular education classes with appropriate supplementary aids and services (as discussed in Chapter 2), and must be based upon the IEP.[69] The latter requirement means that the IEP must be developed *before* a placement is chosen.[70] Thus it is not permissible for a school system to write an IEP to fit a placement it has already selected.

All placements must be chosen by a group of persons knowledgeable about the child, the meaning of the evaluation data, and the placement options.[71] Parents must be part of any group that makes placement decisions.[72] In order to ensure that parents have a meaningful opportunity to participate in this group, schools must notify parents of any meeting far enough in advance to ensure that they will have an opportunity to attend; schedule the meeting at a mutually agreed on time and place; notify them of the purpose, time and location of the meeting, and who will be attending; and inform them of their right to bring others with knowledge or expertise about their child with them to the meeting.[73] If neither parent can participate in a meeting at which a decision relating to placement is to be made, the school system must find other ways to ensure their participation, such as individual or conference telephone calls.[74] The school system must also make reasonable efforts to ensure that the parents can understand and participate in group discussions, including arranging for a translator or sign language interpreter.[75] A placement decision may be made without parents' involvement only if school personnel try, and fail, to involve them. In that case, the school system must keep a record of its efforts, including detailed records of telephone calls made or attempted, and the results; copies of correspondence sent to the parents, and of any responses received; and detailed records of visits made to the home or parent's workplace, and the results.[76]

D. IEP Review and Revision

1. Periodic or Annual Reviews

School districts must periodically initiate and conduct meetings to review and, if appropriate, revise a child's IEP.[77] In addition, parents have the right to request an IEP meeting at any time.[78] IEP review meetings should be held as often as necessary to address the child's needs.[79] At least one review meeting must be held each year.[80] The above-described requirements regarding IEP team members, meeting participants, meeting notice and parent participation rights apply to IEP review meetings as well.[81]

Based upon its review, the IEP team must revise the IEP as needed to address:

- any lack of expected progress in the general curriculum;
- any lack of expected progress towards the annual goals in the IEP;
- new evaluation results, including information provided by parents;
- the student's anticipated needs; or
- other matters.[82]

2. Revisions

Once an IEP has been developed and agreed upon, school personnel may not unilaterally change it. In order to revise an IEP or change a placement, school systems must follow the meeting and team process described above.[83] They must also give parents prior written notice of the proposed change.[84] The IDEA regulations set out detailed requirements governing the content of this notice, which also must be given any time a school system proposes or refuses to initiate or change the identification, evaluation, or educational placement of a child or the provision of a free appropriate public education to a child.[85] These content requirements are discussed in Chapter 8.

Parents may request an IEP or placement change, or a meeting to consider making a change, at any time. When a school system refuses to make a change sought by a parent, it must provide the written notice described above. Parents may challenge any refusal to modify an IEP or change a placement by invoking IDEA's dispute resolution procedures, which include requesting a due process hearing, filing a complaint with the state education agency, seeking mediation and bringing a lawsuit.[86]

For a discussion of these procedures, see Chapter 8.

NOTES

1. 34 C.F.R. §300.342(b)(1)(i); 34 C.F.R. part 300, App. A, question 14.

2. 34 C.F.R. §300.343(b).

3. 20 U.S.C. §1414(d)(2)(A); 34 C.F.R. §300.342(a).

4. 34 C.F.R. §300.346(a)(1).

5. 20 U.S.C. §§1401(8)(D), 1412(a)(4); 34 C.F.R. §§300.13(d), 300.535(b); *Board of Education of the Hendrick Hudson Central School District v. Rowley*, 458 U.S. 176, 206-207, 102 S.Ct. 3034, 3035 (1982).

6. 20 U.S.C. §1401(8); 34 C.F.R. §300.350(a)(1); 34 C.F.R. part 300, App. A, question 31.

7. 34 C.F.R. §104.33(b)(2).

8. *See* 34 C.F.R. part 300, App. A, question 1.

9. *See id.*

10. 20 U.S.C. §1414(d)(A)(iii); 34 C.F.R. §300.347(a)(3).

11. 20 U.S.C. §1414(d)(1)(A)(v)(II); 34 C.F.R. §300.347(5)(ii).

12. 20 U.S.C. §1414(d)(1)(A); 34 C.F.R. §300.347. Note, however, that the IEP team of a child convicted as an adult under state law and incarcerated in an adult prison may modify the child's IEP or placement notwithstanding these requirements *if the State has demonstrated a bona fide security or compelling penological interest that cannot otherwise be accommodated.* 20 U.S.C. §1414(d)(6)(B); 34 C.F.R. §300.311(c).

13. *See, e.g., Todd D. v. Andrews*, 933 F.2d 1576, 1580-81 (11th Cir. 1991) (district court erred by ordering alteration of IEP goals so that IEP could be implemented at existing placement, rather than ordering school system to provide placement that could implement IEP as written).

14. 20 U.S.C. §1401(8)(D); 34 C.F.R. §300.350(a)(1); 34 C.F.R. part 300, Appendix A, question 31.

15. 20 U.S.C. §1414(d)(3)(B); 34 C.F.R. §300.346(a)(2), (c).

16. 34 C.F.R. §300.309(a).

17. *See, e.g., Johnson v. Independent School District No. 4*, 921 F.2d 1022 (10th Cir. 1990), *cert. denied*, 500 U.S. 905, 111 S.Ct. 1685 (1991); *Cordrey v. Eukert*, 917 F.2d 1460 (6th Cir. 1990); *Battle v. Commonwealth of Pennsylvania*, 629 F.2d 269 (3rd. Cir. 1980), *cert. denied*, 452 U.S. 968, 101 S.Ct. 3123 (1981); *Reusch v. Fountain*, 872 F. Supp. 1421 (D. Md. 1994); *Lawyer v. Chesterfield Co. School Bd.*, 19 IDELR 904, 907 (E.D. Va. 1993).

18. *Lawyer, supra.*

19. 34 C.F.R. §300.309(a)(3).

20. 20 U.S.C. §1414(d)(1)(A)(vii)(I); 34 C.F.R. §300.347(b)(1). The mandate to begin transition planning for all youth with disabilities by no later than age 14 was added to IDEA in 1997. Previously, the law allowed schools to delay transition planning for many students until age 16. In making this change, Congress explained that the purpose of the new provision was to supplement the existing requirements for 16-year olds, by focusing attention at an earlier age on how the student's educational program can be planned to make for a successful transition to his or her goals for life after high school. *See* H. R.Report 105-95, 105th Cong., 1st Sess., at 101 (1997).

21. Two federal laws have mandated or encouraged states and school systems to create high quality vocational education and school-to-work programs for *all* students: the Carl D. Perkins Vocational and Applied Technology Education Act, 20 U.S.C. §2301 *et seq.*, and the School-to- Work Opportunities Act, 20 U.S.C. §6101 *et seq.* For a discussion of these laws as they affect students with disabilities, see Eileen L. Ordover and Leslie T. Annexstein, *Ensuring Access, Equity and Quality for Students with Disabilities in School-to-Work Systems* (1999), available from the Center for Law and Education, 1875 Connecticut Ave., N.W., Suite 510, Washington, D.C. 20009 (telephone: 202/986-3000; fax: 202/986-6648).

22. 20 U.S.C. §1414(d)(1)(A)(vii)(II); 34 C.F.R. §300.347(b)(2).

23. 20 U.S.C. §1401(30); 34 C.F.R. §300.29.

24. 20 U.S.C. §1401(30); 34 C.F.R. §300.29.

25. 20 U.S.C. §1414(d)(1)(A)(vii)(II); 34 C.F.R. §300.347(b)(2).

26. 20 U.S.C. §1414(d)(1)(A)(vii)(II); 34 C.F.R. §300.348(a).

27. 20 U.S.C. §1414(d)(6)(A)(ii); 34 C.F.R. §300.311(b)(2). The determination of whether a youth's IDEA eligibility will end prior to release from prison must be based upon consideration of their sentence and eligibility for early release. 34 C.F.R. §300.311(b)(2).

28. 20 U.S.C. §1414(d)(1)(A)(vii)(III); 34 C.F.R. §300.347(c).

29. 20 U.S.C. §1414(d)(2)(B); 34 C.F.R. §300.342(c).

30. *Id.*

31. 34 C.F.R. §300.342(c)(2).

32. 34 C.F.R. §300.342(c)(1).

33. For IFSP content requirements, see 20 U.S.C. §1436(d). For the range of early intervention services required to be made available, see 20 U.S.C. §1432(4) and the early intervention regulations at 34 C.F.R. part 303.

34. 20 U.S.C. §1414(d); 34 C.F.R. §§300.343(a), 300.344.

35. 34 C.F.R. part 300, App. A, question 22.

36. 34 C.F.R. §300.344(c).

37. 20 U.S.C. §1414(d)(1)(B); 34 C.F.R. §§300.343, 300.344.

38. *See Honig v. Doe*, 484 U.S. 305, 311, 108 S. Ct. 592, 598 (1988) ("[e]nvisioning the IEP as the centerpiece of the statute's education delivery system…and aware that schools had all too often denied such children appropriate educations without in any way consulting their parents, Congress repeatedly emphasized throughout the Act the importance and indeed the necessity of parental participation in both the development of the IEP and any subsequent assessments of its effectiveness.") *Rowley, supra,*458 U.S. at 205-06 ("…the importance Congress attached to these procedural safeguards cannot be gainsaid…Congress placed every bit as much emphasis upon compliance with procedures giving parents and guardians a large measure of participation at every stage of the administrative process…as it did upon the measurement of the resulting IEP against a substantive standard…[T]he congressional emphasis upon full participation of concerned parties throughout the development of the IEP…demonstrates the legislative conviction that adequate compliance with the procedures prescribed would in most cases assure much if not all of what Congress wished in the way of substantive content in an IEP.").

39. 34 C.F.R. §300.340(a) (defining "IEP," in part, as a document developed *in a meeting* by certain school personnel and parents) (emphasis added); 34 C.F.R. part 300, App. A, question 32; *Inquiry of Hellmuth*, 16 EHLR 503 (OSEP 1/30/90).

40. *See* 34 C.F.R. part 300, App. A, question 32; *V.W. v. Favolise*, 131 F.R.D. 654, 659 (D. Conn. 1990).

41. 34 C.F.R. §§300.343, 300.345.

42. 34 C.F.R. §300.345(a), (b).

43. 34 C.F.R. §300.345(b)(iii).

44. 34 C.F.R. §300.503(c). See also the discussion below regarding translation of IEPs.

45. 34 C.F.R. §300.345(c).

46. 34 C.F.R. §300.345(d).

47. *Id.*

48. *Id.*

49. 34 C.F.R. §300.345(e).

50. *See* 34 C.F.R. Part 300, App. A, question 21.

51. *E.H. v. Tirozzi*, 735 F. Supp. 53 (D. Conn. 1990); *V.W. v. Favolise*, 131 F.R.D. 654 (D. Conn. 1990).

52. 34 C.F.R. §300.342(b).

53. *Id.*

54. *Id.*

55. 34 C.F.R. §300.345(f).

56. *See, e.g.* 34 C.F.R. §300.345(e) ("[t]he public agency shall take whatever action is necessary to ensure that the parent understands the proceedings at the meeting…."); 34 C.F.R. §300.500(b)(1) (defining "consent"). *See also Rowley, supra,*458 U.S. at 205-06 ("…the importance Congress attached to these procedural safeguards cannot be gainsaid…Congress placed every bit as much emphasis upon compliance with

procedures giving parents and guardians a large measure of participation at every stage of the administrative process...as it did upon the measurement of the resulting IEP against a substantive standard...[T]he congressional emphasis upon full participation of concerned parties throughout the development of the IEP...demonstrates the legislative conviction that adequate compliance with the procedures prescribed would in most cases assure much if not all of what Congress wished in the way of substantive content in an IEP.").

57. *See* 42 U.S.C. §2000d; 34 C.F.R. §100.3(b).

58. *Cf. San Luis Valley (CO) Board of Cooperative* Services, 21 IDELR 304 (OCR 3/4/94) (failure to notify parents of rights and procedural safeguards in language they can best understand violated Title VI, §504 and Title II of the ADA); *Ogden (UT) City School District*, 21 IDELR 387 (OCR 3/23/94) (forms and notices in general); *Dade County (FL) School District*, 20 IDELR 267 (OCR 5/11/93) (failure to translate procedural safeguards notice into Spanish for limited English proficient parents and to provide information and explanations regarding daughter's program violated Title VI, §504 and Title II).

59. 34 C.F.R. §300.345(b)(2), (3).

60. *Id.*

61. 34 C.F.R. §300.344(b)(1).

62. 34 C.F.R. §300.344(b)(2).

63. *See* 20 U.S.C. §1414(d)(1)(A)(vii)(II) (regarding interagency linkages).

64. 34 C.F.R. §300.344(b)(3)(i).

65. 34 C.F.R. §300.344(b)(3)(ii).

66. 20 U.S.C. §1414(d)(1)(A)(vii)(II); 34 C.F.R. §300.347(b)(2).

67. 34 C.F.R. §300.348(a).

68. 34 C.F.R. Part 300, Appendix A, question 1.

69. 34 C.F.R. §300.552.

70. 34 C.F.R. part 300, App. A, para. 14; *Spielberg v. Henrico County Public Schools*, 853 F.2d 256, 259 (4th Cir. 1988). *C.f. Todd D.*, *supra*, 933 F.2d at 1580-81 (district court erred by ordering alteration of IEP goals so that IEP could be implemented at existing placement, rather than ordering school system to provide placement capable of implementing IEP as written).

71. 34 C.F.R. §300.552(a). The regulations implementing Section 504 of the Rehabilitation Act of 1973 also include this requirement. *See* 34 C.F.R. §104.35(c)(3).

72. 20 U.S.C. §1414(f); 34 C.F.R. §300.501(c).

73. 34 C.F.R. §300.501(c)(2) (incorporating by reference §300.345(a) through (b)(1)).

74. 34 C.F.R. §300.501(c)(3).

75. 34 C.F.R. §300.501(c)(5).

76. 34 C.F.R. §300.501(c)(4) (incorporating by reference §300.345(d)).

77. 20 U.S.C. §1414(d)(4)(A); 34 C.F.R. §300.343(c).

78. 34 C.F.R. part 300, App. A, question 20.

79. *Id.*

80. 20 U.S.C. §1414(a)(5); 34 C.F.R. §300.343(d).

81. 34 C.F.R. §300.344(a).

82. 20 U.S.C. §1414(d)(4)(A); 34 C.F.R. §300.343(c).

83. 34 C.F.R. §300.343(a); 34 C.F.R. part 300, App. A, question 20.

84. 20 U.S.C. §1415(b)(3); 34 C.F.R. §300.503.

85. 34 C.F.R. §300.504(a).

86. *See* 20 U.S.C. §1415(b)(6), (e), (f), (g), (i)(2); 34 C.F.R. §§300.660 - 300.662.

CHAPTER 7

PARTICIPATION IN STATE- AND DISTRICT-WIDE ASSESSMENTS

Current state and federal education reform initiatives rely heavily upon large scale testing of students to gather information about how well they are learning. The results of such state- or district-wide assessments may be used to evaluate programs, identify problems, improve instruction and otherwise hold schools accountable for how well they are educating their students; to make high-stakes decisions about individual students (for example, whether a student will receive a high school diploma); or both. The use of such large-scale assessments raises a myriad of legal issues for students with disabilities under IDEA, §504 and the ADA, the U.S. Constitution, Title I of the Elementary and Secondary Education Act, and state laws. Discussed below are some of the legal implications and rights at stake, with a focus on exclusion from/participation in assessments; equitable participation, through accommodations and alternate assessments; and assessments with high-stakes consequences for students.

A. EXCLUSION FROM ASSESSMENTS AS UNLAWFUL DISCRIMINATION

Historically, students with disabilities have been excluded in large numbers from the assessments used to hold public schools accountable for student achievement.[1] As a result, information about the educational achievement of students with disabilities is often absent from the data upon which judgements about the effectiveness of educational programs and services are made, and upon which decisions about policies and reform initiatives are made. Section 504 and Title II of the ADA, however, make it illegal for states and school systems to exclude students from accountability systems and assessment programs on account of disability. In addition, IDEA was amended in 1997 to expressly require inclusion.

1. Section 504 and the ADA

The justification for large-scale assessments is that they will help improve educational quality, whether the results are used to hold schools accountable, to evaluate and improve programs, to measure student progress, or to improve instruction for individual students. When students are excluded from the assessment program because of disability, they are denied these benefits because of disability. This violates both §504, which provides that a qualified individual with a disability may not, on the basis of disability, "be excluded from the participation in, be denied the benefits of, or be subjected to discrimination…,"[2] and the parallel provision of Title II of the ADA.[3]

Further, exclusion from assessment programs violates the §504 and ADA regulations requiring that students with disabilities be provided benefits and services comparable to those provided other students. As noted in Chapter 1, *supra*, the §504 regulations prohibit, as a discriminatory practice, affording students with disabilities "an opportunity to participate in or benefit from an aid, benefit or service that is not equal to that afforded others,"[4] or providing "an aid, benefit or service that is not as effective as that provided to others."[5] The ADA regulations contain parallel provisions.[6] Where assessment results are used to inform educational decision making with respect to, for example, programming, resource allocations or instructional strategies and methodologies, students with disabilities who are excluded from participation in the assessment program are unlawfully afforded just such lesser and less effective benefits and services.

2. IDEA

IDEA requires that, with the exception of youth convicted as adults and incarcerated in adult prisons, students with disabilities be included in general state and district-wide assessment programs, with "appropriate accommodations" and "modifications in administration" where necessary.[7] The state (for state assessment programs) or local educational agency (for district- wide assessments) must also develop and conduct "alternate assessments" for those children who cannot participate in the regular assessment even with appropriate accommodations and modifications.[8] Whether a student will participate in a particular large-scale assessment (or particular part thereof), or in an alternate assessment is to be decided by his or her IEP team.[9] If the IEP team decides that a student will not participate in a particular assessment or part thereof, it must include in the IEP an explanation of why that assessment (or assessment segment) is not appropriate for the student, and how he or she will be assessed instead.[10] As noted previously, these provisions mandating inclusion in large scale assessments were added to IDEA in 1997 — at the same time that Congress made more explicit the requirement that all children with disabilities receive meaningful opportunities to learn in the general curriculum, upon which such assessments are based.[*]

The state must report to the public the number of children with disabilities participating in regular assessments; the number participating in alternate assessments; and the performance of children with disabilities on each.[11] These reports must include aggregated data combining the performance of children with disabilities together with all children; disaggregated data on the performance of children with disabilities alone; and must be made in the same detail and at least as often as are reports on the assessment of children without disabilities.[12]

3. Other relevant laws

Title I of the Elementary and Secondary Education Act Title I of the Elementary and Secondary Education Act, as amended by the Improving America's Schools Act of 1994,[**] provides, as part of its accountability system, for yearly assessments of Title I student progress towards meeting the high standards set by the state for all children in certain academic areas.[13] The statute expressly requires that "all" students participate in these assessments, with "the reasonable adaptations and accommodations for students with diverse learning needs, necessary to measure the achievement of such students relative to State content standards."[14] Thus, students with disabilities who attend schools operating school-wide Title I programs must be included in these assessments, as must individual students with disabilities receiving Title I services in schools operating targeted assistance programs. Further, to ensure accountability, assessment results must be capable of being disaggregated so that the performance of students with disabilities may be compared to that of their nondisabled peers.[15] The U.S. Department of Education has emphasized that the

---

[*] For a discussion of the right to learn in the general curriculum under IDEA as well as under Section 504 and Title II of the ADA, see Chapter 3.

[**] As this book went to press in July 2001, Congress was in the process of reauthorizing and amending Title I. Advocates should check the most recent version of the statute, as well as any regulations interpreting and implementing it, for current requirements.

results for every student who takes an assessment must be reported and integrated into the state's mechanism for evaluating schools, regardless of whether the student has taken the standard administration of the assessment, participated with accommodations, or taken an alternate assessment.[16]

Goals 2000: Educate America Act The Goals 2000 legislation, first enacted in 1994,[17] made grants to states to develop state improvement plans based upon the principles of standards-based education reform. Among other things, states were required to include in their plans a process for developing and implementing state assessments aligned with rigorous state standards for what all children should know and be able to do.[18] These assessments were to provide for the participation of "all students with diverse learning needs," explicitly including students with disabilities.[19] Further, state assessments developed as part of a Goals 2000-funded state improvement plan were to include "the adaptations and accommodations necessary to permit" participation by all students.[20]

State education reform laws Many state education reform laws include provisions regarding large scale testing and assessment. These laws may or may not directly address the participation of students with disabilities. Advocates should consult their state laws and regulations as well as state and local policies, all of which much be consistent with federal law.

B. EQUITABLE PARTICIPATION IN ASSESSMENTS — ACCOMMODATIONS, MODIFICATIONS AND ALTERNATE ASSESSMENTS

Students with disabilities have rights not only to be included in large scale assessments, but to *equitable* participation, meaning participation that affords them an equal opportunity to demonstrate their proficiency and achievement in the area being assessed. For purposes of §504 and Title II of the ADA, this right arises from both the statutory language[21] and from regulations requiring (1) comparable benefits and services, discussed in Chapter 1[22] and (2) the modification of policies and procedures when necessary to avoid discrimination.[23] IDEA addresses equitable participation in assessment through express requirements for accommodations, modifications and alternate assessments, noted above and discussed in further detail below.

Whether in the context of IDEA or of §504 and the ADA, it is a simpler matter to say that students with disabilities, as appropriate, are entitled to accommodations, modifications and alternate assessments than it is to define, or differentiate among, accommodations, modifications and alternate assessments. There are no uniform definitions of these terms, in either law or practice. Thus various federal, state and local laws, assessment policies, legal analyses, policy documents, studies, and practice guides may use the same term to mean very different things. In addition, the IDEA statute and regulations use all three without defining any of them. Regardless of any differences in how each of these terms comes to be used in practice and/or law, however, the requirements of inclusion and equitable participation mean that large scale assessment programs must define and employ them in such a way as to address the needs of *all* students with disabilities who cannot fairly demonstrate what they know and are able to do through a standard administration of the standard assessment. This includes not only those students who can take the standard assessment if provided changes in the logistics of test-taking (e.g., changes in time or setting, use of readers, scribes or assistive technology, braille or large print versions of the test, etc.), but also those who need a different kind of assessment in order to demonstrate the same knowledge and skills to be measured by the standard assessment, as well the small number of students with cognitive impairments so severe that their curriculum permissibly differs substantially in content from what the standard assessment, or part thereof, is testing.

1. Modifications, Accommodations and Alternate Assessments under IDEA

In regard to the details of individual student participation in large scale assessments, the IDEA statute and regulations require that —

- students with disabilities receive "appropriate accommodations and modifications in administration, if necessary";[24]
- states and school districts develop and, by July 1, 2000, conduct "alternate assessments for those children who cannot participate" in a State or district-wide assessment, or part thereof;[25]
- IEPs include a statement of "any individual modifications in the administration of State or district-wide assessments of student achievement that are needed in order for the child to participate";[26] and
- if the IEP team determines that a child will not participate in a par-

ticular assessment (or part thereof), the IEP must explain (1) why the assessment is not appropriate for him or her, and (2) how the child will be assessed.[27]

As an initial matter, it is important to note that IDEA gives significant authority to the IEP team (and consequently, great weight to the resulting IEP) in determining not whether, but *how* a student will participate in assessments — i.e., what kinds of modifications, accommodations, or alternate assessment arrangements he or she will be able to rely upon when taking part in state or district-wide assessments.[28] These decisions can have profound consequences, particularly when assessment results may be used for such purposes as improving the manner in which students are instructed, or for deciding whether a student will be promoted, be admitted to a desired program, or receive a high school diploma. It is thus critical for parents, students and their advocates to pay close attention to these issues while they are developing IEPs. This includes ensuring that evaluations and re-evaluations address the impact of the student's disability on participation in the standard assessment(s), and that the IEP team includes individuals with appropriate professional expertise in identifying the need for, and devising, appropriate assessment modifications and accommodations that will enable the student to be validly assessed, as well as the need for alternate assessment. In addition, some states and school systems have adopted policies limiting assessment accommodations and/or modifications to those used by the student (as per his or her IEP) during the course of the school year for instructional purposes. The legality of applying uniformly such a policy is highly questionable; however, it is nonetheless important to include in the IEP as *instructional* accommodations/modifications any accommodations/modifications anticipated to be needed for assessments.

As previously noted, the statute and regulations neither define nor differentiate among "appropriate accommodations," "modifications in administration" and "alternate assessment." The U.S. Department of Education, however, has made statements partially interpreting "modifications in administration" and "alternate assessment." In regard to alternate assessments, upon releasing the 1999 IDEA regulations, the Department stated that "[a]lternate assessments need to be aligned with the general curriculum standards set for all students and should not be assumed appropriate only for those students with significant cognitive impairment," further stressing that the need for an alternate assessment depends upon the needs of the child, and not the category or severity of his or her disability.[29] It subsequently explained that "the alternate assessment is sufficiently flexible to meet the needs of difficult-to-assess students with disabilities who may need the alternate assessment to demonstrate competency for benefits such as promotion or a diploma."[30] In regard to the term "modifications in administration," the Department of Education has stated that, as used in the statutory and regulatory requirement that IEPs include "modifications in the administration" of assessments, the term encompasses both changes to the assessment in format, response, setting, timing or scheduling that do not alter in any significant way what the test measures or the comparability of scores, and changes in the assessment that do.[31]

2. Section 504 and Title II of the ADA

Equitable participation, or equal opportunity to demonstrate one's knowledge and skill, requires that assessments be administered in such a way that they measure the student's proficiency in the area being assessed, rather than his or her unrelated disability.[32] Towards this end, §504 and the ADA require that students with disabilities be provided with reasonable accommodations when participating in large scale assessments.[33] For §504 and ADA purposes, reasonable accommodations are those that do not fundamentally alter the nature of the assessment program,[34] or impose an undue burden.[35] The U.S. Department of Education/Office for Civil Rights has applied this interpretation, finding that refusing to provide a reader for a student with a learning disability during a high school graduation examination, based on a policy allowing only blind students to have readers, constituted an illegal denial of equal opportunity. On the other hand, OCR found that no violation occurred where elementary school children whose IEPs called for the use of calculators as an educational aid were not permitted to use them on a statewide math proficiency test.[36] In the latter case, allowing the use of calculators on an assessment intended to measure students' computational skills would alter the essential nature of the assessment.

The mandate for equitable participation in large scale assessments also requires the provision of different or alternate assessments for students with disabilities who need them in order to have an equal opportunity to benefit from the assessment program. For students unable to demonstrate their proficiency in the area being tested via the standard assessment, failure to provide a different assessment that *would* enable them to demonstrate their level of achievement in the relevant area would violate the §504 and ADA regulations requiring comparable benefits and services.[37] Here, depending upon the purpose(s) of the assessment, the benefits and services are (1) having accurate data about their educational attainment included in the state or school system's accountability system, and/or (2) in the case of high stakes testing, having an opportunity to demonstrate the proficiency required for the "stakes" involved, e.g., promotion, placement in a particular program or receipt of a high school diploma. The same would be true for the small number of students with cognitive impairments so severe that their curriculum permissibly differs substantially in content from what the standard assessment is measuring. These students, too, must be provided an opportunity to demonstrate what they know and can do, presumably through a performance assessment that measures the different content.

C. ASSESSMENTS WITH HIGH-STAKES CONSEQUENCES FOR STUDENTS

Increasingly, states and some school systems are using student performance on large-scale assessments to make "high stakes" decisions about individual students such as, e.g., whether a student will receive a high school diploma, or be promoted to the next grade. While the above-discussed legal provisions apply with equal force whether an assessment is used to hold schools accountable or to make decisions about individual students, the use of assessments to make high stakes decisions about students implicates additional legal rights.

Assessments used for holding schools accountable are based on the premise that poor student performance indicates that students have not been effectively taught, and have not had an adequate opportunity to learn what is being tested — and that, therefore, schools must improve. Testing with high stakes for students is based on the opposite premise — that students *have* had an adequate opportunity to learn, and that it is therefore fair to subject those who do not meet performance standards to negative consequences (e.g., retention in grade or diploma denial). Where this premise is not correct, i.e. where students with or without disabilities have not had an adequate opportunity to learn what is being tested, the use of high stakes tests should be held to violate due process under the U.S. Constitution.[38]

Two federal appellate court decisions involving high school competency tests make this point. The first, *Debra P. v. Turlington*,[39] held unconstitutional a Florida law requiring that students pass a statewide minimum competency test in order to receive a high school diploma. The court ruled that as a matter of constitutional due process, students must be provided adequate notice that passing such an examination is a condition of receiving a diploma.[40] In addition, the court held that the test was invalid because the state failed to show that it fairly assessed what was actually taught in school.[41] This concept, known as curricular or instructional validity, requires that the test items adequately correspond to the required curriculum in which the students should have been instructed before taking the test, and that the test measure the material and skills actually (not supposed to have been) taught in the schools at issue.[42]

The second case, *Brookhart v. Illinois State Board of Education*,[43] applied an analysis similar to *Debra P.* to hold that the plaintiffs, here students with disabilities, could not be denied high school diplomas for having failed a district-wide Minimum Competency Test (the "M.C.T."), because their programs of instruction had not been developed to meet the goal of passing the test.[44] The court found that since the students and their parents learned that passing the test would be required only one to one and a half years prior to the students' anticipated graduation, the test's objectives could not have been specifically incorporated into the students' IEPs over a period of years.[45] Issuing its ruling in 1983, the court advised that in the future the notice/opportunity to learn requirement could be met in one of two ways: "[t]he School District can, first, ensure that handicapped students are sufficiently exposed to most of the material that appears on the M.C.T. , or, second, they can produce evidence of a reasoned and well-informed decision by the parents and the teachers involved that a particular high school student will be better off concentrating on educational objectives other than preparation for the M.C.T."[46] However, except perhaps as applied to the very small percentage of students with the most severe cognitive impairments, the latter option would appear to be at odds not only with the IDEA requirement that students with disabilities participate in state and district wide assessments (as discussed above), but with IDEA requirements regarding participation in the general curriculum, particularly as made explicit in the 1997 amendments to IDEA.[*]

---

[*] For a discussion of participation in the general curriculum, see Chapter 3.

NOTES

1. *See, e.g.,* Kevin McGrew *et al.*, University of Minnesota, National Center on Educational Outcomes, *Inclusion of Students with Disabilities in National and State Data Collection Programs* 12-13 (1992).

2. 29 U.S.C. §794(a).

3. *See* 42 U.S.C. §12132.

4. 34 C.F.R. §104.4(b)(1)(ii).

5. 34 C.F.R. §104.4(b)(1)(iii).

6. *See* 28 C.F.R. §35.130(b).

7. 20 U.S.C. §§1412(a)(17)(A), 1414(d)(6)(A)(i); 34 C.F.R. §§300.138(a), 300.311(b)(1).

8. 20 U.S.C. §1412(a)(17)(A); 34 C.F.R. §300.138(b). Accommodations, modifications and alternate assessments are discussed below in section B of this Chapter.

9. 20 U.S.C. §1414(d)(1)(A)(v)(II); 34 C.F.R. §300.347(a)(5)(ii).

10. 20 U.S.C. §1414(d)(1)(A)(v)(II); 34 C.F.R. §300.347(a)(5)(ii).

11. 20 U.S.C. §1412(a)(17)(B); 34 C.F.R. §300.139(a). Performance information is to be reported only if doing so would be statistically sound and would not result in the disclosure of results identifiable to individual children. 20 U.S.C. §1412(a)(17)(B)(iii)(I); 34 C.F.R. §300.139(a)(2).

12. 20 U.S.C. §1412(a)(17)(B); 34 C.F.R. §300.139(b). In addition to the provisions regarding participation in general assessments, IDEA aims to hold states accountable for educational quality by requiring states to establish goals for the performance of children with disabilities. Goals must promote the purposes of IDEA, and be consistent, to the maximum extent appropriate, with other goals and standards for children set by the state. The state must also establish performance indicators for assessing progress towards achieving the goals that, at a minimum, address the performance of children with disabilities on assessments, drop-out rates and graduation rates. Finally, the state must report to the public and to the Department of Education once every two years on the progress being made toward meeting the goals. *See generally* 20 U.S.C. §1412(a)(16).

13. *See* 20 U.S.C. §6311(b). For a discussion of Title I accountability requirements, see Margot Rogers and Christine Stoneman, "Triggering Educational Accountability," Center for Law and Education White Paper (1999), available from the Center for Law and Education, 1875 Connecticut Ave., N.W. Suite 510, Washington, D.C. 20009 (telephone: 202/986-3000, fax: 202/986-6648).

14. 20 U.S.C. §6315(b)(3)(F)(i), (ii).

15. 20 U.S.C. §6315(b)(3)(I).

16. *See* Michael Cohen, Assistant Secretary U.S. Department of Education, Memorandum to Chief State School Officers, Update on Review of Final Assessment Systems Under Title I and Reminder of October 1 Deadline for Submission of Evidence, September 7, 2000 at 4.

17. Pub. L. 103-227, 108 Stat. 128 (March 31, 1994).

18. *See* 20 U.S.C. §5886(c)(1)(B).

19. 20 U.S.C. §5886(c)(1)(B)(III)(aa); 20 U.S.C. §5802(a).

20. 20 U.S.C. §5886(c)(1)(B)(i)(III)(bb).

21. *See* 29 U.S.C. §794(a) (otherwise qualified individual with a disability shall not, "solely by reason of her or his disability...be subjected to discrimination....") (Section 504); 42 U.S.C. §12132 ("no qualified individual with a disability shall, by reason of such disability...be subjected to discrimination.....") (Title II ADA).

22. *See* 34 C.F.R. §104.4(b)(1)(ii) (affording qualified individual with a disability an opportunity to participate in or benefit from an aid, benefit or service that is not equal to that afforded others prohibited) (§504); 28 C.F.R. §35.130(b)(ii) (same) (Title II ADA); 34 C.F.R. §104.4(b)(1)(3) (providing qualified individual with a disability with an aid, benefit or service that is not as effective as that provided to others prohibited) (§504); 28 C.F.R. §35.130(b)(iii) (same) (Title II ADA); 34 C.F.R. §104.4(b)(2) ("'to be equally effective, aids, benefits, and services...must afford handicapped persons equal opportunity to obtain the same result, to gain the same benefit, or to reach the same level of achievement....") (§504). *See also* 34 C.F.R. §104.4(b)(4) (prohibiting, *inter alia*, "criteria or methods of administration" that "have the effect of subjecting qualified handicapped persons to discrimination on the basis of handicap," or "have the purpose or effect of defeating or substantially impairing accomplishment of the objectives of the...program with respect to handicapped persons") (§504); 28 C.F.R. §35.130(b)(3) (same) (Title II ADA).

23. 28 C.F.R. §35.130(b)(7) ("[a] public entity shall make reasonable modifications in policies, practices, or procedures when...necessary to avoid discrimination on the basis of disability, unless the public entity can demonstrate that making the modifications would fundamentally alter the nature of the service, program or activity") (Title II ADA).

24. 34 C.F.R. §300.138(a); 20 U.S.C. §1412(a)(17)(A).

25. 20 U.S.C. §1412(a)(17)(A); 34 C.F.R. §300.138(b).

26. 20 U.S.C. §1414(d)(1)(A)(v)(I); 34 C.F.R. §300.347(a)(5)(i).

27. 20 U.S.C. §1414(d)(1)(A)(v)(II); 34 C.F.R. §300.(a)(5)(ii).

28. Of course, parents or students who disagree with the IEP team's determination regarding accommodations, modifications, alternate assessments, etc. may challenge that decision by requesting an IDEA due process hearing, or invoking any of IDEA's other dispute resolution mechanisms. See Chapter 8, *infra*.

29. 64 Fed. Reg. at 12564-65, 12594 (March 12, 1999). *See also* Judith E. Heumann, Assistant Secretary, U.S. Department of Education, Memorandum to State Directors of Special Education, Questions and Answers about Provisions in the Individuals with Disabilities Education Act Amendments of 1997 Related to Students with Disabilities and State and District-wide Assessments, OSEP 00-24 (August 26, 2000) (hereinafter "OSEP Assessment Memo") at 9.

30. OSEP Assessment Memo at 9.

31. *Id.* at 7.

32. *See, e.g., Brookhart v. Illinois State Bd. of Ed.*, 697 F.2d 179, 184 (7th Cir. 1983); *Hawaii State Department of Education*, 17 EHLR 360 (OCR 10/11/90) (citing 34 C.F.R.§104.4(b)(1)(iii), (iv), (2)). *See also* 34 C.F.R. §104.35(b)(3) (tests used in context of evaluation and placement must be selected and administered so as to best ensure that results accurately reflect student aptitude and achievement, rather than reflecting student's impaired sensory, manual or speaking skills). *Cf. Harrison Co. (WV) School District*, EHLR 353:121 (OCR) (regarding grading of a child with disabilities).

33. *Brookhart, supra,* 697 F.2d at 184; *Hawaii State Department of Education, supra*; 34 C.F.R. §104.4(b)(iii), (iv), (2), 104.35(b)(3); 28 C.F.R. §35.130(b)(1)(iii), (iv), (7).

34. *Alexander v. Choate*, 469 U.S. 287, 300 - 301; 105 S. Ct. 712, 719-20 (1985); 28 C.F.R. §35.130(b)(7). *See also Brookhart, supra*, 697 F.2d at 184 ("[a]ltering the content of the…[high school graduation test] to accommodate an individual's inability to learn the tested material because of his handicap would be a ësubstantial modification'…of the diploma requirement" and so is not required) (citations omitted).

35. *Southeastern Community College v. Davis*, 442 U.S. 397, 413; 99 S. Ct. 2361, 2370-71 (1979); 28 C.F.R. §35.130(b)(7).

36. See, respectively, *Hawaii State Department of Education, supra*, and *South Carolina Department of Education*, EHLR 352:475 (OCR 6/23/87).

37. *See* 34 C.F.R. §104.4(b); 28 C.F.R. §35.130(b).

38. *Brookhart, supra*; *Debra P. v. Turlington*, 644 F.2d 397 (5th Cir. 1981).

39. 644 F.2d 397 (5th Cir. 1981).

40. As the basis for finding due process rights applicable, the court found that the state's compulsory attendance law and statewide education program granted students a constitutionally protected expectation that they would receive a diploma if they successfully completed high school. *Id.* at 404. Since the students possessed this protected property interest, the court held that the state was barred from imposing new criteria without adequate notice and sufficient relationship between the test and the curriculum. *Id.*

41. *Debra P., supra*, 644 F.2d. at 405. *See also Crump v. Gilmer Independent School District*, 797 F. Supp. 552, 555-556 (E.D. Texas 1992)(court granting preliminary injunction permitting plaintiff students who had failed minimum competency test to participate in graduation ceremony based, in part, on court's finding that school would not be able to meet significant burden of proof required to show that the examination questions specifically correspond to the school curriculum). *But see Williams v. Austin Independent School District*, 796 F. Supp. 251 (W.D. Tex. 1992) (denying injunction against imposition of test as diploma requirement on ground that, absent denial of educational opportunity to prepare for the test, such decisions should rest with the legislature and education officials).

    Debra P. also involved allegations of racial discrimination. In this regard, the court found, under the Equal Protection Clause of the Constitution, Title VI of the Civil Rights Act of 1964, 42 U.S.C. §2000d, and the Equal Educational Opportunities Act, 20 U.S.C. §1703(f), that where failure rate on the test showed a greater impact on black than white students, in light of the history of de jure segregation in public schools in the state of Florida, minority students must be afforded access to learning opportunities unhindered by the effects of past racial segregation of the schools before a minimum competency test was included as part of a high school graduation requirement. *Debra P.*, 644 F.2d at 408.

42. *Id.* at 405. For a recent decision applying *Debra P.*, see *G.I. Forum v. Texas Education Agency*, 87 F. Supp.2d 267 (W.D. Tex. 2000), where the court rejected a due process challenge to Texas' high school graduation test. Finding significant, *inter alia*, the state's efforts at remediation and the fact that students were given eight opportunities to pass the examination before leaving school, the court held that all Texas students had had a reasonable opportunity to learn the subject matter covered by the exam. *Id.* at 682. *G.I. Forum* was brought on behalf of minority students who additionally claimed, without success, that use of the test to deny diplomas constituted illegal discrimination under the regulations implementing Title VI of the Civil Rights Act of 1964.

43. 697 F.2d 179 (7th Cir. 1983).

44. 697 F.2d at 187. Whereas the *Debra P.* court held that due process rights were implicated based upon its finding that the student plaintiffs had a property interest in receiving a high school diploma, *Brookhart* found due process rights to be triggered because the diploma denial at issue implicated a protected liberty interest of the students. *See Brookhart*, 697 F.2d at 184-5.

45. *Id.*

46. *Id.* at 187-88.

CHAPTER 8

PROCEDURAL SAFEGUARDS AND PARENT OR STUDENT CHALLENGES TO SCHOOL DECISIONS

IDEA contains an elaborate scheme of procedural safeguards designed to ensure that parents are involved in decisions affecting their child's education and, that when disputes develop nonetheless, they can challenge school system decisions.* The Supreme Court has stressed that these procedural requirements are not mere technicalities but, rather, the primary mechanism through which IDEA seeks to guarantee that the "appropriate" education it promises is actually delivered.[1] Critical procedural safeguards concern surrogate parents, notice, informed consent, access to education records, the opportunity to present complaints, mediation, due process hearings and lawsuits.

While less specific than IDEA, the regulations implementing §504 also require entities operating public school programs to establish and implement a system of procedural safeguards meeting certain criteria.[2] Compliance with IDEA procedural safeguards is one way of meeting this §504 obligation.[3]

A. DEFINING "PARENTS"

As discussed in previous Chapters and below, IDEA affords "parents" strong rights to participate in making, and to challenge, educational decisions. Under IDEA, "parent" means a natural or adoptive parent, a guardian (but not the state if the child is a ward of the state), a person acting in the place of a parent (such as a grandparent or stepparent with whom the child lives, or a person who is legally responsible for the child's welfare), or, as explained below, someone appointed as a "surrogate parent."[4] In addition, a state may allow a foster parent to act as a par-

---

* As discussed below, these rights ordinarily transfer to students when they reach their state's legal age of adulthood.

ent for purposes of IDEA if four conditions exist: (1) the natural parents' power to make educational decisions has been terminated under state law; (2) the foster parent has an ongoing, long-term parental relationship with the child; (3) the foster parent is willing to make the educational decisions required of parents under IDEA; and (4) the foster parent has no interest that would conflict with the interest of the child.[5]

B. Surrogate Parents

Consistent with its emphasis on parent participation in decision making and, as described below, advocacy by parents to ensure that their children receive the education to which they are entitled, IDEA requires states to ensure that all children with disabilities have the equivalent of a parent to act on their behalf. If a child's parents or guardian are not known or cannot be located after reasonable efforts, or if a child is a ward of the state, a "surrogate parent" must be appointed to fulfill the role otherwise played by parents under IDEA.[6] The surrogate parent cannot be an employee of the state educational agency, the local educational agency, or any other agency that is involved in the education or care of the child; must have no interest that conflicts with the child's interest; and must have the knowledge and skills necessary to ensure that the child will be adequately represented.[7]

Once appointed a surrogate parent may — and has a responsibility to — represent the child in all matters relating to the child's identification, evaluation, IEP, placement and right to a free appropriate public education.[8]

C. Transfer of Rights at Age of Majority

Amendments made to IDEA in 1997 provide for the transfer of IDEA rights from parents to students when students reach the legal age of adulthood, or the age of majority, under state law (most commonly, age 18). Rights transfer so long as the student has not been declared incompetent in a legal proceeding under state law. Under the statute, schools must provide all IDEA-required notices to both the parent and the student. All other rights ordinarily afforded parents under IDEA transfer to the student.[9] This includes the rights discussed below, as well as those discussed in previous Chapters. States may further provide that *all* rights — including the right to receive notice of school actions and proposals — transfer *completely* to incarcerated youth (whether in juvenile or adult correctional institutions) who have reached the age of majority.[10]

Schools must notify the student and parents when rights transfer, and also must include in the student's IEP, beginning at least one year before the child will reach the age of majority, a statement indicating that the student has been informed of the rights that will transfer to him or her when he or she becomes an adult.[11]

In addition, the 1997 amendments to IDEA attempt to address educational decision-making for adult students who have *not* been declared incompetent in a legal proceeding, but who are unable to give informed consent regarding their educational programming.[12] IDEA provides that under such circumstances, the state must establish procedures for appointing the student's parent (or, if the parent is not available, another appropriate individual) to represent his or her educational interests. This provision, however, raises a number of serious questions. Ordinarily, only a court may deprive an adult of the right to make his or her own decisions, and only then after a legal proceeding that meets constitutional standards. The language in the IDEA statute does not address these constitutional issues. It also does not address *who* may determine that a legally competent adult student cannot make informed decisions about his education, *who* has the authority to take that decision-making power away from him or her (or on what basis), or who may initiate procedures for taking away decision-making rights. Nor does it create any standards for deciding that a student is not capable of giving informed consent. The regulations do not address these difficulties, providing instead that "[i]f, under Sate law a state has a mechanism" for determining that adult students with disabilities who have not been declared incompetent cannot make informed educational decisions, the state must establish procedures for appointing the parent or (if the parent is unavailable) other appropriate individual to make those decisions.[13]

D. RIGHT TO PRIOR WRITTEN NOTICE OF SCHOOL DECISIONS

1. Notice in General

Under IDEA, parents must be given prior written notice *any time* a school system proposes or refuses (usually in response to a parent's request) to initiate or change the identification, evaluation or educational placement of a child with disabilities or the provision of a free appropriate public education to the child.[14] This includes providing notice when school authorities decide to take certain actions under the discipline provisions of the statute.[15] The §504 regulations require notice of actions regarding the identification, evaluation or educational placement of students with disabilities.[16] The §504 regulations do not specify how, or at what point in time, the notice must be given. They do, however, provide that notice meeting IDEA requirements will satisfy §504 as well.[17]

The notice required by IDEA must include:

- a description of the action proposed or refused by the school system;
- an explanation of why the school system proposes or refuses to take the action;
- a description of alternatives the school system considered along with an explanation of why those alternatives were rejected;
- a description of each evaluation procedure, test, record or report the school system used as a basis for its proposal or refusal;
- a description of any other factors that are relevant to the proposal or refusal;
- a statement that the parents have rights under IDEA's procedural safeguards, and an explanation of how parents can obtain more information about procedural safeguards; and
- sources for parents to contact for help in understanding IDEA.[18]

The notice must be written in language that the general public can understand and provided in the language or other mode of communication used by the parent.[19] If the parent's native language or other mode of communication is not a written one, the school system must ensure that the notice is translated, that the parent understands it and that there is written evidence that these two requirements have been met.[20]

Notice meeting these criteria can be of enormous value to parents and their advocates in enforcing education rights. Unfortunately, these notice provisions are probably among the most often-violated of IDEA requirements. When schools fail to provide proper notice, parents and advocates should consider demanding it as a matter of course.

2. Procedural Safeguards Notice

As noted above, notice under IDEA must include a statement that parents have rights under the procedural safeguards created by the statutes, along with information about how to obtain a description of those rights. In addition, under certain circumstances schools must automatically give parents this detailed description — called "procedural safeguards notice" — regardless of whether parents request it. Procedural safeguards notice must be given:

- when a child is referred for an IDEA evaluation for the first time;
- each time the school system notifies the parents of an IEP meeting;
- whenever the child is to be reevaluated;
- whenever parents (or the school system) file a request for a due process hearing to resolve a dispute concerning the child's education under IDEA; and
- whenever school authorities decide to take certain actions under IDEA's discipline provisions.[21]

The procedural safeguards notice must include a full explanation of all of the IDEA procedural safeguards concerning:[*]

- independent educational evaluations;[**]
- prior written notice;
- parental consent;
- access to education records;
- opportunity to present complaints and to initiate due process hearings;
- the child's placement while due process hearings and appeals to court are pending;
- procedures for students who are placed in interim alternative educational settings;[***]
- requirements for parents who place their children in private schools at public expense;
- mediation;
- due process hearings, including requirements for disclosing evaluation results and recommendations;
- state-level appeals;
- lawsuits;

---

[*] Unless otherwise noted, the following procedural safeguards are discussed in this chapter.

[**] See Chapter 5.

[***] For a discussion of interim alternative educational settings and other discipline matters, see Chapter 9.

- attorneys' fees; and
- procedures for filing a complaint for investigation by the state educational agency.[22]

The procedural safeguards notice, too, must be written in language that the general public can understand, and provided in the language or other mode of communication used by the parent.[23] If the parent's native language or other mode of communication is not a written one, the school system must ensure that the notice is translated, that the parent understands it and that there is written evidence that these two requirements have been met.[24]

E. CONSENT

Consent requirements IDEA requires school systems to obtain informed parental consent before evaluating a child for the first time, conducting a re-evaluation, or providing a child with special education and related services for the first time.[25] Note that consent is *not* required for tests or other evaluations administered to *all* children, unless, of course, the school system seeks consent from all parents.[26] A parent who consents to an evaluation is *not* also consenting to have the child receive special education and related services. Therefore, if the evaluation results in a finding that the child is eligible for services under IDEA, separate, informed consent must be obtained before such services can be provided.[27]

In addition to these IDEA requirements, IDEA permits states to require parental consent for other IDEA services and activities, for example, changes in IEPs or placement.[28] However, states with additional parental consent requirements must ensure that a parent's refusal to consent does not result in a failure to provide the child with a free appropriate public education.[29] Thus, for example, if a parent refuses to consent to a particular IEP or placement change in a state that requires consent for such changes, school personnel should work with the parent to find another way to address the educational need that prompted the proposed change.

Failure or refusal to consent If a parent *fails to respond* to a request for consent to a *re-evaluation*, the school system may proceed anyway if it has taken "reasonable measures" to obtain consent, including telephone calls, correspondence and visits, and has documented its efforts and the results.[30]

If a parent does respond and refuses to consent to an *initial evaluation or re-evaluation*, a number of possibilities might follow. School personnel may, and should, discuss the issue with the parent in order to understand the parent's reasons for withholding consent, explain the school system's concerns, and try to come to a mutually agreeable resolution. Indeed, some *state* laws, regulations or policies may require this process. In addition, the IDEA regulations permit schools to request mediation (see discussion below) in an attempt to resolve the impasse, or to seek a due process hearing (see below) and request that the hearing officer allow the evaluation (or re-evaluation) to proceed over the parent's objection.[31] If, however, state law does not allow schools to do so, and/or gives parents an absolute right to refuse consent, the matter ends there, and the evaluation or re-evaluation cannot proceed.[32]

Finally, schools may not use a parent's refusal to consent to one thing (e.g. a re-evaluation, or a particular IEP provision in a state that requires consent for the latter) as a reason to deny a child other services or benefits due him or her under IDEA.[33]

F. ACCESS TO EDUCATION RECORDS

IDEA , the §504 regulations and the Family Educational Rights and Privacy Act ("FERPA") guarantee parents the right to inspect and review education records concerning their children.[34] The IDEA and FERPA regulations on this topic go into greater detail than do the §504 regulations which, for example, do not define "record" and do not detail the scope of access rights.[35] However, it is important to remember that FERPA rights apply to *all* parents and students, regardless of whether the student is eligible for services under IDEA, or even has a disability. Thus parents of children who are protected by §504 but not by IDEA enjoy the full range of access rights afforded by FERPA.

Under both IDEA and FERPA, school systems must honor a request to review education records without unnecessary delay; in no event can a system take more than 45 days to comply.[36] IDEA further provides that education records must be made available before any meeting concerning an IEP, before any hearing, and in connection with certain disciplinary matters.[37]

For purposes of IDEA and FERPA, "education records" means those records that are directly related to a student.[38] "Record," in turn, means any information recorded in any way and includes, among other things, handwriting, print, tape and film.[39] Upon request, a school system must provide parents with a list of the types and locations of the education records it collects, maintains or uses.[40] Access rights, or the right to inspect and review records, include the rights to:

- receive a response from school officials to reasonable requests for explanations and interpretations of the records;
- have a representative of the parent inspect and review the records; and
- obtain copies of records, if a lack of copies would effectively prevent the parent from exercising the right to inspect and review the records.[41]
    - A school system may not charge a fee for copies if the fee would effectively prevent the parent from exercising the right to inspect and review the records, and in no event can the system charge for searching for or retrieving records.[42]

Either parent, including a non-custodial parent, may review and inspect records under both laws, unless that right has been revoked by state law, court order or other legally binding document relating to matters such as divorce, separation, custody or guardianship.[43]

FERPA grants all of the above rights to students who have reached age 18 or are in postsecondary education. When a student thus becomes eligible to exercise FERPA rights himself, these rights transfer from the parent and become the student's, exclusively.[44] In addition, as discussed above, under IDEA many rights, including the above, transfer from parent to student when the student reaches the age of majority under state law.[45]

G. ADMINISTRATIVE COMPLAINTS UNDER IDEA, §504 AND THE ADA

As explained in the following section, parents have the right to request an impartial due process hearing in order to vindicate IDEA and §504 rights as well as the right to bring an action in court. Parents may also file administrative complaints regarding IDEA, §504 and Americans with Disabilities Act ("ADA") violations with their state department of education (in regard to IDEA) or the U.S. Department of Education Office for Civil Rights ("OCR") (in regard to §504 and the ADA). Complaints of this sort do *not* trigger a due process hearing. Rather, they are investigated by the responsible agency, which then makes a determination as to whether rights have been violated.

1. IDEA Complaints to a State Educational Agency

As a condition of receiving IDEA funds, each state educational agency ("SEA") must operate a complaint management system for accepting, investigating and resolving complaints of IDEA violations. While complaints generally are received, investigated and resolved by the SEA, states may, at their discretion, create a system in which complaints are initially filed at the local level (or with whatever public agency is directly responsible for the child's education), with decisions reviewable at the state level.[46]

The IDEA regulations set out mandatory standards that these state complaint systems must meet. Individuals and organizations may file a signed, written complaint, which must specify that an IDEA violation has occurred, and include the supporting facts.[47] Complaints must be filed within a year of the violation, unless a longer period is reasonable because the violation is continuing.[48] Complaints seeking compensatory education services must be filed within three years.[49]

Once it receives a complaint, the SEA must carry out an independent on-site investigation, if necessary; give the individual or organization filing the complaint an opportunity to submit additional information; review all relevant information; and determine whether a violation of IDEA has occurred.[50] The SEA must issue a written decision that responds to each one of the allegations in the complaint, and contains findings of fact, conclusions, and the reasons for the decision.[51] All of these steps must take place within 60 days of when a complaint is filed, unless a particular complaint presents exceptional circumstances.[52]

In resolving a complaint that involves a failure to provide appropriate services, the SEA must fashion a way to compensate the affected child (or children) for the denial of those services, including, for example, by an award of compensatory education, financial reimbursement or other corrective action.[53] The SEA must also address future provision of services for all children with disabilities in light of the particular violation(s) found, and ensure effective implementation of all aspects of its final decision through technical assistance, negotiations and corrective actions aimed at the offending school system.[54]

Finally, the IDEA regulations address the relationship between this kind of complaint to the SEA and the due process hearings discussed below. If a complaint to the SEA raises issues that are also part of a due process hearing, the SEA must set aside those *common* issues until the due process hearing ends, while going on to resolve any issues that are *not* part of the hearing.[55] If an issue in a complaint has *already* been decided in a due process hearing, the due process hearing decision is binding and the SEA cannot take on the issue.[56] However, when a complaint to the SEA alleges that a school system has failed to implement a due process hearing decision, the SEA must entertain and resolve the complaint.[57]

2. Complaints to OCR Under §504 and the ADA

OCR is responsible for §504 and Title II ADA enforcement in the context of education. Any person who believes a school system has discriminated against a student in violation of §504 or the §504 regulations may file a written complaint.[58] ADA complaints may be filed by an individual who believes that he or she or a specific class of individuals has been discriminated against on the basis of disability.[59] Ordinarily, a complaint must be filed within 180 days of the date that the §504 or ADA violation occurred.[60] Complaints may be filed with the appropriate OCR regional office.[61]

OCR will investigate the complaint and, if it finds a violation, attempt to resolve the matter through informal means and obtain voluntary compliance from the offending school district.[62] Where informal resolution is not possible, OCR has the authority to terminate federal funding for §504 violations, and take other legal action in regard to both §504 and ADA issues.[63] As a practical matter, however, OCR resolves most complaints without resort to such remedies.

Department of Education regulations expressly forbid school systems from intimidating, threatening, coercing, discriminating against or otherwise retaliating against anyone who has filed a §504 complaint or cooperated with a complaint investigation.[64] These regulations also generally prohibit retaliation against students and parents and others for engaging in activities protected by §504.[65] The regulations implementing Title II of the ADA contain similar protections.[66]

In responding to complaints, OCR does not ordinarily review the result of individual placement and other educational decisions but, rather, looks to see if school systems used correct procedures in reaching them.[67] Thus, for example, while OCR might examine whether a school followed the procedures in the §504 regulations in deciding upon the least restrictive environment for a chid, as long as those procedures were followed, it would not decide whether or not the placement chosen actually *is* the least restrictive environment for him or her. OCR has also stated that, as a policy matter, it will not investigate matters that are also the subject of a pending due process hearing.[68] Rather, OCR will entertain such complaints if filed *after* the due process hearing concludes, review them to see whether the hearing decision addressed the issues raised using legal standards comparable to those under §504 and the ADA, and proceed accordingly.[69]

H. DUE PROCESS HEARINGS AND REVIEWS

IDEA entitles parents and students to an impartial due process hearing on any matter related to the provision of a free appropriate public education including — but not limited to — identification, evaluation, and placement issues.[70] School districts, too, may initiate hearings.[71] Regardless of who requests the hearing, the educational agency must inform the parent of any free or low-cost legal and other relevant services available in the area.[72] Parents must also be provided this information upon request, even where no hearing is pending.[73]

The §504 regulations also require entities operating public school programs to establish an impartial administrative hearing and review system to address the complaints of students with disabilities regarding identification, evaluation or educational placement.[74] Although the regulations do not set out specific criteria that hearing procedures must meet, they do provide that procedures meeting IDEA criteria will fulfill the §504 requirement as well.[75] In addition, the §504 regulations require school systems to adopt grievance procedures that "incorporate appropriate due process standards and…provide for prompt and equitable resolution of complaints" alleging *any* violation of §504 or the §504 regulations,[76] and to designate at least one person to coordinate its §504 compliance efforts.[77] The regulations implementing Title II of the ADA contain a comparable provision.[78]

1. Single Versus Two Tiered Hearing/Review Systems

IDEA gives states two options for due process hearing systems. Under the first, due process hearings are conducted by the local school district.[79] Any party aggrieved by the decision can appeal to the state educational agency, which must conduct an impartial review of the hearing and make an independent decision on the case.[80] The official conducting the review must examine the entire record of the due process hearing; ensure that hearing procedures were consistent with due process; give the parties an opportunity for written and/or oral argument; seek additional evidence if necessary; and make an independent decision, including written findings and a written decision.[81]

If the reviewing officer seeks additional evidence, the hearing rights described below apply.[82] The decision of the reviewing official is final and binding unless appealed to a court.[83]

Under the second permissible system, due process hearings are conducted by the state educational agency.[84] Where this is the case, the hearing officer's decision *must* be final and binding (subject to the right to bring an action in court), and *cannot* be subject to any form of administrative review.[85]

2. Hearing Rights and Obligations

A request for a due process hearing must be accompanied by a complaint, albeit a different sort of complaint than that discussed above in regard to complaints to the SEA. A complaint seeking a due process hearing must include:

- the name and address of the child;
- the name of the school he or she attends;
- a description of the problem(s) prompting the complaint, including the related facts; and
- a proposed resolution of the problem, to the extent known and available to the parents at the time the complaint/hearing request is filed.[86]

However, a state or school system cannot deny or delay a parent's right to a due process hearing simply because the parent fails to provide this information.[87]

In addition to providing this information in the complaint, at least five business days before the hearing parents, school systems and other parties to a due process hearing must disclose to all of the other parties all completed evaluations, and recommendations based on those evaluations, that will be used at the hearing.[88] A hearing officer may bar any party that fails to do so from introducing the undisclosed evaluation or recommendation at the hearing without the consent of the other party.[89]

Regardless of whether the hearing is conducted at the local level or at the state level, the hearing officer cannot be an employee of the state agency or local school system involved in the education or care of the child.[90] Anyone with a personal or professional interest that would undermine his or her objectivity is likewise disqualified from serving.[91] Hearings and reviews involving oral arguments must be conducted at a time and place reasonably convenient to the parents and student involved.[92]

In addition to the right to an impartial hearing officer, parties to due process hearings have the following rights:

- to be represented by an attorney;
- to be accompanied and advised by individuals with special knowledge or training in the needs of children with disabilities;
- to present evidence;
- to confront and cross-examine witnesses;
- to compel the attendance of witnesses;
- to a written or, at the parent's option, electronic, verbatim record of the hearing (at no cost); and
- to written or, at the parent's option, electronic findings of fact and decisions (at no cost).[93]

Either party may prohibit the other from presenting evidence it did not disclose at least five business days before the hearing.[94] Parents but not other parties have the rights to have the child present at the hearing, and to open the hearing to the public.[95]

3. Timelines

The IDEA regulations provide that a final decision in an impartial due process hearing must be rendered no later than 45 days after the hearing request is received.[96] In states that have opted for the local hearing/state-level review system, review decisions must be rendered no later than 30 days after the request for review is received.[97] Hearing and reviewing officers, however, may extend these deadlines at the request of either party.[98]

4. Advocacy Considerations

IDEA sets forth the minimum criteria state due process hearing schemes must meet. Most states have statutes or regulations that also address these issues. Parents and advocates should check state law for additional requirements governing hearing procedures, rights and logistics.

In preparing for a hearing, it is crucial to plan for the possibility that the dispute might ultimately become the subject of an action in court. Should this occur, the rule requiring exhaustion of administrative remedies (discussed in further detail below) may prevent parents from raising issues they did not raise at the due process hearing.[99] Parents and advocates should thus be careful to raise all issues and claims at the hearing.

A similar consideration exists in regard to testimony and other evidence. As discussed below, some courts have held that there is only a limited right to introduce new evidence when an IDEA case reaches court. Under this view, under certain circumstances failure to present certain witnesses (or their complete testimony) or other evidence at the due process hearing means that they cannot be presented in court.[100] Thus ordinarily all relevant testimony and evidence should be presented at the hearing, and none "saved" for trial.

Parents and advocates should also be aware that courts are required to give "due weight" to due process hearing outcomes under IDEA.[101] In addition, the party challenging the due process decision in court will have the burden of proving that the decision was wrong.[102] These factors underscore the importance of planning for due process hearings with court in mind.

I. MEDIATION

The IDEA Amendments of 1997 provided for the first time in federal law for mediation of special education disputes. State educational agencies, local school systems and other public agencies that educate children must ensure that opportunities exist to mediate disputes involving the identification, evaluation, educational placement or provision of a free appropriate public education to a child with a disability.[103] At a minimum, mediation must be available whenever a due process hearing is requested.[104] Parents must be informed of the availability of mediation whenever they or a school system request a hearing.[105]

Mediation is much less formal than a due process hearing. In mediation, a neutral third party meets with the parent and school system and attempts to assist them in discussing the dispute and reaching a mutually agreeable solution to their disagreement. Unlike a due process hearing officer, a mediator does not serve as a judge, and does not make decisions.

Under IDEA, mediation is *voluntary* for both parties, and *cannot be used to deny or delay a parent's right to a due process hearing.*[106] Note that mandatory mediation violates §504 as well as IDEA.[107]

Mediation must be conducted by a qualified and impartial mediator who is trained in effective mediation techniques.[108] A mediator may not be an employee of any school system (or other local educational agency), of any state agency that receives an IDEA grant from the state educational agency, or of the state educational agency if it is providing direct services to the child involved in the mediation; nor may he or she have any personal or professional conflict of interest.[109] The state must keep a list of qualified mediators who are knowledgeable about the education rights, under laws and regulations, of students with disabilities.[110] The mediator who will serve in a particular case must be chosen either by random from the list, or with the involvement and agreement of both parties.[111]

Other key IDEA provisions concerning mediation include the following:

- Each mediation session must be held at a time and place convenient for both parties.
- An agreement reached during mediation must be put into a written mediation agreement.
- Discussions during mediation are confidential, and may not be used as evidence in a later due process hearing or lawsuit.[112]

J. Civil Action in Court

IDEA provides that any party aggrieved by a due process hearing decision (or, in states with a local hearing/state review system, the review decision) may bring a lawsuit in federal district court or in a state court of competent jurisdiction.[113] The court must receive the records of the administrative proceedings, hear additional evidence at the request of a party and base its decision on the preponderance of the evidence.[114] While courts must give "due weight…to…[state administrative] proceedings,"[115] they must also make an independent decision based upon the evidence before them, and are free to reject the findings of the due process hearing or review after careful consideration.[116] Where IDEA violations are found, courts are to grant such relief as they deem appropriate.[117]

Section 504 does not expressly state that private individuals may sue in court for §504 violations. However, courts have generally held that they may bring a civil action to enforce §504, finding an implied right of action.[118]

1. Statute of Limitations/Time Within Which to Sue

IDEA does not specify the time within which an aggrieved party must file suit. Courts must therefore "borrow" the statute of limitations for the most closely analogous state law claim, provided that it is consistent with the intent of IDEA.[119] The statute of limitations for bringing §504 claims in court is also "borrowed" from state law.[120]

Application of this rule in IDEA cases has resulted in statutes of limitations that vary widely from state to state. And even *within* a state, statutes of limitations may vary depending upon the particular IDEA claim.[121] Some courts have adopted limitation periods as short as 30[122] or 60[123] days or 4 months.[124] It is thus important for parents who have gone to due process without an attorney to seek the advice of one as soon as possible after an unfavorable due process hearing or review decision is issued, and for the non-attorney advocates who may have assisted them to advise them accordingly.

2. Exhaustion of Administrative Remedies

IDEA   IDEA provisions regarding civil actions and jurisdiction ordinarily prohibit parents from bringing IDEA claims to court without first exhausting administrative remedies.[125] Although exhaustion may be excused if resort to administrative remedies would be "futile or inadequate,"[126] courts apply the exhaustion rule very strictly, and usually read these exceptions narrowly.

The exhaustion requirement applies to particular *issues* as well as to the matter as a whole.[127] Filing an administrative complaint to the state educational agency — as opposed to the kind of complaint that triggers a due process hearing — does not ordinarily constitute "exhaustion"; parents must go through due process hearings (and, in states with a local hearing/state review system, the review phase) in order to fulfill this requirement.[128]

Section 504 and the ADA   Ordinarily, individuals enforcing §504 rights or ADA rights under Title II of that law are not required to exhaust administrative remedies before going to court.[129] However, under certain circumstances parents and students with *§504 or ADA* claims regarding public elementary or secondary education must exhaust *IDEA* administrative remedies before suing. If the §504 or ADA action seeks relief that is also available under IDEA, the plaintiffs must fulfill IDEA exhaustion requirements *even if they had not intended to raise IDEA claims in court.*[130]

3. Additional Testimony and Evidence

Although IDEA provides that courts "shall hear additional evidence at the request of a party,"[131] the right to introduce new evidence is not absolute. Federal appellate courts have ruled, for example, that "additional" evidence means only "supplemental" evidence, and/or that valid reasons for supplementing the evidence already presented at the due process hearing will vary from case to case.[132] Courts also have held that witnesses cannot be presented in court simply to "repeat or embellish" their due process hearing testimony.[133]

K. CHILD'S STATUS DURING IDEA HEARINGS AND LAWSUITS

While due process or judicial proceedings are pending, the child is to remain in his or her then current educational placement unless the state or local education agency and her parents agree upon some other arrangement.[134] This IDEA provision is often referred to as the "stay put" provision, and has been characterized as "unequivocal" by the Supreme Court.[135] Stay-put rights apply to all changes in placement, including graduation.[136] There are, however, limited exceptions to the stay-put rule for some children involved in certain kinds of disciplinary incidents involving dangerous weapons, illegal drugs, or behavior substantially likely to cause injury to self or others.[137] These exceptions are discussed in Chapter 9.

Where a parent challenges a school system's placement proposal and prevails at the due process hearing level (or, where relevant, the state-level review), the favorable placement decision becomes an agreement between the parents and the State or local education agency within the meaning of the stay-put rule.[138] The placement thus must be implemented at public expense *even if the school system appeals the hearing or review decision in court.*[139]

It is important to note that the stay-put provision prohibits *school systems* from unilaterally changing a student's placement pending due process and judicial proceedings. Parents have more latitude. As the Supreme Court has observed, the stay-put provision "is located in a section [of the statute] detailing procedural safeguards which are largely for the benefit of the parents and the child," and it is doubtful "that this pro-vision would authorize a court to order parents to leave their child in a particular placement."[140] For example, and as explained below, parents who disagree with the school's placement choice, and who have the resources to do so, may place their child in a private program at their own expense and, if they succeed in establishing that the school system's pro-posed placement did not provide FAPE, and that their own placement is "appropriate" within the meaning of IDEA, obtain reimbursement from the school system.

L. REMEDIES

IDEA requires courts to order such relief as is "appropriate."[141] Similarly, §504 entitles students who successfully pursue their rights under that law to a variety of remedies as relief for having suffered dis-crimination. Due process hearing officers and courts can order a school system to take any number of actions in order to correct violations of IDEA and §504, as well as of the ADA, including modifying an IEP, implementing an existing IEP it has failed to carry out, providing a par-ticular placement, providing a particular related service(s), etc. Complaints to OCR can result in similar relief. In addition, compensatory education and reimbursement for special education and related services paid for by parents are available remedies under proper circumstances. Damages may also be available (see below).

1. Reimbursement

The Supreme Court approved retroactive reimbursement as an IDEA remedy in *School Committee of the Town of Burlington v. Department of Education*.[142] In that case, the court ruled that courts' broad power to award "appropriate" relief under IDEA includes the power to order a school system to reimburse parents for the cost of obtaining an appropri-ate education when the school system has failed to provide one.[143] Parents who win their IDEA case at the due process hearing level do not have to go to court to obtain an order requiring reimbursement; IDEA hearing officers the authority to order this remedy, and states must permit them to do so.[144] Under and since *Burlington*, reimbursement has been awarded to remedy a wide variety of IDEA violations. Reimbursement for private school tuition, for example, may be available where a hearing officer or a court determines that a school district failed to provide or offer the free appropriate public education required by IDEA, and that the private education obtained by parents was "appropriate."[145] Parents may also obtain reimbursement under IDEA for related services a school district should have, but did not, provide.[146] Transportation (including compensation for the expenditure of time and effort in providing transportation as well as out-of-pocket expenses),[147] summer programming[148] and tutoring,[149] as well as interest on loans obtained to finance educational costs,[150] have all been ordered reimbursed. As the Supreme Court held in *Florence Co. School District No. 4 v. Carter*,[151] parents need not precisely replicate the placement or services a school district should have provided in order to obtain reimbursement, and need not meet the same standards that a school system must meet in selecting a placement. Rather, parents may receive reimbursement for the costs incurred in providing special education or related services so long as these educational services meet the standard of "appropriateness" established by IDEA.[152]

The 1997 amendments to IDEA added provisions regarding reimbursement to the statute for the first time; prior to 1997, the law on this topic came solely from *Burlington* and subsequent judicial decisions. The new statutory provision applies to children *who have previously received special education and related services from a public education system*, and provides that if their parents enroll them in a private school, a court or a hearing officer may order reimbursement after finding that the public system failed to make a free appropriate public education available to the child in a timely matter.[153] Reimbursement in this situation may be reduced or denied under any of the following circumstances:

- If at the last IEP meeting before removing their child from the public school, the parents did not inform the IEP team that they were rejecting the school system's proposed placement, state their concerns, and announce their intent to enroll their child in a private school at public expense, or did not provide this information in writing 10 business days before removing the child.
- If the school system notified the parents that it proposed to evaluate the child before the parents removed him or her from school, but the parents did not make the child available for the evaluation.
- If a judge finds that the parents acted unreasonably.[154]

However, reimbursement may *not* be reduced or denied for failure to notify the school as described above if providing the notice before enrolling the child in a private school would likely result in physical or serious emotional harm to the child; if the school prevented the parent from providing notice; if the parents were never informed of the notice requirement; or if the parent is illiterate and cannot write in English.[155]

As the U.S. Department of Education has noted, these 1997 provisions *supplement* the broad authority courts and hearing officers enjoy under *Burlington* and *Carter* to award reimbursement whenever appropriate; they do not diminish it. [156] Thus the new statutory language notwithstanding, hearing officers and courts retain their pre-existing authority to award reimbursement in situations where a child has *not* yet been provided services, by virtue of the broad equitable powers to award "appropriate" relief granted elsewhere in the statute.[157]

Although most court cases seeking reimbursement have been decided under IDEA, reimbursement is available for §504 violations as well, and a number of OCR complaint investigations have resulted in reimbursement by offending school districts.[158]

2. Compensatory Education

Since the Supreme Court's decision in *Burlington*, courts have consistently held that compensatory education, meaning additional educational and/or related services to make up for the time during which a school system failed to provide a free appropriate public education, is also an appropriate remedy under IDEA.[159] Comparing compensatory education to the reimbursement approved in *Burlington*, these courts have recognized that without compensatory education, students whose parents lack the resources to place them in private programs and seek reimbursement have no way to vindicate their IDEA rights.[160] Compensatory education should therefore be available whenever necessary to secure the right to a free appropriate public education. IDEA grants due process hearing officers the authority to award compensatory education.[161] Parents should not have to go to court simply to secure this particular remedy.

Depending upon the circumstances, the particular IDEA violation and the student's needs, compensatory education may take the form of additional special education or related services during the school day, after usual school hours, or during the summer or other vacation periods. It may also take the form of additional *years* of special education and related services, requiring school systems to continue educational services beyond the age at which a student's entitlement to public education would otherwise end — including education beyond age 21.[162]

As is the case with reimbursement, most reported judicial decisions awarding compensatory education have done so under IDEA, with no discussion of §504.[163] Resolutions of OCR complaints, however, have resulted in the provision of compensatory education to remedy §504 violations in a number of cases, including education beyond age 21.[164]

3. Damages

Whether damages are available as a remedy for violations of IDEA rights is an unsettled question. Most of the judicial decisions stating that damages are *not* available pre-date the Supreme Court's 1992 decision in *Franklin v. Gwinnett Co. Public Schools*,[165] and so should no longer be considered good law. *Franklin*, which involved the availability of damages for intentional violations of Title IX of the Education Amendments of 1972 (prohibiting sex discrimination), held that as a "general rule," "absent clear direction to the contrary by Congress, the federal courts have the power to award any appropriate relief in a cognizable cause of action brought pursuant to a federal statute."[166]

Based upon *Franklin*, courts increasingly are holding that damages may be awarded for violations of IDEA rights.[167] Post-*Franklin* cases stating or holding to the contrary generally have done so without addressing or acknowledging *Franklin*. [168]

Courts generally agree that damages are available for at least intentional discrimination under §504.[169]

M. ATTORNEY FEES

Parents who prevail in IDEA disputes may recover reasonable attorneys fees (at prevailing market rates) and costs, subject to certain conditions.[170] Under 1997 amendments to the statute, courts are to reduce the amount of an attorneys' fee award if (1) the parent unreasonably protracted the final resolution of the dispute; (2) the amount of the fees unreasonably exceeds the prevailing hourly rate in the community for similar services by attorneys with similar skills, experience and reputation; (3) the attorney time spent and the services rendered were excessive under the circumstances; or (4) the attorney representing the parent did not provide the school system with the information ordinarily required to be provided in a complaint and due process hearing request (see above).[171] However, fees cannot be reduced for any of these reasons if the court finds that the state or local educational agency unreasonably protracted the final resolution of the dispute, or violated any of the provisions of 20 U.S.C. §1415, regarding procedural safeguards.[172]

In addition, fees and costs may not be awarded for services performed after a written settlement offer is made to the parents if:

- the offer was made more than 10 days before the start of the due process hearing or, in the case of court proceedings, within the time specified by Rule 68 of the Federal Rules of Civil Procedure (currently more than 10 days before trial starts)

AND

- the offer is not accepted within 10 days

AND

- the court or administrative officer finds that the relief finally obtained by the parents is not more favorable than the settlement offer, unless the parent was substantially justified in rejecting the offer.[173]

Attorneys' fees are available for parents who prevail in due process hearings (with no subsequent appeal to court) as well as for those who prevail in court.[174] In addition, at least two courts have held that parents may recover attorneys' fees for work done in connection with a successful administrative complaint to the state educational agency.[175] Courts have also awarded fees for work done in settling IDEA disputes prior to a due process hearing.[176] Fees may also be available for mediation.[177] Fees relating to an IEP team meeting may not be awarded unless the meeting was convened as a result of an administrative proceeding or judicial action.[178]

NOTES

1. *Board of Education of the Hendrick Hudson Central School District v. Rowley*, 458 U.S. 176, 205-06, 102 S. Ct. 3034, 3050-51 (1982). *See also Pasatiempo v. Aizawa*, 103 F.3d 796, 802 (9th Cir. 1996) ("Congress intended the procedural protections to counteract the tendency of school districts to make decisions regarding the education of disabled children without consulting their parents, and to require school districts to respond adequately to parental concerns about their children.").

2. 34 C.F.R. §104.36.

3. *Id.*

4. 20 U.S.C. §1401(19); 34 C.F.R. §300.20(a).

5. 34 C.F.R. §300.20(b).

6. 20 U.S.C. §1415(b)(2); 34 C.F.R. §300.515.

7. 20 U.S.C. §1415(b)(2); 34 C.F.R. §300.515(c)(2). However, the IDEA regulations, but not the statute, state that an employee of a private agency that provides only non-educational care for the child may serve as a surrogate parent. *See* 34 C.F.R. §300.515(c)(3).

8. 34 C.F.R. §§300.515(e); *see also* 34 C.F.R. part 300, App. A, question 5.

9. 20 U.S.C. §1415(m)(1)(A), (B); 34 C.F.R. §300.517(a).

10. 20 U.S.C. §1415(m)(1)(D); 34 C.F.R. §300.517(a).

11. 20 U.S.C. §§1414(d)(1)(A)(vii)(III), 1414(m)(1)(C); 34 C.F.R. §§300.347(c), 300.517(a)(3).

12. *See* 20 U.S.C. §1415(m)(2); 34 C.F.R. §300.517(b).

13. *See* 34 C.F.R. §300.517(b). Further complicating matters, in its Notice of Interpretation accompanying the regulations, the Department of Education states that "[t]he IDEA Amendments of 1997 also *permit, but do not require*, States to establish a procedure for appointing the parent...." 34 C.F.R. part 300, Appendix A, question 4 (emphasis added).

14. 20 U.S.C. §1415(b)(3); 34 C.F.R. §300.503(a).

15. *See* 20 U.S.C. §1415(k)(4)(A)(i); 34 C.F.R. §300.523(a)(1). The discipline provisions of IDEA are discussed in detail in Chapter 9.

16. 34 C.F.R. §104.36.

17. *Id.*

18. 20 U.S.C. §1415(c); 34 C.F.R. §300.503(b).

19. 20 U.S.C. §1415(b)(4);34 C.F.R. §300.503(c)(1).

20. 34 C.F.R. §300.503(c)(2).

21. 20 U.S.C. §1415(d)(1), (k)(4)(A)(i); 34 C.F.R. §§300.504(a), 300.523(a)(1).

22. 20 U.S.C. §1415(d)(2); 34 C.F.R. §300.504(b).

23. 20 U.S.C. §1415(d)(2);34 C.F.R. §300.504(c).

24. 20 U.S.C. §1415(d)(2);34 C.F.R. §300.504(c).

25. 20 U.S.C. §§1414(a)(1)(C), 1414(c)(3); 34 C.F.R. §300.505(a). Note that while the IDEA statute provides that the review of existing evaluation data discussed above in Chapter 5 is "part of" the evaluation or re-evaluation — and, so, arguably, requires parental consent — the IDEA regulations state that schools need not obtain consent before conducting the review. *Compare* 20 U.S.C. §§1414(a)(1)(C), 1414(c)(1), (3) *and* 34 C.F.R. §300.505(a)(3)(i).

26. 34 C.F.R. §300.505(a)(3)(ii).

27. 34 C.F.R. §300.505(a)(2).

28. 34 C.F.R. §300.505(d), incorporating by reference §300.345(d).

29. *Id.*

30. 20 U.S.C. §1414(c)(3); 34 C.F.R. §300.505(c).

31. 34 C.F.R. §300.505(b). Neither the IDEA regulations nor the statute itself describe the circumstances under which it would be permissible for a hearing officer to order that an evaluation proceed over parental objection. Given the constitutional rights at stake, the lack of standards and resulting orders may be problematic. See *Troxel v. Granville*, 530 U.S. 57, 120 S.Ct. 2054, 2060 (2000), discussing parents' fundamental, constitutionally-protected liberty interest in controlling the care, education and upbringing of their children, and Supreme Court precedent on the issue cited therein.

32. *See id.*

33. 34 C.F.R. §300.505(e).

34. 20 U.S.C. §1415(b)(1); 20 U.S.C. §1232g(a)(1)(A); 34 C.F.R. §§300.501(a)(1), 300.562-300.569; 34 C.F.R. §104.36; 34 C.F.R. §§99.10 - 99.12.

35. The §504 regulations do provide, however, that compliance with IDEA access requirements will fulfill §504 requirements. *See* 34 C.F.R. §104.36.

36. 34 C.F.R. §300.562(a); 34 C.F.R. §99.10(b).

37. 34 C.F.R. §300.562(a).

38. 34 C.F.R. §99.3, incorporated into the IDEA regulations by reference at 34 C.F.R. §300.560(b). Note that FERPA's definition of the "educational records" that parents have a right to inspect and review excludes some kinds of material, including records of instructional, supervisory, and administrative personnel and educational personnel ancillary to those persons that are kept in the sole possession of the maker of the record, and are not accessible or revealed to any other person except a temporary substitute for the maker of the record; records of the law enforcement unit of an educational agency or institution; certain records relating to employees of an educational agency or institution; and certain records regarding students who are 18 years of age or older, or who are attending an institution of postsecondary education. See 34 C.F.R. §99.3.

39. *Id.*

40. 34 C.F.R. §300.565.

41. 34 C.F.R. §300.562(b); 34 C.F.R. §99.10(c), (d)..

42. 34 C.F.R. §300.566; 34 C.F.R. §99.11.

43. 34 C.F.R. §300.562(c); 34 C.F.R. §99.4.

44. 34 C.F.R. §§99.1, 99.5.

45. In regard to access to education records in particular, see 34 C.F.R. §300.574(c).

46. 34 C.F.R. §300.660(a).

47. 34 C.F.R. §§300.660(a)(1), 300.662(a), (b).

48. 34 C.F.R. §300.662(c).

49. *Id.*

50. 34 C.F.R. §300.661(a).

51. *Id.*

52. 34 C.F.R. §300.661(b).

53. 34 C.F.R. §300.660(b).

54. *Id.*; 34 C.F.R. §661(b)(2).

55. 34 C.F.R. §661(c).

56. *Id.*

57. *Id.*

58. 34 C.F.R. §100.7(b). 34 C.F.R. §104.61 makes 34 C.F.R. §§100.6-100.10 applicable to §504 violations.

59. 28 C.F.R. §35.170(a).

60. 34 C.F.R. §100.7(b); 28 C.F.R.§35.170(b).

61. To find the OCR regional office responsible for a particular state, contact OCR headquarters in Washington, D.C. at 1- 800- 421-3481. This information is also available on OCR's site on the world wide web, <www.ed.gov/offices/OCR>. Although §504 complaints are investigated by the appropriate regional office, OCR has stated that the decisions of one regional office are binding on other regions. *See Inquiry by Rhys*, EHLR 305:26 (OCR 4/14/85).

62. 34 C.F.R. §100.7(c), (d); 28 C.F.R. §35.173.

63. 34 C.F.R. §100.8(a); 28 C.F.R. §35.174.

64. 34 C.F.R. §100.7(e).

65. *Id. See, e.g., Modoc County (CA) Office of Education*, 24 IDELR 580 (OCR 1/28/96) (schools official's threats to order additional evaluation and attempt to have student's physician reverse recommendation were unlawful retaliation for parent's request for independent evaluation); *Pueblo (CO) School Dist. No. 60*, 20 IDELR 1066 (OCR 9/1/93) (limitations placed by school system on parents' phone calls and classroom visits, and enforcement of policy regarding administration of eye drops not usually enforced, constituted unlawful retaliation for parents' filing of OCR complaint); *Auburn (AL) City School District*, EHLR 353:374 (OCR 8/7/89) (school district reversal of prior eligibility determination was, under the circumstances, illegal retaliation against parent and student for parent's participation in meetings and filing of complaints with OCR and state department of education); *Bethpage (NY) Union Free School District*, EHLR 353:147 (OCR 1988) (under the circumstances, referring parent to Child Protective Services for educational neglect constituted impermissible retaliation for exercise of §504 rights); *Frederick County (MD) School District*, EHLR 352:407 (OCR 3/25/87) (treating complainant's requests for records differently than all others constituted retaliation for her protected advocacy activities on behalf of her sons and others).

66. *See* 28 C.F.R. §35.134.

67. *See* 34 C.F.R. part 104, App. A, para. immediately preceding para. 22.

68. *See, e.g., Burlington (MA) Public Schools*, 29 IDELR 848 (OCR 7/8/97).

69. *Id.*

70. 20 U.S.C. §§1415(b)(6), (f); 34 C.F.R. §300.507(a).

71. 34 C.F.R. §300.507(a).

72. 34 C.F.R. §300.507(a)(3).

73. *Id.*

74. 34 C.F.R. §104.36.

75. *Id.*

76. 34 C.F.R. §104.7(b).

77. 34 C.F.R. §104.7(a).

78. *See* 28 C.F.R. §35.107.

79. 20 U.S.C. §1415(f)(1).

80. 20 U.S.C. §1415(g).

81. 20 U.S.C. §1415(g); 34 C.F.R. §300.510(b)(2).

82. *See* 34 C.F.R. §§300.510(b)(2).

83. 20 U.S.C. 1415(i)(2)(B); 34 C.F.R. §300.510(d).

84. 20 U.S.C. §1415(f).

85. 20 U.S.C. §§1415(i)(1)(A), (2).

86. 20 U.S.C. §1415(b)(7); 34 C.F.R. §300.507(c)(1), (2).

87. 34 C.F.R. §300.507(c)(4). If a parent is represented by counsel, however, a court may later reduce the award of attorney fees which the parent might otherwise receive if the attorney failed to provide this information. *See* 20 U.S.C. §1415(i)(3)(F).

88. 20 U.S.C. §1415(f)(2)(A); 34 C.F.R. §300.509(b).

89. 20 U.S.C. §1415(f)(2)(B); 34 C.F.R. §300.509(b)(2).

90. 20 U.S.C. §1415(f)(3); 34 C.F.R. §300.508(a)(1).

91. 34 C.F.R. §300.508(a)(2).

92. 34 C.F.R. §300.511(d).

93. 20 U.S.C. §1415(h); 34 C.F.R. §300.509(a), (c)(2).

94. 34 C.F.R. §300.509(a)(3).

95. 34 C.F.R. §300.509(c).

96. 34 C.F.R. §300.511(a).

97. 34 C.F.R. §300.511(b).

98. 34 C.F.R. §300.511(c).

99. *See, e.g., Jeremy H. v. Mt. Lebanon School District,* 95 F.3d 272 (3rd Cir. 1996); *Leonard v. McKenzie,* 869 F.2d 1558, 1563 (D.C. Cir. 1989); *Howell v. Waterford Public Schools,* 731 F. Supp. 1314, 1315-1316 (E.D. Mich. 1990).

100. *See, e.g., Ojai Unified School District v. Jackson,* 4 F.3d 1467 (9th Cir. 1993); *Anderson v. District of Columbia,* 877 F.2d 1018, 1025 (D.C. Cir. 1989); *Town of*

Burlington v. Department of Education, 736 F.2d 773, 790-791 (1st Cir. 1984), *aff'd. on other grounds*, 471 U.S. 359, 105 S. Ct. 1996 (1985).

101. *Rowley, supra,* 458 U.S. at 206, 102 S.Ct. at 3051; *see also Town of Burlington, supra*, 736 F.2d at 791-792.

102. *E.g., Roland M. v. Concord School Committee*, 910 F.2d 983, 991 (1st Cir. 1990), *cert. denied*, 499 U.S. 912, 111 S. Ct. 1122 (1991).

103. 20 U.S.C. §1415(e)(1); 34 C.F.R. §300.506(a).

104. 20 U.S.C. §1415(e); 34 C.F.R. §300.506(a).

105. 34 C.F.R. §300.507(a)(2).

106. 20 U.S.C. 1415(e)(1); 34 C.F.R. §300.506(b)(1).

107. *Bristol-Plymouth Regional Vocational-Technical School District*, EHLR 353:241 (OCR 6/27/89) (mandatory 30 day mediation period violated 34 C.F.R. §104.36 by delaying parent's right to due process hearing immediately after rejection of IEP).

108. 20 U.S.C. §1415(e)(1); 34 C.F.R. §300.506(b)(1).

109. 34 C.F.R. §300.506(c).

110. 20 U.S.C. §1415(e)(2)(C); 34 C.F.R. §300.506(b)(2)(i).

111. 34 C.F.R. §300.506(b)(2)(ii).

112. *See* 20 U.S.C. §1415(e)(2); 34 C.F.R. §300.506(b).

113. 20 U.S.C. §1415(i)(2)(A).

114. 20 U.S.C. §1415(i)(2)(B).

115. *Rowley, supra,* 458 U.S. at 206, 102 S. Ct. at 3051.

116. *See, e.g., Town of Burlington, supra,* 736 F.2d at 792 ("The court, in recognition of the expertise of the administrative agency, must consider the findings carefully and endeavor to respond to the hearing officer's resolution of each material issue. After such consideration, the court is free to accept or reject the findings in part or in whole.") . *See also Rowley, supra,* 458 U.S. at 205, 102 S.Ct. at 3050 (quoting legislative history to the effect that "courts were to make ëindependent [decisions] based on preponderance of the evidence.'").

117. 20 U.S.C. §1415(i)(2)(B).

118. *See, e.g., Consolidated Rail Corporation v. Darrone*, 465 U.S. 624, 630 (1984) ("...§504 authorizes a plaintiff who alleges intentional discrimination to bring an equitable action for back pay").

119. *Wilson v. Garcia*, 471 U.S. 261, 266-67, 105 S.Ct. 1938 (1984); *Spiegler v. District of Columbia*, 866 F.2d 461 (D.C. Cir. 1989); *Tokarcik v. Forest Hills School District*, 665 F. 2d 443 (3rd Cir. 1981), *cert. denied*, 458 U.S. 1121, 102 S.Ct. 3508 (1982).

120. *See, e.g., Andrews v. Consolidated Rail Corporation*, 831 F.2d 678 (7th Cir. 1987); *Alexopulos v. San Francisco Unified School District*, 817 F.2d 551 (9th Cir. 1987); *Doe v. Southeastern University*, 732 F. Supp 7 (D. D.C. 1990); *Bush v.*

Commonwealth Edison Co., 732 F. Supp. 895 (N.D.Ill. 1990); *Wallace v. Town of Stratford Board of Education*, 674 F. Supp. 67 (D. Conn. 1986).

121. *Compare, e.g., Janzen v. Knox County Board of Education*, 790 F.2d. 484 (6th Cir. 1986) (Tennessee statute of limitations governing actions for reimbursement under IDEA is 3 year period applicable to actions for money owed for personal services rendered) *with* Doe v. Smith, 16 EHLR 65 (M.D. Tenn. 1988) (Tennessee statute of limitations applicable to non-reimbursement matters under IDEA is 60 days).

122. *Spiegler, supra*; *Livingston School District v. Kenan*, 82 F.3d 912 (9th Cir. 1996); *Amann v. Town of Stow*, 991 F.2d 929 (1st Cir. 1993).

123. *Doe v. Smith, supra* (for non-reimbursement cases in Tennessee).

124. *Adler v. New York Department of Education*, 760 F.2d 454 (2nd Cir. 1985) (New York); *Thomas v. Staats*, 633 F. Supp. 797 (S.D. W.Va. 1985) (120 days, West Virginia).

125. *Honig v. Doe*, 484 U.S. 305, 108 S.Ct. 592, 606 (1988).

126. *Id.*

127. *Leonard, supra*, 869 F.2d at 1558; *Howell, supra*, 731 F. Supp. at 1315-1316.

128. *Christopher W. v. Portsmouth School Committee*, 877 F.2d 1089 (1st Cir. 1989); *Richards v. Fairfax*, 798 F. Supp. 338 (E.D. Va. 1992), *aff'd*, 7 F.3d 225 (4th Cir. 1993). *But see Hoeft v. Tucson Unified School District*, 967 F. 2d 1298 (9th Cir. 1992).

129. In regard to section 504, see, e.g., *Mrs. W. v. Tirozzi*, 832 F.2d 748 (2nd Cir. 1987); *Georgia State Conference of Branches of the N.A.A.C.P. v. State of Georgia*, 775 F.2d 1403 (11th Cir. 1985); *New Mexico Association for Retarded Citizens v. State of New Mexico*, 678 F.2d 847 (10th Cir. 1982). In regard to Title II of the ADA, see 28 C.F.R. part 35, App. A (discussing §35.172).

130. 20 U.S.C. §1415(l).

131. 20 U.S.C. §1415(i)(2)(B)(ii).

132. *See, e.g., Walker County School District v. Bennett,* 203 F.3d 1293 (11th Cir.), *cert. denied,* 69 U.S.L.W. 3398 (U.S. 2000); *Springer v. Fairfax County School Board*, 134 F.3d 659 (4th Cir. 1998); *Monticello School District No. 25 v. George L.*, 102 F.3d 895 (7th Cir. 1996); *Independent Sch. Dist. No. 283 v. S.D.*, 88 F.3d 556 (8th Cir. 1996); *Susan N. v. Wilson School District*, 70 F.3d 751, 759-60 (3d Cir.1995); *Ojai, supra*; *Metropolitan Gov't of Nashville and Davidson County v. Cook*, 915 F.2d 232, 234 (6th Cir. 1990); *Town of Burlington, supra*. In *Town of Burlington*, for example, the court offered the following as examples of reasons for supplementation: gaps in the hearing transcript due to mechanical failure; unavailability of a witness; improper exclusion of evidence by the hearing or review officer; and evidence concerning relevant events occurring after the due process hearing. *Id.*, 736 F.2d at 790.

133. *E.g, Town of Burlington, supra; Ojai, supra*.

134. 20 U.S.C. §1415(j). The Court of Appeals for the D.C. Circuit has held that §1415(e)(3) applies only during the pendency of administrative due process and

trial court level proceedings, and not pending further review by appellate courts. *See Andersen v. District of Columbia*, 877 F.2d 1018, 1093 (D.C. Cir. 1989).

135. *Honig, supra*, 484 U.S. at 323, 108 S. Ct. at 604.

136. *Cronin v. Board of East Ramapo Central School District*, 689 F. Supp. 197 (S.D.N.Y. 1988); *Stock v. Massachusetts Hospital School*, 392 Mass. 705, 467 N.E.2d 448 (1984), *cert. denied*, 474 U.S. 844 (1985); *Inquiry of Richards*, 17 EHLR 288 (OSEP 1991).

137. *See generally* 20 U.S.C. §1415(k)(7); 34 C.F.R. §300.526.

138. *School Committee of the Town of Burlington v. Department of Education,* 471 U.S. 359, 372, 105 S. Ct. 1996 (1985).

139. *See, e.g., St. Tammany Parish School Board v. State of Louisiana*, 142 F.3d 776 (5th Cir. 1998); *Susquenita School District v. Raelee S.*, 96 F.3d 78 (3rd Cir. 1996); *Clovis Unified School District v. California Office of Administrative Hearings*, 903 F.2d 635 (9th Cir. 1990); *Chester Township Bd. Of Ed. V. J.R.*, 33 IDELR 218 (D. N.J. 2000) (denying motion for stay); *Mohawk Trail Regional School District v. Shaun D.*, 35 F. Supp.2d 34 (D. Mass. 1999); *A.P. v. McGrew,* 28 IDELR 19 (N.D. Ill. 1998); *T.H. v. Bd. of Ed. of Palatine Community Consolidated School District*, 29 IDELR 471 (N.D. Ill. 1998); *Board of Education of Montgomery Co. v. Brett Y.*, 959 F. Supp. 705 (D. Md. 1997); *Grace B. v. Lexington School Committee*, 762 F. Supp. 416 (D. Mass. 1991); *Kantak v. Liverpool Central School District*, 16 EHLR 643 (N.D.N.Y. 1990); *Department of Education of Hawaii v. Mr. and Mrs. S.*, 632 F. Supp. 1268 (D. Hawaii 1986); *Blazejewski v. Board of Education of Allegany Central School District,* 560 F. Supp. 701 (W.D.N.Y. 1983).

The IDEA regulations issued on March 12, 1999 purport to limit the right to implementation of a favorable administrative decision pending appeal to those hearing decisions rendered in a hearing conducted by the state education agency (as opposed to those conducted at the local level), and review decisions rendered by a state review official. *See* 34 C.F.R. §300.514(c). This interpretation appears inconsistent with the language of 20 U.S.C. §1415(j), as well as the analysis underlying *Town of Burlington* and the other cited cases, particularly *A.W.* and *T.H. But see Murphy v. Arlington Central School District*, 86 F. Supp. 2d 354 (S.D.N.Y. 2000) (applying 34 C.F.R. §300.514(c)); *Bd. of Oak Park and River Forest High School District v. Illinois State Bd. of Ed.*, 10 F. Supp. 971 (N.D. Ill. 1998) (using, without analysis, review decision rather than due process hearing decision as critical date for implementation purposes).

140. *Burlington, supra*, 471 U.S. at 373, 105 S.Ct. at 2004. *See also Susquenita, supra,* 96 F.3d at 84 (stay-put provision "was drafted to guard the interests of parents and their children").

141. 20 U.S.C. §1415(i)(2)(B)(iii). The statute does not define "appropriate."

142. 471 U.S. 359, 105 S. Ct. 1996 (1985).

143. 471 U.S. at 370, 105 S. Ct. at 2003.

144. *Inquiry of Armstrong*, 28 IDELR 303 (OSEP 6/11/97); *Inquiry of Van Buiten*, EHLR 211:429 (Office of Special Education and Rehabilitative Services 6/17/87). *See also S-1 v. Spangler*, 650 F. Supp. 1427 (M.D.N.C. 1986), *vacated as moot*, 832 F.2d 294 (4th Cir. 1987).

145. *Burlington*, 471 U.S. at 370, 105 S. Ct. at 2002-2003. *See also Florence Co. School District No. 4 v. Carter*, 510 U.S. 7, 114 S.Ct. 361 (1993).

146. *See, e.g., Rapid City School District 51-4 v. Vahle*, 733 F. Supp. 1364 (D.S.D. 1990), *aff'd.* 922 F.2d 476 (8th Cir. 1990).

147. *Hurry v. Jones*, 734 F.2d 879 (1st Cir. 1984). *See also Alamo Heights Independent School District v. State Board of Education*, 790 F.2d 1153 (5th Cir. 1986).

148. *Alamo Heights, supra.*

149. *Hall, supra.*

150. *Board of Education of the County of Cabell v. Dienelt*, 1986-87 EHLR DEC. 558:305 (S.D.W.V. 1987), *aff'd.*, 843 F. 2d 813 (4th Cir. 1988).

151. 510 U.S. 7, 13-14, 114 S.Ct. 361, 365-6.

152. *See Carter, supra; Alamo Heights*, 790 F.2d at 1153 (program in which parent enrolled child, "although it might not have been adequate under the EAHCA, was better than no summer program at all...*Burlington* rule is not so narrow as to permit reimbursement only when the interim placement chosen by the parent is found to be the exact proper placement required under the Act"). *See also Garland Independent School District v. Wilks*, 657 F. Supp. 1163, 1166-67 (N.D. Tex. 1987) (finding that a low income parent was entitled to reimbursement for furnishing those services intended, to the extent the parent could afford, to create a "facsimile" of the residential placement ultimately ordered by the court).

    Parents and their advocates should be aware that reimbursement is not necessarily available in all cases. In *Burlington*, the Supreme Court stated that courts may take "equitable considerations" into account in deciding whether to order reimbursement in a particular case and, if so, in what amount. *Id.* The lower court opinion in *Burlington* stated that such considerations might include whether or not parents consulted the school district before placing their child in a private school, or whether parents attempted to reach an agreement or compromise before doing so. 736 F.2d at 799; see also 736 F.2d at 801-802 ("...whether to order reimbursement, and at what amount, is a question to be determined by balancing the equities...[f]actors that should be taken into account include the parties' compliance or noncompliance with state and federal regulations pending review, the reasonableness of the parties' positions, and like matters"). *See also Carter, supra,* 510 U.S. at 15-16, 114 S.Ct. at 366 ("...equitable considerations are relevant in fashioning relief...and the court enjoys broad discretion in so doing...Courts fashioning discretionary equitable relief under IDEA must consider all relevant factors, including the appropriate and reasonable level of reimbursement that should be required.") (Citations omitted). See also 20 U.S.C. §1412(a)(10)(C)(ii)(III), added to IDEA in 1997 and discussed below.

153. 20 U.S.C. 1412(a)(10)(C)(ii).

154. 20 U.S.C. §1412(a)(10)(C)(iii); *see also* 34 C.F.R. §300.403.

155. 20 U.S.C. §1412(a)(10)(C)(iv); *see also* 34 C.F.R. §300.403(e).

156. For the Department's interpretation, see Analysis of Comments and Changes, 64 Fed. Reg. 124537, 12602 (March 12, 1999), quoted in note 153, below.

157. *See* 20 U.S.C. §1415(i)(2)(B)(iii). This provision, as formerly codified at 20 U.S.C. §1415(e)(2), was held by the Supreme Court in *Burlington* to vest courts with broad equitable powers to fashion relief. The U.S. Department of Education interprets this provision as continuing to empower courts and hearing officers to award tuition reimbursement to parents of IDEA-eligible children who have not been provided with services. *See* Analysis of Comments and Changes, 64 Fed. Reg. 12536, 12602 (March 12, 1999) ("As one commenter noted, hearing officers and courts retain their authority, recognized in *Burlington* and *Florence County School District Four v. Carter*...to award "appropriate" relief if a public agency has failed to provide FAPE, including reimbursement...under section 615(i)(2)(B)(iii) [20 U.S.C. §1415(i)(2)(B)(iii)] in instances in which the child has not yet received special education and related services. This authority is independent of their authority under section 612(a)(10)(C)(ii) [20 U.S.C. §1412(a)(19)(C)(ii)] to award reimbursement for private placements of children who previously were receiving special education and related services from a public agency.").

158. *See, e.g.*, *Boston (MA) Renaissance Charter* School, 26 IDELR 889 (9/5/97); *Northwest Jefferson County (MO) R-I School District*, EHLR 257:354 (OCR 3/31/82); *Clark County (NV) School District*, EHLR 257:245 (OCR 1/16/81); School District #220 (IL), EHLR 257:200 (OCR 2/12/81); *Fremont (CO) School District RE-3*, EHLR 257:273 (OCR 10/27/80). *See also* Memorandum to Gary D. Jackson, Regional Civil Rights Director, Region X from William L. Smith, Acting Assistant Secretary for Civil Rights of June 28, 1989, reprinted at EHLR 307:10 (responding to request for policy guidance and discussing reimbursement as remedy for §504 violations).

159. *See, e.g.*, *M.C. v. Central Regional School District*, 81 F.3d 389 (3rd Cir. 1996); *Pihl v. Massachusetts Department of Education*, 9 F.3d 184 (1st Cir. 1993); *Lester H. v. Gilhool*, 916 F.2d 865 (3rd Cir. 1990), *cert. denied*, 499 U.S. 923, 111 S. Ct. 1317 (1991); *Burr v. Sobol*, 863 F.2d 1071 (2nd Cir. 1989), *vacated and remanded* 492 U.S. 902, 109 S. Ct. 3209 (1989), *on remand, aff'd. per curiam*, 888 F.2d 258 (2nd Cir. 1989), *cert. denied, 494 U.S. 1005* (1990); *Jefferson County Board of Education v. Breen*, 853 F.2d 853 (11th Cir. 1988); *Miener v. Missouri*, 800 F.2d 749 (8th Cir. 1986); *Max M. v. Thompson*, 592 F. Supp. 1450 (N.D. Ill. 1984). *See also Jackson v. Franklin County School Board*, 806 F.2d 632,631 (5th Cir. 1986) (on remand "...the district court must determine what damages, either monetary, or in the form of remedial education services...would be appropriate at this time"). For a pre-*Burlington* case awarding compensatory education, see *Campbell v. Talladega County Board of Education*, 518 F. Supp. 47 (N.D. Ala. 1981).

160. *See, e.g., Meiner, supra*, 800 F.2d at 753; *Breen, supra*, 853 F.2d at 857-58; *Burr, supra*, 863 F.2d at 1078.

161. *Inquiry of Kohn*, 17 EHLR 522 (OSEP 2/13/91).

162. *See Pihl, supra; Todd D. v. Andrews*, 933 F. 2d 1576, 1584 (11th Cir. 1991); *Burr, supra; Breen, supra; Lester H., supra; Campbell, supra; Max M., supra. But see also Alexopulos v. Riles*, 784 F.2d 1408 (9th Cir. 1986) (finding claim to be time-barred and beyond statutory cut- off intended by Congress); *McDowell v. Fort Bend Independent School District*, 737 F. Supp. 386 (S.D. Tex. 1990) (finding IDEA claim of 23 year-old student moot).

163. *Lester H., supra*, is one exception. While the Third Circuit's opinion discussed only IDEA, the district court opinion awarding compensatory education notes §504 as well as IDEA violations. *See Lester H. v. Carroll*, 16 EHLR 10 (E.D. Penn. 1989). The Second Circuit has explicitly recognized the availability of compensatory education under §504. *See Mrs. C. v. Wheaton*, 916 F.2d 69, 75-76 (2nd Cir. 1990). For examples of administrative complaints to the Office for Civil Rights that have resulted in awards of compensatory education, see. e.g., *Tift Co. (GA) School District*, 31 IDELR 59 (OCR 1998); *Chatham Co. (GA) School District*, 26 IDELR 29 (OCR 11/6/96); *Calcasieu Parish Public School System*, 20 IDELR 762 (8/3/93); *Anderson CO. (TN) School District*, 16 IDELR 760 (2/26/90).

164. *See, e.g., Augusta County (VA) School Division*, EHLR 352:233 (OCR 8/21/86); *Chicago (IL) Board of Education*; EHLR 257:568 (OCR 7/9/84); *Clermont (OH) Northeastern Schools*, EHLR 257:577 (OCR 7/23/84); *Kanawha County (WV) School District*, EHLR 257:439 (OCR 9/28/83) (beyond age 21); *Chicago (IL) Board of Education*, EHLR 257:453 (OCR 3/11/83).

165. 503 U.S. 60, 112 S.Ct. 1028 (1992).

166. *Id.*, 503 U.S. at 70-71, 112 S.Ct. at 1035.

167. *See W.B. v. Matula*, 67 F.3d 484 (3rd Cir. 1995); *Butler v. South Glen Falls Central School District*, 106 F. Supp. 2d 414 (N.D.N.Y. 2000) (damages available in action linking IDEA and 42 U.S.C. §1983, but not directly under IDEA); *Cappillino v. Hyde Park Central School District*, 40 F. Supp. 2d 513 (S.D.N.Y. 1999); *Padilla v. School District No. 1*, 35 F. Supp.2d 1260 (D. Colo. 1999), *rev'd. in part on other grounds,* 233 F.3d 1268 (10th Cir. 2000); *Searles v. Bd. of Ed. of Ellenville Central School District*, 29 IDELR 787 (N.D.N.Y. 1999) (IDEA/§1983claim); *Walker v. District of Columbia*, 969 F. Supp. 794 (D.DC 1997) (IDEA/§1983 claim); *Emma C. v. Eastin*, 985 F. Supp. 940 (N.D. Cal. 1997) (damages available directly under IDEA as well as for IDEA/§1983 claim).

168. *See, e.g., Sellers v. School Bd. of Manassas*, 141 F.3d 524, n.3 (4th Cir.), *cert. denied*, 525 U.S. 871, 119 S.Ct. 168 (1998) (dismissing *Franklin* holding in one-sentence footnote); *Hoekstra v. Independent School District No. 283*, 103 F.3d 624 (8th Cir. 1996).

169. *See, e.g., W.B. v. Matula, supra*; *Sellers, supra*; *Wenger, supra*; *Walker, supra*; *Asbury v. Missouri Dept. of Elementary and Secondary Education* , 29 IDELR 877 (E.D. Mo. 1999) *T.J.W. v. Dothan City Bd. of Ed.*, 26 IDELR 999 (M.D. Ala. 1997); *McKay v. Winthrop Bd. of Ed.*, 26 IDELR 1100 (D. Maine 1997); *Jonathan G. v. Caddo Parish School Board*, 875 F. Supp. 352 (W.D. La. 1994).

 29 U.S.C. §794a(a)(2) provides that "[t]he remedies, procedures and rights set forth in Title VI of the Civil Rights Act of 1964 [which bars discrimination on the basis of race, color or national origin in programs or activities receiving Federal financial assistance]…shall be available to any person" aggrieved by violations of §504. Title IX of the Education Amendments of 1972, which bars gender discrimination in education programs receiving federal funds, similarly incorporates Title VI remedies. As noted above, the Supreme Court held in *Franklin* that damages are available to remedy at least intentional Title IX violations.

170. 20 U.S.C. §1415(i)(3)(B) - (G); *see also* 34 C.F.R. §300.513.

171. 20 U.S.C. §1415(i)(3)(F).

172. 20 U.S.C. §1415(i)(3)(G).

173. 20 U.S.C. §1415(i)(3)(D), (E).

174. *See, e.g., Moore v. D.C. Board of Education*, 907 F.2d 165 (D.C. Cir.), *vacating* 886 F.2d 335, *cert. denied*, 498 U.S. 998, 111 S. Ct. 556 (1990); *Mitten v. Muscogee County School District*, 877 F.2d 932 (11th Cir. 1989), *cert. denied*, 493 U.S. 1072, 110 S. Ct. 1117 (1990); *McSomebodies v. Burlington Elementary and Secondary School District*, 886 F.2d 1558 (9th Cir. 1988), *supplemented* March 2, 2990, 897 F.2d 974; *Duane M. v. Orleans Parish School Board*, 861 F.2d 115 (5th Cir. 1988); *Eggers v. Bullitt County School District*, 854 F.2d 892 (6th Cir. 1988).

175. *See Lucht v. Molalla River School District,* 225 F.3d 1023 (9th Cir. 2000); *Upper Valley Association for Handicapped Citizens v. Blue Mountain Union School District No. 21*, 973 F. Supp. 429 (D. Vt. 1997). *But see Megan C. v. Independent School District No. 626*, 57 F. Supp. 2d 776 (D. Minn. 1999) (fees not available in connection with complaints under 34 C.F.R. §§300.660 - 300.662).

176. *See, e.g.*, *Barlow-Gresham Union High School District No.2 v. Mitchell*, 940 F.2d 1280 (9th Cir. 1991); *Shelly C. v. Venus Independent School District*, 878 F.2d 862 (5th Cir. 1989), *cert. denied*, 493 U.S. 729, 110 S. Ct. 729 (1990). Note that these cases pre-date the 2001 U.S. Supreme Court decision in *Buckhannon Board and Care Home v. West Virginia Department of Health and Human Resources*, ___ U.S. ___, 121 S.Ct. 1835 (2001), which involved claims under the federal Fair Housing Amendments Act and the Americans with Disabilities Act, and held that a party that has not secured a judgement on the merits or a court-ordered consent decree is not a "prevailing party" for purposes of an award of attorney fees. The extent to which courts may apply *Buckhannon* to fee claims based upon IDEA is unclear.

177. The 1997 amendments to IDEA give states the discretion to bar attorneys fees for mediation conducted *prior to* the filing of a complaint. 20 U.S.C. §1415(i)(3)(D)(ii).

178. *Id. See also Daniel S. v. Scranton School District*, 230 F.3d 90) (3rd Cir. 2000) (affirming award of fees for meeting found by the lower court to have been an IEP meeting); *Lucht, supra* (affirming award of fees for IEP meeting attendance).

CHAPTER 9

DISCIPLINE

The law protecting the education rights of children with disabilities recognizes that in school, the behavioral manifestations of disability are often inappropriately treated as discipline problems. As discussed in Chapter 4, securing appropriate education for children with disabilities labeled "behavior problems" and excluded from school for "discipline" reasons was a primary impetus for the 1975 enactment of what is now called IDEA. As also discussed in Chapter 4, the 1997 amendments to IDEA underscored schools' longstanding obligation to treat behavioral manifestations as education issues, by responding with appropriate services and supports. The 1997 law also made explicit the IDEA requirement that even children with disabilities suspended or expelled from school be provided a free appropriate public education. Furthermore, both IDEA and §504 limit schools' ability to subject children to punitive measures for disability-related behavior.[1]

Notwithstanding this history and context — and notwithstanding legal limits on the ability of school officials to exclude students from their educational placements for discipline reasons — suspension and expulsion, often without appropriate educational services (or any education at all) continue to an alarming degree. This Chapter focuses on protections against such disciplinary exclusion under IDEA and §504. It also briefly discusses the procedural rights of *all* students faced with suspension or expulsion from school, and IDEA provisions regarding the filing of criminal charges by school officials against children with disabilities.[*]

---

[*] As this book went to press in July, 2001, Congress had before it proposed legislation that would alter IDEA's discipline provisions. Parents and advocates should check current law for any changes.

A. RIGHTS OF ALL STUDENTS

1. The Right to Procedural Due Process

In the context of school discipline, students with disabilities not only have rights under IDEA and §504 but, as do all other public school students, they have the right under the Fourteenth Amendment to the U.S. Constitution to "due process of law" before being suspended or expelled from school. This right was recognized in 1975 by the U.S. Supreme Court in *Goss v. Lopez*,[2] where the court held that even a student faced with a suspension of less than ten days is entitled to notice of the charges, an explanation of the evidence against him or her, and a hearing.[3] Even where the fact of the misconduct is not in dispute, the Court held, a student must still have "the opportunity to characterize….[the] conduct and put it in what he deems the proper context."[4]

The Court further ruled that in the case of suspensions of ten days or less, ordinarily the notice may be oral or written, the hearing may consist of an informal opportunity for the student to explain his or her side of the story, and the notice and hearing may occur simultaneously.[5] Longer suspensions, and short ones involving what the Court termed "unusual situations," require more formal due process protections and procedures.[6] The type of notice and kind of hearing, the rights accorded the student at the hearing and the formality of the hearing depend upon the nature of the charge and the seriousness of the penalty.[7]

Under *Goss*, unless a student's presence in school poses "a continuing danger to persons or property or an ongoing threat of disrupting the academic process," the notice and hearing should precede the student's removal from school.[8] Where a student's presence does pose such a continuing danger or ongoing threat, the necessary notice and hearing must follow as soon as practicable.[9]

2. The Relevance of State Law

Some states have enacted laws that mandate specific, and sometimes extensive, safeguards in school discipline proceedings, such as rights to legal counsel, presentation of evidence, and cross-examination of witnesses. In addition, some state courts have issued decisions requiring more extensive procedures than federal courts have required as a matter of federal constitutional due process. Finally, in many states state law, by statute or judicial decision, addresses matters such as the kind of discipline that can be imposed for particular kinds of conduct, the particular officials who can mete out certain forms of discipline, disciplinary procedures, and the scope of schools' power to suspend, expel and otherwise discipline students. Thus it is important for parents and their advocates to examine state law when faced with school discipline matters.

B. SUSPENSION, EXPULSION AND DENIAL OF EDUCATION FOR DISCIPLINE REASONS

1. IDEA

Denial of education Congress explicitly amended IDEA in 1997 to state that a free appropriate public education must be provided to all children with disabilities, "including children with disabilities who have been suspended or expelled from school."[10] This clear language requires schools to continue to provide education during *all* periods of suspension and expulsion.

The U.S. Department of Education regulations implementing IDEA, however, contradict the statute on this point. Under the regulations, schools do not have to provide FAPE — or any educational services at all — until a child has already been suspended for a total of ten school days in the same school year.[11] Or, in other words, until the eleventh total day of suspension. The regulations thus purport to allow schools to deny a child up to two weeks of education and related services per school year. However, even under the regulations, denial of education is only allowed if children without disabilities are also suspended from school with no educational services.[12]

Limits to and procedures for suspension and expulsion The IDEA statute and regulations allow school personnel to suspend a child for up to ten school days (if children without disabilities are similarly treated) without determining whether the alleged misconduct is a manifestation of disability.[13] The statute does not specify whether this limit means ten consecutive school days, or ten cumulative (total) school days in a school year. The regulations are specific, providing that these suspensions may last up to ten consecutive school days.[14] However, the regulations recognize that a series of suspensions that are each less that ten days, when taken together, may constitute a pattern of exclusion requiring that they be treated, for purposes of IDEA rights, as if they were a single, continuous suspension.[15] Where such a pattern exists,[*] the upper limit on suspension without a manifestation determination is ten *cumulative* school days.[16]

As soon as a school system decides to initiate a suspension of more than ten consecutive school days, a suspension that would include the eleventh cumulative suspension day in a school year where a pattern exists, or an expulsion, it must notify the child's parents and provide written notice of all the procedural safeguards available to them and their child under IDEA.[17] Before the school system can actually proceed with any such suspension or expulsion, however, it must — immediately, and no later than within ten days of its decision to take that disciplinary action — conduct a review of the relationship between the behavior at issue and the child's disability, and determine whether the behavior was a manifestation of his or her disability.[18] The procedures and other requirements governing these reviews and determinations are discussed below.

If the result of the review is a determination that the behavior at issue was *not* a manifestation of the child's disability, he or she can be subjected to the same disciplinary measures as are children without disabilities who engage in similar behavior, including suspension or expulsion.[19] However, as discussed above, the school system must continue to provide FAPE during the suspension or expulsion. And as discussed below, a determination that behavior was not a manifestation of disability may be appealed through IDEA's complaint and due process hearing procedure.

If the review determines that the behavior *was* a manifestation of disability, the child may not be suspended or expelled.[20] However, the school system may, if appropriate, propose changes in the child's IEP and/or placement. Except in certain cases involving weapons or drugs or other particular kinds of dangerous behavior, as discussed below, the usual IDEA procedures for making such changes apply, including prior notice to parents, IEP team meeting and parent participation requirements, as do the rights of parents to reject the school's proposal and chal-

---

[*] The regulations do not include criteria for determining whether a pattern exists, or provide examples. However, as discussed below, the U.S. Department of Education/Office for Civil Rights has long applied a similar rule in enforcing §504. The circumstances under which OCR has found patterns of exclusion should provide guidance in interpreting this provision of the IDEA regulations. Examples of cases in which OCR has found patterns are discussed below.

lenge any decision with which they disagree.*

Functional behavior assessment The IDEA *statute* requires that the school system convene the IEP team to plan a functional behavior assessment,** arrange for the assessment to be conducted, and develop and implement a plan of appropriate interventions to address the behavior either before, or within ten days of making a "change in the placement of a child with a disability" for discipline reasons, including suspensions of ten school days or less.[21] Contrary to this requirement, the *regulations* state that these steps regarding functional behavior assessment need only be taken if the child will be excluded for eleven or more days, total, in a school year.[22]

If a child has already had a functional behavior assessment and has a behavioral intervention plan, the IEP team must meet to review the plan and its implementation, and modify it as necessary to address the behavior that prompted the exclusion.[23] If a child with a new or modified behavioral intervention plan is later again excluded from his or her placement, the IEP team members must review the plan and its implementation to determine if changes are necessary.[24] If *any* member of the team — *including the parent* — believes the plan should be changed, the team must meet and change the plan to the extent the team determines necessary.[25]

2. §504

Much like IDEA, the § 504 regulations require that certain procedures be followed before a child's educational placement may be changed. For

---

* IDEA procedures for making IEP and placement changes are discussed in Chapter 6. Rights to reject school proposals and challenge school decisions are discussed in Chapter 8.

** Neither the statute nor the regulations define "functional behavior assessment." Experts in the field describe it as an approach that uses multiple strategies and techniques to understand the causes of behavior, i.e., the "functions" particular behavior serves for the child engaging in it, and to design interventions intended to address the problem behavior. Rather than simply focusing on the behavior itself, functional behavior assessment looks for the motivation behind the behavior, including the biological, social, affective and environmental factors that trigger, sustain or end it. See, e.g., Center for Effective Collaboration and Practice, Addressing Student Problem Behavior: An IEP Team's Introduction to Functional Behavioral Assessment and Behavior Intervention Plans (January 1998) (available from American Institutes for Research, 1000 Thomas Jefferson St., N.W., Suite 400, Washington, D.C. 20007, 202/944-5400, 888/457-1551, www.air-dcorg/cecp).

example, a comprehensive evaluation by appropriate, qualified personnel must be conducted prior to any "significant change in placement."[26] A suspension exceeding 10 consecutive (or, as discussed below, sometimes 10 cumulative) days or an expulsion constitutes a "significant change of placement" under the regulations.[27] The school system therefore must conduct a comprehensive evaluation meeting all of the requirements of the §504 regulations *before* attempting to exclude a student for more than ten days.[28] The evaluation must also include a determination of whether there is a connection between the behavior for which discipline is to be imposed and the student's disability.[29]

If the behavior is found *not* to be a manifestation of disability, the student may be subjected to the same disciplinary measures as are nondisabled students, including suspension or expulsion without education. However, by judicial decision, educational services should continue in at least those states covered by the Fifth, Sixth and Eleventh Circuit U.S. Courts of Appeals.[30] This includes Alabama, Florida, Georgia, Kentucky, Louisiana, Michigan, Mississippi, Ohio Tennessee and Texas.

A series of short-term (ten days or less) suspensions that cumulate to more than ten days may constitute a pattern of exclusion tantamount to a "significant change in placement" for §504 purposes, triggering the prior evaluation and manifestation determination requirements.[31] According to the U.S. Department of Education/Office for Civil Rights ("OCR"), which enforces §504, factors to be considered in determining whether such a pattern exists include, but are not limited to, the length of each suspension; the proximity of the suspensions to one another; and the total amount of time that the child is excluded from school.[32] Other factors, such as the pattern of exclusions from the previous school year, other disciplinary sanctions imposed, or the student's history may also be relevant.[33] Cases in which OCR has found an impermissible pattern of short-term suspensions under the totality of the circumstances include cases where suspensions totaled 15 days over a three month period; 16 days from the start of the school year to March; 18 days from mid-December through May; 12 days from mid-November through early February; 20 days from mid-January through May; and 22 days between September and March.[34]

According to OCR policy, a suspension of ten days or less does not, in and of itself, constitute a "significant change in placement" triggering re-evaluation rights, including a manifestation determination. However, the overriding prohibition against disability-based discrimination of both §504 and the Americans with Disabilities Act, and their implementing regulations, should preclude imposition of *any* punitive discipline for conduct that is a manifestation of disability.[35]

C. INCIDENTS INVOLVING WEAPONS OR ILLEGAL DRUGS

1. IDEA

IDEA contains explicit provisions concerning children who (1) carry or possess a weapon to or at school, on school premises, or to or at a school function, or (2) knowingly possess or use illegal drugs or sell or try to sell a controlled substance while at school or at a school function.[36] For purposes of these provisions, "weapon" means

> "a weapon, device, instrument, material, or substance, animate or inanimate, that is used for, or is readily capable of, causing death or serious bodily injury, except that such term does not include a pocket knife with a blade of less than 2 Ω inches in length."[37]

The term "controlled substance" means a drug or other substance identified in certain sections of the federal Controlled Substances Act.[38] It does not include alcohol. "Illegal drug" means a controlled substance, unless the child's possession or use is legal by virtue of being under the supervision of a licensed health-care professional, or by virtue of any other provision of federal law.[39]

Students with disabilities involved in this kind of behavior may be suspended or expelled from school under the same terms described above: for up to ten days without a manifestation determination, and for longer upon a finding that the behavior was *not* a manifestation of disability — subject, of course, to the school system's obligation to continue to provide a free appropriate public education (albeit in another setting). The difference in legal rights comes when the behavior *is* found to be a manifestation of the child's disability.

As discussed above, ordinarily when behavior is a manifestation of disability, not only can the school system not suspend for more than 10 days or expel, but any change in placement can be accomplished only by following all of the usual IDEA procedures and procedural safeguards. These include the right of parents to participate in placement decisions, to object, and to request a due process hearing and invoke stay-put rights (as discussed in Chapter 8), in order to stop the placement change pending resolution of the dispute.[40]

In contrast, if a child is involved in one of the kinds of drug- or weapon-related incidents described above, school officials may, acting alone and over parental objection, temporarily place him or her in an appropriate "interim alternative educational setting" — despite the fact that the behavior is a manifestation of disability.[41] However, school officials may do so *only if* (1) keeping the child in his or her current placement is substantially likely to result in injury to the child or to others, *and* (2) this substantial likelihood remains despite the fact that the school system has made reasonable efforts to minimize the risk of harm in that placement, including the use of supplementary aids and services.[42]

The placement in an interim alternative educational setting may last up to 45 calendar days or for the same amount of time that a child without disabilities would be subject to discipline, whichever is shorter.[43] The child must be returned to the prior placement at the end of this period, or to another placement to which his or her parents agree. If the school system wishes to place the child in another placement *not* acceptable to the parents, the parents may object, file a complaint and request a due process hearing, thereby triggering the child's right to return to, and remain in, his or her prior placement until the dispute is resolved.[44] Should the school system believe that returning the child to that placement would be dangerous, it may request an expedited due process hearing and seek permission to keep him or her in the interim alternative educational setting pending resolution of the dispute.[45] This should rarely be necessary or appropriate, however, as the initial 45 day placement period is ample time for schools to collaborate with parents to develop long-term strategies for addressing the child's educational needs, including any changes in the services or supports the child receives.

Consistent with the duty to provide a free appropriate public education to *all* students, the interim alternative educational setting must provide FAPE, including meeting the quality requirements described below regarding the content of education during periods of disciplinary exclusion.

2. §504

Students with disabilities involved in weapons incidents are treated no differently under §504 than students with disabilities accused of other discipline infractions. Students involved with illegal drugs or alcohol, in contrast, *are* treated differently. School officials may discipline a student with a disability for "the use or possession of illegal drugs or alcohol" to the same extent that a non-disabled student would be disciplined if he or she "currently is engaging in the illegal use of drugs or in the use of alcohol."[46] Furthermore, while such students will have a right to a hearing of some sort consistent with the constitutional due process rights discussed above and any other pertinent laws, they do not have a right to the kind of hearing ordinary required under the §504 regulations for students with disabilities contesting a placement change.[47] However, provided that they are also "children with disabilities" within the meaning of IDEA, they retain all of the IDEA rights and protections described in this Chapter.

D. Students with Other Kinds of Behavior Schools Deem Dangerous

1. IDEA

IDEA also permits a child whose behavior is a manifestation of disability to be placed in an appropriate "interim alternative educational setting" over parental objection for other, dangerous behavior under certain circumstances. This aspect of the law, however, does not allow school officials to take action on their own. Rather, they must request a due process hearing and seek an order from an IDEA due process hearing officer placing the child in an interim alternative educational setting.[48] The hearing officer may order placement in such a setting for no more than 45 calendar days.[49]

Before ordering a child placed in an interim alternative educational setting, the hearing officer must:

- Determine that the school system has proven by more than a preponderance of the evidence that keeping the child in his or her current placement is substantially likely to result in injury to the child or others;
- Consider the appropriateness of the child's placement;
- Consider whether the school system has made reasonable efforts to minimize the risk of harm in the current placement, including through the use of supplementary aids and services; and
- Determine that the interim alternative educational setting meets IDEA requirements (discussed below).[50]

Where parents and school system disagree as to the child's placement at the end of the 45 day (or shorter) interim alternative placement, the same rules, options and procedures discussed above in connection with weapon and drug incidents apply.[51]

2. §504

Students with disabilities whose behavior schools deem dangerous are treated no differently under §504 than students with disabilities accused of other discipline infractions.

E. MANIFESTATION DETERMINATIONS

1. IDEA

As noted above, a manifestation review must be conducted, and a manifestation determination made, before a child with a disability may be excluded from his or her current educational placement for more than ten days, including where a shorter suspension is part of a pattern of exclusions that together exceed ten days in a school year. The purpose of the review is to explore the relationship between the behavior at issue and the child's disability and educational program and services. It is conducted, and the manifestation determination made, by the IEP team (which by definition includes the child's parents) and "other qualified personnel."[52]

Information to be reviewed and determinations to be made In performing its task, the group must consider all relevant information, including evaluation and diagnostic results (whether obtained by the school system or the parent); observations of the child; and the content, characteristics and implementation of his or her IEP and placement.[53] It may determine that the behavior was *not* a manifestation of disability *only if*:

- in relationship to the behavior at issue, the child's IEP and placement were appropriate, and that all services were implemented consistent with the IEP; *and*
- the child's disability did not impair his or her ability to understand the impact and consequences of the behavior at issue; *and*
- the disability did not impair his or her ability to control the behavior.[54]

If the group finds that *any* of these criteria have *not* been met, it *must* find that the behavior *was* a manifestation of disability.[55] In addition, if the group discovers any deficiency in the child's IEP or placement, or in their implementation, it must take immediate steps to remedy the situation.[56]

"Other qualified personnel" As noted above, the manifestation review and determination are to be carried out by the IEP team and "other qualified personnel." Neither IDEA itself nor the regulations specify who these qualified professionals must be. However, this provision reflects Congress' recognition that IEP teams alone do not have the expertise needed to determine the relationship between disability and behavior. The "qualified personnel" who supplement the IEP team must bring this expertise to the group, of which they must be an integral part, and enable it to evaluate the factors listed above *in regard to this particular child.* At a minimum, it would seem that in order to do so, these qualified personnel must include individuals with expertise in the child's disability (or disabilities), including it's potential developmental, cognitive, educational and behavioral consequences; in interpreting (and understanding the limits of) existing evaluation data and other information about the child; in identifying and understanding what triggered the behavior, including expertise in functional behavior analysis; in appropriate behavioral supports and strategies for children with his or her particular disability, strengths and needs; in assessing the appropriateness of the services being provided to the child, any issues regarding their implementation, and the impact on the child and his or her behavior; any cultural or related issues or concerns; and, where the child has limited English proficiency, in any language issues that may be relevant to the behavior or incident at issue.

2. §504

OCR required manifestation determinations as a §504 matter long before they became a part of IDEA. In order to comply with §504, a group of people knowledgeable about the student, the meaning of the evaluation data, and the placement options must determine whether the behavior in question is related to the student's disability, and whether the student was appropriately placed and served at the time of the incident.[57] This group of professionals must base their determination upon the kind of current information that competent professionals would require, including psychological evaluation data related to behavior.[58]

IDEA provisions concerning the factors to be considered in making manifestation determinations, while relevant, do not limit the inquiry under §504, and parents and advocates should remain aware of the many ways in which disability and behavior may be related.[59]

F. Content of Education During Disciplinary Exclusion

1. IDEA

Meaning and content of FAPE As previously discussed, all children with disabilities are entitled to a free appropriate public education, or FAPE, including those who have been suspended or expelled from school.[60] The term "free appropriate public education" has a technical legal meaning. As defined in the IDEA statute, it means special education and related services that are provided at public expense, under public supervision, at no charge; meet the standards of the state educational agency; include an appropriate preschool, elementary or secondary education in the state involved; and are provided in accordance with an IEP that meets IDEA requirements.[61] In addition, FAPE requires that the IEP be developed in accordance with the procedures set forth in IDEA, including those governing educational decision making and the resolution of disputes between parents and school systems.[62]

The education provided to children excluded from their usual educational placement for discipline reasons must meet all of these criteria. Compliance with these criteria should ensure that these children receive a full, high quality education, with qualified instructors, in a school setting. For example, the mandate that FAPE include an appropriate elementary or secondary education in the state involved means that children must be provided the entire curriculum — not simply the isolated "special education" services listed in their IEPs, such as speech and language therapy or reading skills assistance. Ordinarily, this will be virtually impossible to accomplish through home tutoring, or limited numbers of hours per week of instruction.

In addition to these general rules regarding the content of FAPE, the IDEA statute speaks in detail to the situation of children excluded from their usual placements and placed in an "interim alternative educational setting" as a result of either involvement in certain kinds of incidents involving weapons or illegal drugs, or because a hearing officer has so ordered after finding that keeping the child in his or her current placement would be dangerous (as discussed above). The selected interim alternative educational setting must be one that enables the child to continue to participate in the general curriculum; to continue to receive the services and modifications, including those described in the IEP, that will enable him or her to meet the IEP goals; and include services and modifications designed to address the behavior that prompted placement in the interim alternative educational setting so that it does not recur.[63]

These details *elucidate* some of the general statutory rules regarding FAPE. They are not a substitute for them. It is important to keep in mind that these requirements would be components of FAPE even if *not* expressly listed in connection with interim alternative educational settings.[*] Therefore, they are required for *all* children excluded from their usual educational placement for discipline reasons, even if they are not placed in an interim alternative educational setting, and even if the behavior for which they are being suspended, expelled, or otherwise excluded is not a manifestation of disability.

In addition, the IDEA regulations further clarify that even the education provided to a child during short-term suspensions,[**] or to a child permissibly suspended or expelled for longer periods because the behavior is not related to disability, must enable him or her to appropriately progress in the general curriculum and advance towards achievement of IEP goals.[64]

Educational decision makers When a child is to be placed in an interim alternative educational setting due to an incident involving weapons or illegal drugs, the IEP team, which includes the parent, chooses the setting.[65] Similarly, and consistent with general IDEA requirements regarding IEP development and revision (discussed in Chapter 6), the IEP team is responsible for planning services for children subjected to long-term suspension or expulsion because their behavior has been found to be unrelated to disability.[66] The IEP team also plans services for a child subjected to a series of short-term (10 days or less) suspensions that, because they exceed ten days in total and create a pattern of exclusion, are to be treated as a long-term suspension (see discussion above).[67]

---

[*] See Chapters 3 and 4 discussing, respectively, the right to learn in the general curriculum and the duty to address behavior as an education issue.

[**] As discussed above, the IDEA statute provides that all children, including those who have been suspended, are entitled to FAPE. The IDEA regulations would narrow this right for children subjected to short-term suspensions (ten days or less), stating that the right to FAPE does not begin until the eleventh total day of suspensions in a school year.

In the case of a child to be placed in an interim alternative educational setting by order of a hearing officer (to address dangerous behavior) the hearing officer must approve the setting, after determining that it meets IDEA requirements.[68] Ordinarily, schools seeking such an order will propose a particular placement as the interim alternative educational setting. As the IDEA statute mandates that parents be "members of any group that makes decisions on the educational placement of their child,"[69] provisions must be made to include parents when schools develop these proposals.

The IDEA regulations confuse the issue, however, by referring to hearing officers determining that "the interim alternative educational setting that is proposed by school personnel who have consulted with the child's special education teacher" meets legal requirements.[70] The regulations thus erroneously imply that the usual process under IDEA for developing placement proposals does not apply in this situation. The regulations also state that "school personnel, in consultation with the child's special education teacher" determine services to be received during periods of short-term suspension that are not part of a pattern of exclusion.[71] Thus the regulations appear to attempt to excuse schools from following usual IDEA procedures in regard to these two groups of children, contrary to the U.S. Supreme Court's ruling in *Board of Education of the Hendrick Hudson Central School District v. Rowley* that compliance with IDEA procedures is a critical, required, aspect of FAPE.[72]

2. §504

As explained above, §504 permits suspension and expulsion without services for behavior unrelated to disability, and for certain behavior involving illegal drugs or alcohol (except in those states noted above, where judicial decisions have held otherwise), provided that students without disabilities are excluded without services for comparable behavior.

G. Challenging Discipline Decisions

1. IDEA

Hearing rights Parents who disagree with discipline decisions have the right to a due process hearing. A parent may request a hearing to challenge a manifestation determination, placement in an interim alternative educational setting by either school personnel or a hearing officer, any other placement decision, the nature or quality of education and services a child receives during periods of exclusion, or any other matter concerning the provision of a free appropriate public education.[73] If the parent's complaint concerns the manifestation determination or placement, an expedited hearing must be held.[74] Parents who do not prevail in the hearing may appeal to the state educational agency (if in a state with a two-level hearing system, as discussed in Chapter 8), or file a lawsuit in state or federal district court.[75]

Operation of "stay-put" provision As discussed in Chapter 8, ordinarily when a parent files a complaint and requests a due process hearing, the child has the right to remain in his or her current educational placement until the dispute is resolved, unless the state or local educational agency and the parent agree otherwise.[76] The same is ordinarily true when a parent requests a hearing to challenge a change in placement proposed or made for discipline reasons.[77]

The 1997 amendments to IDEA, however, created a limited exception to this rule. When the hearing request challenges the interim alternative educational setting (whether that placement was made by school officials following an incident involving weapons or drugs, or ordered by another hearing officer to address dangerous behavior) or the manifestation determination, the child remains in the interim alternative educational setting until the decision is issued or until the interim alternative placement expires, whichever comes first — unless the parent and the state or local educational agency agree otherwise.[78]

2. §504

The §504 regulations entitle students to an impartial hearing with opportunity for participation by the student's parents and representation by counsel on any discipline matters implicating identification (as an individual with a disability), evaluation or placement.[79] These include challenges to the evaluation results, the manifestation determination, any resulting placement decision, or any other actions regarding the identification, evaluation or educational placement of the student. As noted above, certain students possessing or using illegal drugs or alcohol may lose these hearing rights.

The §504 regulations have no stay-put provision. However, it should be possible to obtain a temporary restraining order and/or preliminary injunction requiring a child's reinstatement in school by filing an action in court and meeting the usual criteria for preliminary relief.

H. Students Not Previously Identified as Having a Disability

1. IDEA

Students who are or may be "children with disabilities" within the meaning of IDEA may be fully protected against suspension and expulsion as described above, even if the school system has not yet identified them as such. A student may assert IDEA protections if the school system "had knowledge" that he or she was a child with a disability before the behavior in question occurred.[80] Under the statute itself, the school system will be deemed to have had such knowledge if:

- the parent expressed concern in writing (or orally if the parent does not know how to write or has a disability that prevents a written statement) to school system personnel that the child needs special education and related services; *or*

- the child's behavior or performance demonstrates the need for such services; *or*

- the parent has requested an evaluation; *or*

- the child's teacher or other school system personnel has expressed concern about the child's behavior or performance "to the director of special education…or to other personnel of the agency."[81]

Note that the law requires that the parent have requested an evaluation or expressed concerns about possible special education and related services needs even though, her child not yet being part of the IDEA system, she would not have had any way of knowing about special education, evaluation, or other IDEA rights.

The regulations on this topic undermine the statute — and curtail students' statutory rights — by imposing additional restrictions on the circumstances under which a school system can be deemed to have had knowledge that a student has a disability. *First*, if the basis of holding the school system responsible is that the child's teacher or other staff expressed concern about the child's behavior or performance, the concern, if not expressed to the director of special education, must have been raised in accordance with the "child find" or special education referral system.[82] *Second*, the regulations create two exceptions to the rule that schools will be considered to have had knowledge that a child has a disability under any of the circumstances listed above. Under the regulations, the school system will *not* be considered to have had knowledge that the child is a child with a disability if, after receiving any of these pieces of information, the system:

- either conducted an evaluation meeting all IDEA requirements and found that the child was not eligible for services, or
- determined that an evaluation was not necessary, *and*
- in either case, provided the parents with written notice of its decision that met all IDEA notice requirements.[83]

If the school district did not "have knowledge," the child can be subjected to the same disciplinary measures to which nondisabled children are subjected.[84] However, if the parent (or anyone else) requests an evaluation it must be performed on an expedited basis, and a free appropriate public education — including all discipline protections — provided if the child is found to be a child with a disability.[85] Pending the results of the evaluation, the child remains in the "educational placement determined by school authorities."[86] The statute's use of the phrase *educational* placement should mean that educational services must be provided during this period, even if the child has been suspended or expelled from school. In contrast, however, the IDEA regulations state that the "educational placement" determined by school authorities may include suspension or expulsion without education.[87]

2. §504

Any student who is or may be an "individual with a disability" within the meaning of §504 is fully protected against improper suspension and expulsion as described above, *regardless* of whether the school district has yet identified him or her as such.[88] Generally, some reason on the school's part to believe that a child may have a disability is required before a school is found to have violated these §504 rights.[89] However, IDEA limits on the circumstances under which schools will be deemed to have knowledge of a child's disability do not apply.

I. School-filed Crime Reports and Delinquency Petitions

Perhaps because faced with the above-discussed limits on their ability to exclude students directly, perhaps in enforcement of "zero tolerance" policies, or perhaps for other reasons, schools frequently turn to the juvenile courts or the police, filing delinquency petitions or crime reports based upon in-school behavior. Often this behavior is related not only to disability, but to the consequences of the school system's past or present (or continuing) failure to provide appropriate education and related services. Two 1997 legal developments are particularly relevant to this issue: a favorable decision by the U.S. Court of Appeals for the Sixth Circuit in the case of *Morgan v. Chris L.* and a new provision added to IDEA shortly thereafter regarding school crime reports and related disclosures of education records.

1. Reporting "Crimes"

The IDEA Amendments of 1997 added to the statute for the first time language addressing the reporting of "crimes" allegedly committed by students with disabilities. This addition was made shortly after a student against whom school officials had filed a juvenile delinquency petition for in-school, disability-related conduct, won a significant legal victory in *Morgan v. Chris L.*[90] Entitled "Referral to and Action By Law Enforcement and Judicial Authorities," the 1997 provision states, "[n]othing in this part shall be construed to prohibit an agency from *reporting* a crime committed by a child with a disability to *appropriate* authorities...."[91] The legislative history of the 1997 law explains that schools may *not* "report" crimes to even "appropriate" authorities *where doing so would circumvent the school's obligations to the child under IDEA.*[92]

The provision on crime reports thus raises three key questions: (1) what constitutes "reporting a crime," (2) what are "appropriate authorities," and (3) when does "reporting" to "appropriate authorities" circumvent a school's obligations under IDEA?

The term "reporting a crime" is not defined in the statute, and therefore must be given its ordinary meaning. So understood, this provision limits schools to notifying the law enforcement entities to which crimes ordinarily are reported, i.e., police. The 1997 law thus does not authorize school officials to file juvenile delinquency petitions, nor does it condone such actions. The use of the phrase "*appropriate* authorities" reinforces this limitation, as law enforcement entities such as police are the appropriate authorities to receive crime reports — not the courts.[93] In addition, the dictate that the reporting of crimes by schools be limited to reports to "appropriate" authorities means that reports may only be made to such authorities as are appropriate in light of the purposes of IDEA.[94] Depending upon the particular situation, reporting behavior to police (or using the behavior as a basis for a delinquency petition) may not be appropriate in light of the purposes of IDEA, and so would not constitute the reporting to "appropriate" authorities.

In regard to the requirement that a school's reporting behavior as a crime not circumvent its IDEA obligations to the child, it is possible to imagine many situations in which such reporting would do just that. Responding to the behavioral manifestations of disability by filing crime reports rather than by providing appropriate special education and related services is one, as is failing to provide appropriate services and then treating the disability-related behavior that follows as a discipline problem and a crime. Both were the case in *Morgan v. Chris L.*, where the school system filed a juvenile delinquency petition against a student with Attention Deficit Hyperactivity Disorder ("ADHD") accused of kicking a water pipe. Even after school staff recommended private counseling and private evaluation for possible ADHD — and after Chris L. was privately diagnosed with ADHD, informed school personnel of the diagnosis, and began having medication administered to him in school — school personnel continued to treat the student's longstanding academic and behavioral difficulties as a discipline problem, rather than evaluating him under IDEA and providing appropriate special education and related services. A special education evaluation, requested by his parents, was pending at the time of the alleged incident, at his parents' request. When the student challenged the school's filing of the petition, he prevailed at an IDEA due process hearing, in federal district court, and before the U.S. Court of Appeals for the Sixth Circuit. All found that the school system had attempted to circumvent its obligations under IDEA.[95]

2. Disclosing Education Records

With the 1997 amendments, IDEA now further provides that when a school reports a crime alleged to have been committed by a child with a disability, it must send copies of the child's special education and disciplinary records to the "appropriate authorities" to whom it reports the alleged crime.[96] However, schools may transmit these records *only to the extent permitted by the Family Educational Rights and Privacy Act* ("FERPA").[97] FERPA ordinarily prohibits disclosure of education records without the prior written consent of the parent or of a student 18 years of age or older.[98] The exceptional circumstances under which FERPA allows protected education records to be disclosed *without* prior written consent are very narrow. They include disclosure to comply with a court order or lawfully issued subpoena — provided that parents and students are notified in advance — and disclosure "to appropriate parties" in connection with a health or safety emergency, "if knowledge of the information is necessary to protect the health or safety of the student or other individuals."[99] The latter exception is to be strictly construed.[100] Note that there is no broad exception for crime reports.[101]

FERPA was, however, amended in 1994 to address the limited circumstances under which school systems may disclose information from education records to juvenile authorities. Education records or the personally identifiable information they contain may be released to state and local officials or authorities to whom such information is specifically allowed to be reported or disclosed pursuant to a state statute adopted *before* November 19, 1974 if the allowed reporting or disclosure concerns the juvenile justice system and it's ability to effectively serve the student in question. If the relevant state statute was adopted *after* November 19, 1974, then reporting or disclosure is only permissible if it concerns the juvenile justice system's ability to effectively serve the student *prior to adjudication*, and the officials or authorities to whom the information is released certify in writing to the school system that the information will not be disclosed to any other party without the prior written consent of the student's parent, except as provided under state law.[102]

NOTES

1. Even prior to enactment of IDEA and §504, courts recognized the right of children with disabilities to receive a publicly supported education and established the principle that exclusion on the basis of disability is unconstitutional on federal due process and equal protection grounds, and on a variety of state law grounds. *See, e.g., Frederick L. v. Thomas*, 408 F. Supp. 832, 419 F. Supp. 960 (E.D. Pa. 1976), *aff'd* 557 F.2d 373 (3rd Cir. 1977); *Pennsylvania Association for Retarded Citizens v. Pennsylvania*, 334 F. Supp. 279 (1972); *Mills v. Board of Education of District of Columbia*, 348 F. Supp. 866 (D.D.C. 1972); *In re G.H.*, 218 N.W.2d 441 (North Dakota Supreme Ct. 1974). *Mills*, one of the early, successful, lawsuits vindicating this right was brought on behalf of children with disabilities labeled "behavior problems," and excluded from public education on that ground.

2. 419 U.S. 565, 95 S.Ct. 729 (1975).

3. *Id.*, 419 U.S. at 581, 95 S.Ct. at 739-40.

4. *Id.*, 419 U.S. at 584, 95 S.Ct. at 741. *See also Strickland v. Inlow*, 519 F.2d 744, 746 (8ᵗʰ Cir. 1975) (recognizing due process right to a hearing on the appropriateness of penalty where students admitted to misconduct).

5. *Goss, supra*, 419 U.S. at 581, 95 S.Ct. at 739-40.

6. *Id.*, 419 U.S. at 584, 95 S.Ct. at 741; *Jackson v. Franklin County School District*, 806 F.2d 623, 631 (5ᵗʰ Cir. 1986).

7. *Goss, supra,* 419 U.S. at 578-80, 584, 95 S.Ct. at 737, 741; *Mathews v. Eldridge,* 424 U.S. 319, 333-35, 96 S.Ct. 893 (1976). A substantial body of case law has developed as parties seek to contest the specific elements of due process that are in fact due. There is disagreement as to what procedural protections school officials should provide students who are expelled from school. For the most part, courts have been reluctant to expand students' procedural rights. Recently, for example, the Eighth Circuit Court of Appeals admonished that courts should exercise "care and restraint" in reviewing a school's disciplinary decisions for due process violations. *See Woodis v. Westark Community College*, 160 F.3d 435, 438 (8ᵗʰ Cir.1998). Another federal appellate court, in an earlier decision, ruled that a student expelled for the remainder of a semester on drug allegations was not entitled to cross-examine student accusers, learn their identities, or cross-examine school officials. *See Newsome v. Batavia Local School Dist.*, 842 F.2d 920, 924-26 (6th Cir. 1988) . On the other hand, another recently decided case was characterized by the court as one of the "unusual" cases involving a short-term suspension that requires something more than rudimentary procedures. In this case, a high school student challenged the multiple disciplinary sanctions imposed upon him (suspension for three days, placement in an alternative education program for five days, probation for the balance of the semester, and participation in graduation conditioned on writing two letters of apology), after being accused by the principal of having taken a photograph of the principal's automobile parked outside the home of a female teacher, being the source of rumors of a sexual nature, and making for distribution T-shirts with a photograph of principal. The court allowed the student to proceed with claims that he was denied the rights to adequate prior notice informing him of the charges against him; to have a meaningful opportunity to present evidence and to present witnesses; to prior notice of the school's evidence against him and to review evidence being relied upon; to an impartial decision-maker; to a fair hearing (untainted by bias); to confront and cross examine witnesses; to review through a grievance procedure that was capable of curing prior denials of rights; to have the proper presumption/burden of proof applied in his disciplinary hearing; and to First Amendment free speech protections. *See Riggan v. Midland Independent School District*, 86 F. Supp. 2d 647 (W.D. Tex. 2000).

8. *Goss, supra,* 419 U.S. at 582, 95 S.Ct. at 740.

9. *Id.*, 419 U.S. at 582-83, 95 S.Ct. at 740.

10. 20 U.S.C. §1412(a)(1)(A).

11. 34 C.F.R. §§300.121(d)(1), 300.520(a)(1)(ii).

12. 34 C.F.R. §300.121(d)(1).

13. 20 U.S.C. §§1415(k)(1)(A)(i), (k)(4)(A); 34 C.F.R. §300.523(a).

14. 34 C.F.R. §§300.520(a)(1)(i), 300.519(a), 300.523(a).

15. *See* 34 C.F.R. §300.519.

16. 34 C.F.R. §§300.519, 300.523(a).

17. 20 U.S.C. §1415(k)(4)(A)(i); 34 C.F.R. §300.523(a)(1).

18. 20 U.S.C. §1415(k)(4)(A); 34 C.F.R. §300.523(a).

19. 20 U.S.C. §1415(k)(5)(A); 34 C.F.R, §300.524(a). If, after a finding of no manifestation, a child is to be subjected to the disciplinary procedures applicable to all children, his or her special education and disciplinary records must be sent for consideration to the person who will make the final decision concerning disciplinary action. 20 U.S.C. §1415(k)(5)(B); 34 C.F.R. §300.524(b).

20. *See* 20 U.S.C. §1415(k)(5)(A); 34 C.F.R. §300.524(a).

21. 20 U.S.C. §1415(k)(1)(B)(i).

22. *See* 34 C.F.R. §300.520(b).

23. 20 U.S.C. §1415(k)(1)(B)(ii); 34 C.F.R. §300.520(b)(ii).

24. 34 C.F.R. §300.520(c).

25. *Id.*

26. 34 C.F.R. §§ 104.35, 104.36.

27. *See, e.g.*, Memorandum of Oct. 28, 1988 to OCR Senior Staff from L.S. Daniels, Assistant Secretary for Civil Rights, reprinted at EHLR 307:05 (hereinafter "OCR Memo").

28. Note that IDEA does not necessarily require a re-evaluation prior to a disciplinary change in placement. As virtually all children covered by IDEA are also protected by §504, this §504 right is an important supplement to IDEA rights. Parents and advocates should not hesitate to invoke it.

29. OCR Memo, *supra.*

30. *Kaelin v. Grubbs*, 682 F.2d 595 (6th Cir. 1982); *S-1 v. Turlington*, 635 F.2d 342 (5th Cir. 1981); *Bonner v. City of* Prichard, 661 F.2d 1206, 1207 (11th Cir. 1981) (decisions of the Fifth Circuit issues prior to 10/1/81 are binding precedent in the Eleventh Circuit). *See also* OCR Memo, *supra.*

31. OCR Memo, *supra.*

32. *See, e.g.*, Memorandum of February 24, 1989 to J.L. High, Regional Civil Rights Director, Region IV. from L.S. Daniels, Assistant Secretary for Civil Rights, reprinted at EHLR 307:07.

33. *See, e.g., id.*; *Roane Co. (TN) School District*, 27 IDELR 853 (OCR 8/8/97); *San Juan (CA) Unified School District*, 20 IDELR 549 (OCR 7/6/93).

34. *See Roane County (TN) School District, supra*; *Mobile County (AL) School District*, 19 IDELR 519 (OCR 11/6/92); *Templeton (CA) Unified School District*, 17 EHLR 859 (OCR 3/19/91); *San Juan (CA) Unified School District, supra*; *York (SC) School District*, 17 EHLR 475 (OCR 11/13/90); *Niagra Falls City (NY) School District*, EHLR 352:472 (OCR 2/6/87).

35. *See* 29 U.S.C. §794; 34 C.F.R. §§104.3(j), 104.4(b), 104.33, 104.35; 42 U.S.C. §12132; 28 C.F.R. §38.130(a),(b) (implementing the ADA). See also the following U.S. Department of Education/Office of Civil Rights complaint decisions: *Oakland (CA) Unified School* District, 20 IDELR 1338 (OCR 11/3/93) (taping closed student's mouth for excessive talking related to mental retardation); *School Administrative Unit #38 (NH)*, 19 IDELR 186 (OCR 7/23/92) (repeatedly sending child to principal's office for conduct related to attention deficit disorder and emotional disturbance); *Compliance Review of Riverview (WA) School District*, EHLR 311:103 (OCR 6/30/87) (student dropped from school rolls for disability-related tardiness); and *Nash County (NC) School District*, EHLR 352:37 (8/12/85) (corporal punishment). *See also Thomas v. Davidson Academy*, 846 F. Supp. 611 (M.D. Tenn. 1994) (§504 and the ADA require modifications to school discipline policies to avoid discrimination).

36. *See* 20 U.S.C. §1415(k)(1)(A)(ii) as amended by the Educational Flexibility Partnership Act of 1999, Pub. L. No. 106-25, §6, 113 Stat. 41, 49.

37. 20 U.S.C. §1415(k)(10)(D), incorporating by reference 18 U.S.C. §930(g).

38. *See* 20 U.S.C. §1415(k)(10)(A), incorporating by reference portions of 21 U.S.C. §812(c).

39. 20 U.S.C. §1415(k)(10)(B).

40. *Honig v. Doe*, 484 U.S. 305, 108 S.Ct. 592 (1988); 20 U.S.C. §1415(j).

41. 20 U.S.C. §1415(k)(1)(A)(ii), (k)(5)(A); 34 C.F.R. §§300.520(a)(2), 300.524(a).

42. *See* 20 U.S.C. §1415(k)(6)(B)(ii), incorporating by reference §1415(k)(2); 34 C.F.R. §300.525(b)(2), incorporating by reference §300.521.

43. 20 U.S.C. §1415(k)(1)(A)(ii); 34 C.F.R. §§300.9, 300.520(a)(2).

44. 20 U.S.C. §1415(k)(7)(B); 34 C.F.R. §300.526(b).

45. 20 U.S.C. §1415(k)(7)(C); 34 C.F.R. §300.526(b).

46. 29 U.S.C. §705(20)(C)(iv).

47. *Id.*

48. 20 U.S.C. §1415(k)(2); 34 C.F.R. §300.521. The provisions allowing a hearing officer to order that a child behaving dangerously be moved to an interim alternative educational setting over parental objection were added to IDEA in 1997. The Supreme Court in 1988 held that, when faced with dangerous behavior and unable to reach agreement with parents on an appropriate course of action, school officials may not unilaterally remove a child from his or her current educational placement but, rather, may seek a court order allowing the change. *See Honig v. Doe, supra*. It is unclear whether, in light of the 1997 addition to the statute, schools may still proceed directly to court under such circumstances, or must first exhaust administrative remedies by seeking an order from an IDEA due process hearing officer.

49. 20 U.S.C. §1415(k)(2); 34 C.F.R. §300.521.

50. 20 U.S.C. §§1415(k)(2), 1415(k)(10)(C); 34 C.F.R. §300.521.

51. *See* 20 U.S.C. §1415(k)(7)(B).

52. 20 U.S.C. §1415(k)(4)(B); 34 C.F.R. §300.523(b).

53. 20 U.S.C. §1415(k)(4)(C)(i); 34 C.F.R. §300.523(c)(1).

54. 20 U.S.C. §1415(k)(4)(C)(ii); 34 C.F.R. §300.523(c)(2).

55. 34 C.F.R. §300.523(d).

56. 34 C.F.R. §300.532(f).

57. *William S. Hart (CA) Union School District*, 26 IDELR 181 (OCR 12/13/96); Memorandum of Nov. 13, 1989 to OCR Senior Staff from William Smith, Acting Assistant Secretary for Civil Rights, reprinted at 16 EHLR 491, 493 (hereinafter "OCR Memo II"). For cases recognizing that a school's failure to provide appropriate services may contribute to inappropriate behavior, *see, e.g., Chris D. v. Montgomery Bd. of Ed.*, 753 F. Supp. 922 (M.D. Ala. 1990) (school failed to provide appropriate educational program to emotionally disturbed student where, rather than employing strategies to teach him appropriate behavior with the goal of ultimately returning him to the regular education setting, IEP merely described classroom rules and punishments and rewards for breaking them or following them; student had repeatedly been subject to disciplinary sanctions); *Lamont X. v. Quisenberry*, 606 F. Supp. 809, 813 n.2 (S.D. Ohio 1984)("….we cannot help but be troubled by the decision to prosecute the minor plaintiffs for the August disturbances, particularly when prosecution was combined with removal from the classroom for several months. Plaintiffs' handicap by definition includes a likelihood for behavioral disturbances, and the fact that defendants chose criminal prosecution as an appropriate response to such behavior leads us to question whether the school may have simply decided that it was time to take harsh action in such instances as a policy matter, a result which we do not perceive as wholly in keeping with the spirit and purpose of the EAHCA [now IDEA]"); *Stuart v. Nappi*, 443 F. Supp. 1235, 1241 (D. Conn. 1978) (school's "handling of the plaintiff may have contributed to her disruptive behavior"); *Howard S. v. Friendswood School District*, 454 F. Supp. 634, 640 (S.D. Tex. 1978)(finding that plaintiff, whom school officials sought to expel following a suicide attempt and hospitalization, "was not afforded a free, appropriate public education during the period from the time he enrolled in high school until December of 1976, [which] was…a contributing and proximate cause of his emotional difficulties and emotional disturbance"); *Frederick L. v. Thomas*, 408 F. Supp. 832, 835 (E.D. Penn. 1976) (recognizing that an inappropriate educational placement can cause antisocial behavior). *C.f. Inquiry of Fields*, EHLR 211:437 (OSEP 1987) (as an IDEA matter, OSEP "would encourage States and localities to be alert to the possibility that repeated discipline problems may indicate that the services being provided to a particular child with a handicap should be reviewed or changed….").

58. OCR Memo II.

59. *See e.g., School Board of Prince William County v. Malone*, 762 F.2d 1210, 1216 (4th Cir. 1985) (student with specific learning disabilities acted as a go-between in drug deals for fellow students; district court had properly reasoned that "'[a] direct result of Jerry's learning disability is a loss of self image, an awareness of lack of peer approval occasioned by ridicule or teasing from his chronological age group…These emotional disturbances make him particularly susceptible to peer pressure. Under these circumstances he leaps at a chance for peer approval'"); *S-1 v. Turlington*, 635 F.2d 342, 346-47 (5th Cir. 1981), ("a determination that a handicapped student knew the difference between right and wrong is not tantamount to a determination that his misconduct was or was not a manifestation of his handicap":

for example, "a child with low intellectual functioning who might respond to stress or respond to a threat in the only way that they feel adequate, which may be verbal aggressive behavior," or an orthopedically disabled child might behave aggressively towards other children, provoking fights, as a way of dealing with stress and feelings of physical vulnerability). *See also* OCR Memo II.

60. 20 U.S.C. §1412(a)(1).

61. 20 U.S.C. §1401(8).

62. *Board of Education of the Hendrick Hudson Central School District v. Rowley*, 458 U.S. 176, 206-207, 102 S.Ct. 3034, 3051 (1982).

63. 20 U.S.C. §1415(k)(3)(B); 34 C.F.R. §300.522(b).

64. 34 C.F.R. §300.121(d)(2).

65. 20 U.S.C. §1415(k)(3)(A); 34 C.F.R. §300.522(a).

66. 34 C.F.R. §300.121(d)(3)(ii).

67. *See* 34 C.F.R. §300.121(d)(3)(i). See also the discussion of decision making procedures and personnel in general in Chapter 6.

68. 20 U.S.C. §1415(k)(2)(D).

69. 20 U.S.C. §1414(f).

70. 34 C.F.R. §300.521(d).

71. 34 C.F.R. §300.121(d)(3)(i).

72. *See Rowley, supra,* 458 U.S. at 206-207, 102 S.Ct. at 3034, 3051. See also the discussion of procedural appropriateness and *Rowley* in Chapter 2.

73. 20 U.S.C. §§1415(b)(6), (f), (k)(6)(A)(i); 34 C.F.R. §§300.507(a)(1), 300.525(a)(1).

74. 20 U.S.C. §1415(k)(6)(A)(ii); 34 C.F.R. §300.525(a)(2). The statute does not provide time frames for expedited hearings, but clearly requires them. Nonetheless, the regulations state that an "expedited" hearing must result in a written decision being mailed within 45 days of receipt of the hearing request — the same time frame that applies to routine hearings. *See* 34 C.F.R. §300.528(b)(1) (expedited hearings) and 34 C.F.R. §300.511(a) (routine hearings).

75. 20 U.S.C. §1415(i)(1).

76. 20 U.S.C. §1415(j).

77. 20 U.S.C. §1415(j); *Honig, supra.* Note that *Honig* held that a court of competent jurisdiction under certain limited circumstances may issue an injunction temporarily excluding a child from his or her current educational placement, over parental objection, for behavior substantially likely to result in injury to the child or to others. As discussed above, the 1997 IDEA amendments grant this authority to hearing officers.

78. 20 U.S.C. §1415(k)(7)(A); 34 C.F.R. §300.526(a).

79. 34 C.F.R. §104.36.

80. 20 U.S.C. §1415(k)(8)(A); 34 C.F.R. §300.527(a).

81. 20 U.S.C. §1415(k)(8)(B); 34 C.F.R. §300.527(b).

82. 34 C.F.R. §300.527(b)(4).

83. 34 C.F.R. §300.527(c).

84. 20 U.S.C. §1415(k)(8)(C)(i); 34 C.F.R. §300.527(d)(1).

85. 20 U.S.C. §1415(k)(8)(C)(ii); 34 C.F.R. §§300.527(d)(2)(i), (iii).

86. 20 U.S.C. §1415(k)(8)(C)(ii).

87. 34 C.F.R. §300.527(d)(2)(ii).

88. *See, e.g., Templeton (CA) Unified School District,* 17 EHLR 859 (OCR 3/19/91); *Prince George's County (MD) Public Schools,* 17 EHLR 875 (OCR 3/22/91); *Lumberton (MS) Public School District,* 18 IDELR 33 (OCR 6/24/91).

89. *See, e.g., Napa Valley (CA) Unified Sch. Dist.,* 27 IDELR 505 (OCR 6/5/97); *Akron (OH) City Sch. Dist.,* 19 IDELR 542 (OCR 11/18/92); *Mineral County (NV) Sch. Dist.,* 16 EHLR 668 (OCR 3/16/90).

90. 927 F. Supp. 267 (E.D. Tenn. 1994), *aff'd without published opinion,* 106 F.3d 401 (6th Cir. 1997), *Sixth Circuit decision reported in full,* 25 IDELR 227, 1997 U.S. App. Lexis 1041.

91. 20 U.S.C. § 1415(k)(9)(A) (emphasis added).

92. See statement of Sen. Harkin, one of the legislation's co-sponsors, at Cong. Rec. May 14, 1997 at S4403 ("The bill also authorizes…proper referrals to police and appropriate authorities when disabled children commit crimes, so long as the referrals, do not circumvent the school's responsibilities under IDEA").

93. In regard to the judiciary, the 1997 amendment simply provides that nothing in IDEA "shall be construed…to prevent…judicial authorities from exercising their responsibilities with regard to the application of Federal and State law to crimes committed by a child with a disability." 20 U.S.C. § 1415(k)(9)(A).

94. *Cf. Burlington School Committee v. Department of Education Commonwealth of Massachusetts,* 471 U.S. 359, 105 S.Ct. 1996 (1985) (where IDEA, then known as the Education of the Handicapped Act, grants courts authority to "grant such relief as the court determines is appropriate," "appropriate" relief is relief that is appropriate in light of the purposes of the Act).

95. The Sixth Circuit found that the school system had breached its duty under IDEA to identify, evaluate and provide Chris with a free appropriate public education; had unlawfully attempted to secure a program for the student from the juvenile court, instead of providing services itself; and had, by filing the petition, improperly sought to change Chris' educational placement without following IDEA's change-in-placement procedures. *See* 25 IDELR at 230, 1997 U.S. App. Lexis 1041 at 14-17. In addition, the court, like the lower court and hearing officer, expressly held that the filing of the delinquency petition constituted a change in educational placement, entitling Chris to IDEA procedural protections, including the convening of an IDEA team meeting prior to such a proposed placement change. *Id.*

A number of other courts have found school-initiated juvenile court proceedings inappropriate where the underlying dispute in essence is an educational one regarding appropriate special education and related services — thus suggesting that such action by schools circumvent their IDEA obligations. Note that these cases did not involve alleged "crimes" and delinquency petitions but, rather, other kinds of juvenile proceedings. *See, e.g., North v. District of Columbia Bd. of Ed.*, 471 F. Supp. 136, 140 (D.D.C. 1979) (it would be inappropriate to proceed with neglect proceedings where real issue concerned school district's failure to provide special education and related services to which child was entitled); *In the Matter of Ruffel P.*, 582 N.Y.S.2d 631 (Family Court Orange Co. 1992) (dismissing "in the interests of justice" Person In Need of Services petition brought by school principal alleging violent behavior by student, where school had refused to certify child as eligible for special education, failed to try different teaching approaches, and responded solely with disciplinary actions); *In the Matter of Shelly Maynard*, 453 N.Y.S.2d 352 (Family Court Monroe Co. 1982) (where child was found to have a disability after being adjudicated a Person in Need of Services on the basis of truancy at the behest of school officials, school would be required to fulfill its obligation to provide appropriate special education and related services; court would renew involvement only if child failed to attend an appropriate placement made pursuant to special education law); *Flint Bd. of Ed. v. Williams*, 276 N.W.2d 499 (Mich. App. 1979) (school system may not ask probate court to take jurisdiction over children with disabilities pursuant to state statute regarding students who repeatedly violate school rules or are truant until proceedings under special education law have terminated and a final decision made that no program within the school system can serve the child's needs). *Cf. Murphy v. Timberlane Regional School District*, 22 F.3d 1186, 1196 n. 13 (1st Cir. 1994) ("Timberlane's misconceptions about the IDEA are betrayed…by the contention that its institution of truancy proceedings should be considered the rough equivalent of the administrative adjudication required under [special education regulations]…[A] coercive adversarial proceeding against a parent is no substitute for a substantive review of the special educational needs of a handicapped child"); *Lamont X., supra*, 606 F. Supp. at 813 n.2 ("…we cannot help but be troubled by the decision to prosecute the minor plaintiffs….Plaintiffs' handicap by definition includes a likelihood for behavioral disturbances, and the fact that defendants chose criminal prosecution as an appropriate response to such behavior leads us to question whether the school may have simply decided that it was time to take harsh action…as a policy matter, a result which we do not perceive as wholly in keeping with the spirit and purpose of the EAHCA [renamed the EHA and then IDEA]").

96. 20 U.S.C. §1415(k)(9)(B); 34 C.F.R. §300.529(b)(1).

97. 34 C.F.R. §529(b)(2).

98. *See* 20 U.S.C. §1232g(b), (d); 34 C.F.R. §99.30.

99. *20 U.S.C. §1232g(b)(2)(B); 34 C.F.R. §99.31(9).*

100. 20 U.S.C. §1232g(b)(2)(B); 34 C.F.R. §99.31(9).

101. For additional exceptions to FERPA consent requirements, see 34 C.F.R. §99.31.

102. See 20 U.S.C. §1232g(b)(1)(E); 34 C.F.R. §99.38.

CHAPTER 10

IDEA AND EARLY CHILDHOOD DEVELOPMENT

The aspects of IDEA discussed in the previous Chapters are found largely in Part B of the statute, which applies to the education of three through twenty-one year olds. Part C of IDEA addresses the needs of younger children, providing for early intervention services for infants and toddlers. Taken together and implemented properly, Parts B and C should create a seamless system of developmentally appropriate early childhood services for infants, toddlers and preschool children, from birth through age 5.[*]

A. PART C — STATEWIDE EARLY INTERVENTION SYSTEMS

Part C of IDEA provides states with funds to assist in maintaining and implementing "a statewide, comprehensive, coordinated, multidisciplinary, interagency system to provide early intervention services for infants and toddlers with disabilities and their families."[1] Congress initially enacted what is now Part C in 1986 as part H of IDEA based upon its finding of "an urgent and substantial need" to, among other things, enhance the development of infants and toddlers with disabilities and minimize their potential for developmental delay; minimize the need for special education and related services when infants and toddlers with disabilities reach school age; enhance the capacity of families to meet the needs of their infants and toddlers with disabilities; and enhance the ability of states and local agencies and service providers to meet the needs of members of historically underrepresented populations, minority, low-income, inner-city and rural populations in particular.[2] Early intervention

---

[*] As of July 1, 2001, proposed changes to the Part C regulations published in the Federal Register on September 5, 2000 were still pending. *See* 65 Fed. Reg. 53808 *et seq.* Advocates should ascertain whether final regulations affecting the topics discussed in this Chapter have since been issued.

services under IDEA are family-centered and voluntary on the part of parents.[3]

All states and jurisdictions accept Part C funds, and so must operate statewide systems that meet its requirements. Chief among these is that appropriate early intervention services be made available to *all* eligible infants and toddlers with disabilities in the state.[4] Waiting lists are not acceptable.[5] In addition to those discussed below, other required components of the statewide system include policies, practices and procedures to ensure that traditionally underserved groups, including minority, low-income and rural families, are meaningfully involved in planning and implementing the early intervention system, and have access to culturally competent services within their local geographic areas; a comprehensive child find system; policies regarding contractual and other arrangements with service providers to provide early intervention services; a state interagency coordinating council; and a comprehensive system of personnel development.[6]

The statewide system mandated by Part C is administered in each state by a "lead agency" designated by the governor. The lead agency may or may not be the state educational agency otherwise responsible for IDEA implementation. Whatever the lead agency, it is responsible for the general administration and supervision of the early intervention system, including ensuring that the public and private service providers that are part of the system comply with IDEA.[7]

B. Eligibility

As noted above, appropriate early intervention services must be made available to all infants and toddlers with disabilities in the state and their families. An otherwise-eligible child may not be denied services because he or she is not a citizen, or because of the child's immigration status.[8] For purposes of Part C, the term "infant or toddler with a disability" means a child from birth through age 2 "who needs early intervention services because… [he or she] —

> (i) is experiencing developmental delays, as measured by appropriate diagnostic instruments and procedures, in one or more of the areas of cognitive development, physical development, communication development, social or emotional development, and adaptive development; or

(ii) has a diagnosed physical or mental condition which has a high probability of resulting in developmental delay…"[9]

The statute does not specify what constitutes a "developmental delay" sufficient to trigger eligibility but, rather, allows each state to define this term itself.[10] In doing so, the state must describe (1) the procedures, including the use of informed clinical opinion, that will be used to measure a child's development, and (2) the levels of functioning or other criteria that constitute a developmental delay, in each of the areas of cognitive, physical, communication, social or emotional, and adaptive development.[11]

At a state's discretion, "infant or toddler with a disability" may also include infants and toddlers who are at risk of experiencing a substantial developmental delay if early intervention services are not provided.[12] IDEA leaves it to states choosing to serve this group to define who is "at risk" for developmental delay.[13] State definitions may include biological factors (e.g., low birth weight, respiratory distress as a newborn) and/or environmental ones.[14] Apparently concerned with the small number of states choosing to serve at-risk infants and toddlers, Congress in 1997 added to Part C a statement that "[i]t is…the policy of the United States to provide financial assistance to States…to encourage States to expand opportunities for children under 3 years of age who would be at risk of having substantial developmental delay if they did not receive early intervention services."[15] Congress also added a provision allowing states that do not serve at risk infants and toddlers in their Part C system to use Part C funds for collaborative efforts related to this population, specifically including identifying and evaluating at-risk infants and toddlers; referring such children to other (non-Part C) services; and conducting periodic follow-ups on each referral to determine if the child has become eligible for Part C services by virtue of developmental delay or having been diagnosed with a condition which has a high probability of resulting in developmental delay.[16]

C. EARLY INTERVENTION SERVICES

Under Part C, the appropriate early intervention services to which all infants and toddlers with disabilities in the state have a right include:

- family training, counseling, and home visits;
- special instruction;
- speech-language and audiology services;

- occupational therapy; physical therapy;
- psychological services;
- service coordination services;
- medical services for diagnostic or evaluation purposes;
- early identification, screening and assessment services;
- health services necessary to enable a child to benefit from other early intervention services;
- social work services;
- vision services;
- assistive technology devices and services;
- transportation and related costs
- nursing services;
- nutrition services; and
- other developmental services designed to meet the needs of an infant or toddler with a disability in physical, cognitive, communication, social, emotional or adaptive development.[17]

Early intervention services must be selected in collaboration with the child's parents; be designed to meet the individual developmental needs of the child and the needs of the family related to enhancing the child's development; be provided under public supervision, by qualified personnel; meet state standards and IDEA requirements; and be provided in conformity with an individualized family service plan ("IFSP").[18] Decisions regarding the particular services a child will receive must be made through the IFSP development process (discussed below), based upon evaluations and assessments of the child and his or her unique needs.[19] In addition, each eligible child and his or her family must be provided a single service coordinator responsible for the implementation of the IFSP, coordinating all services across agency lines and helping parents obtain the services and assistance they need.[20]

D. SETTING FOR SERVICES — "NATURAL ENVIRONMENTS"

Early intervention services must be provided in "natural environments" to the maximum extent appropriate in light of the child's needs; a particular service may be provided in another setting only when the desired early intervention outcome cannot be achieved satisfactorily for the child in a natural environment.[21] "Natural environments" are "settings that are natural or normal for the child's age peers who have no disabilities,"[22] and include the home and community settings in which children without disabilities participate.[23] Programs that provide early intervention services in a center, classroom or other setting limited to infants and toddlers with disabilities are not natural environments.[24] On the contrary, "to comply with Part C's natural environment requirement, States must ensure that, to the maximum extent appropriate to the needs of the child, infants and toddlers with disabilities receive services in settings that include typically developing age peers."[25]

The determination of what constitutes the natural environment for provision of a particular service to a particular child must be made on an individual basis through the IFSP process.[26] The same is true of any decision that a particular service will not be provided in a natural environment because the desired early intervention outcome cannot be achieved satisfactorily there.[27]

E. EVALUATION AND ASSESSMENT

1. Evaluation and Assessment of the Child

Part C provides for both comprehensive, multidisciplinary *evaluation* of infants and toddlers, and multidisciplinary *assessment*.[28] "Evaluation" refers to procedures used to determine a child's eligibility for early intervention services; "assessment" refers to the ongoing procedures used to identify an eligible child's unique strengths and needs and the services appropriate to meet those needs in the context of the family.[29] The evaluation and assessment of each child must be conducted by personnel trained to use appropriate methods and procedures; be based on informed clinical opinion; and include each of the following:

- a review of pertinent records regarding the child's medical history and current health status;
- an evaluation of the child's level of functioning in the areas of cognitive development, physical development (including vision and hearing), communication development, social or emotional development, and adaptive development; and
- an assessment of the child's unique needs in each of the above-mentioned areas of development, including identification of services appropriate to meet those needs.[30]

2. Family Assessments

Part C requires the early intervention system to make available to all families of eligible children "a family-directed assessment of the resources, priorities, and concerns of the family and the identification of the supports and services necessary to enhance the family's capacity to meet the developmental needs of the infant or toddler."[31] Family assessments must be voluntary on the part of the family; they cannot be required, and cannot be made a condition for a child's receipt of early intervention services.[32] When a family assessment is carried out, it must:

- be conducted by personnel trained to utilize appropriate methods and procedures;
- be based upon information provided by the family through a personal interview; and
- incorporate the family's description of its resources, priorities and concerns regarding enhancing the child's development.[33]

3. Safeguards Against Discrimination

As does Part B of IDEA, the Part C regulations include provisions intended to ensure that evaluation and assessment are nondiscriminatory. Tests and other evaluation materials and procedures must be administered in the parents' native language or other mode of communication, unless clearly not feasible; assessment and evaluation procedures and materials must be chosen and administered so as not to be racially or culturally discriminatory; no single procedure may be used as the basis for determining a child's eligibility for services; and evaluations and assessments must be conducted by qualified personnel.[34]

F. The Individualized Family Service Plan ("IFSP")

1. IFSP Development

An individualized family service plan, or IFSP, is a written plan for providing early intervention services to a child and his or her family. IFSPs are developed at a meeting that includes the child's parent or parents; other family members at the parent's request; an advocate or other non-family member, at the parent's request; the child's service coordinator; at least one person directly involved in conducting the evaluations and assessments; and, as appropriate, individuals who will be providing services to the child or family.[35] IFSP meetings must be conducted in places and at times that are convenient for families, and in the native language or other mode of communication used by the family, unless clearly not feasible.[36] Meeting arrangements must be made, and written notice provided to the family and other participants, far enough in advance to ensure that they will be able to attend.[37]

2. Content

The IFSP must include the following components:

- a statement of the child's present levels of physical (including vision, hearing and health status), cognitive, communication, social or emotional, and adaptive development, based on professionally acceptable objective criteria;
- with the agreement of the family, a statement of the family's resources, priorities, and concerns relating to enhancing the child's development;
- a statement of the major outcomes expected to be achieved for child and the family, and the criteria, procedures, and timelines that will be used to determine the degree to which progress toward achieving the outcomes is being made and whether the outcomes or services need to be changed
- a statement of the specific early intervention services necessary to meet the unique needs of the child and family (to achieve the expected outcomes), including the frequency, intensity, and method of delivering services;
- a statement of the natural environments in which each early intervention service will be provided, including a justification of the extent, if any, to which any service will not be provided in a natural environment;
- the projected dates for initiation of services, which must be as soon as possible after the IFSP meeting, and the anticipated duration of the services;
- the payment arrangements, if any;[*]
- the name of the family's assigned service coordinator;
- the steps to be taken to support the transition of the toddler with a disability to preschool or other appropriate services at age 3, including

---

* Part C provisions regarding payment for services are discussed below.

- parent training and discussions regarding future placements and other matters related to the child's transition,

- procedures to prepare the child for changes in service delivery, including steps to help the child adjust to, and function in, a new setting, and

- with prior, written parental consent, sending information about the child to the local school system in order to ensure continuity of services, including evaluation and assessment information and copies of IFSPs;[*] and

- medical and other services that the child needs but that are not required to be provided under Part C, and the funding sources that will be used to pay for them, or the steps that will be taken to secure them from public or private sources.[38]

3. Timeframes

Evaluations and assessments must be completed and a meeting held to develop an initial IFSP within 45 days of when the responsible public agency receives a referral seeking the child's evaluation.[39] Ordinarily, an IFSP is not developed, and early intervention services are not provided, until the evaluation and assessment have been completed (within the 45-day time frame). However, where a child has obvious immediate needs, services may begin before completion of the evaluation and assessments if the parents consent and an interim IFSP is developed.[40] The evaluation and assessment must still be completed within the otherwise- applicable timeframe.[41]

4. Review and Revision

The IFSP must be reviewed every six months, and more frequently if conditions so warrant or the family requests a review, to determine (1) how much progress is being made towards achieving the outcomes in the IFSP, and (2) whether the outcomes or services need to be changed.[42] The review is to be carried out by the same group required for developing the IFSP, and may be accomplished through a meeting or other means accept-able to the parents and other participants.[43] In addition to this periodic review, a meeting must be held at least annually to evaluate the IFSP and revise it as appropriate.[44] The results of any current evaluations and the

---

[*] Transition from early intervention services under Part C to preschool services under Part B of IDEA is discussed in further detail below.

information available from ongoing assessment must be used in determining what services are needed and will be provided.[45] The annual meeting must include the same group required for initial IFSP development and periodic review.[46] Both periodic reviews, if carried out by a meeting, and annual IFSP meetings must be conducted in places and at times that are convenient for families, and in the native language or other mode of communication used by the family, unless clearly not feasible.[47] Meeting arrangements must be made, and written notice provided to the family and other participants, far enough in advance to ensure that they will be able to attend.[48]

G. COST

Early intervention services must be provided at no cost "except where Federal or State law provides for a system of payments by families, including a schedule of sliding fees."[49] Even where a state has adopted a system of payments, families cannot be charged for implementing child find requirements; evaluation and assessment; service coordination; administrative activities related to development, review and evaluation of IFSPs; state administration of the early intervention system; or implementation of Part C procedural safeguards (discussed below), all of which must be at public expense.[50] Further, no child or family may be denied services because of parents' inability to pay an otherwise permissible fee.[51]

Neither the statute nor the regulations explicitly address the use of a family's health insurance to pay for early intervention services. However, the U.S. Department of Education/Office of Special Education Programs has taken the position that the use of private insurance must be voluntary if it would entail any financial cost to the family (e.g., a decrease in available lifetime coverage or other benefit under the policy, an increase in premiums, discontinuation of the policy, or deductibles or other out-of-pocket expenses).[52]

H. PROCEDURAL RIGHTS AND SAFEGUARDS

1. Voluntary Participation

Participation in early intervention services is voluntary; parents have an explicit right under Part C to determine whether they, their infant or toddler, or any other family member will accept or decline any particular service(s) in accordance with state law. Parents are free to decline any service without jeopardizing their or their child's receipt of other Part C services.[53]

2. Prior Notice

Parents must be given written notice a reasonable amount of time before a public agency or service provider proposes or refuses to initiate or change the identification, evaluation, or placement of the child, or the provision of early intervention services to the child or family.[54] The notice must be detailed enough to inform the parents of the action being proposed or refused, the reasons supporting the proposed or refused action, all procedural safeguards, and how to file a complaint.[55] Notice must be written in language understandable to the general public and provided in the parents' native language (unless clearly not feasible).[56] If a parent's native language or other mode of communication is not a written one, the notice must be translated orally or by other means.[57] For parents who are deaf or blind or have no written language, the mode of communication used to provide notice must be that normally used by the parent.[58]

3. Consent

Written parental consent must be obtained before conducting the initial evaluation and assessment of a child, and before beginning early intervention services.[59] In addition, the contents of each IFSP must be fully explained to the parents, and informed written consent obtained before the services in the plan are provided.[60] If the parent does not consent to a particular service, that service may not be provided. The services to which the parent does consent, however, must be provided. A parent may revoke consent at any time.[61]

"Consent" means that the parent has been fully informed of all relevant information in his or her native language or other mode of communication, understands the activity for which consent is sought, agrees in writing and understands that consent is voluntary and revocable at any time.[62] Where consent to release records is sought, the consent must list the records in question and to whom they will be released.[63]

4. Confidentiality and Access to Records

Families have the right to confidentiality of personally identifiable information, including the right of parents to written notice of and consent to the exchange of such information among agencies (consistent with federal and state law).[64] Parents have the right to examine records relating to evaluations and assessments, screening, eligibility determinations, the development and implementation of IFSPs, individual complaints dealing with the child, and any other matter involving records about the child or the family.[65]

5. Dispute Resolution

Administrative complaints: Like Part B of IDEA, Part C provides for two kinds of administrative complaints. First, parents have the right to file a complaint and have an impartial due process hearing on any matter regarding the identification, evaluation, placement or provision of early intervention services to their child, and to have the complaint timely resolved.[66] Parents (or other parties) aggrieved by the outcome may bring a lawsuit in court.[67] Second, the lead agency must operate a complaint management system for accepting, investigating and resolving complaints that a public agency or private service provider is violating any requirement of Part C or the Part C regulations.[68] The Part C regulations set out minimum standards that such complaint systems must meet.[69] Among other things, in resolving a complaint in which a child has been denied appropriate services, the lead agency must (1) ensure that the denial is remediated, including through monetary reimbursement or other corrective action appropriate to the needs of the child and the family, and (2) address future appropriate provision of services for *all* infants and toddlers and their families.[70]

Mediation: Parents who so choose must be allowed to use mediation as provided for parents of older children under Part B (discussed above in Chapter 8).[71] States may use the Part B mediation system for Part C, or establish a separate system meeting regulatory requirements for early intervention matters.[72] As is the case with Part B, mediation must be voluntary on the part of all parties, and may not be used to deny or delay parents' right to a due process hearing, or to deny any other rights afforded under Part C.[73]

Child's status during disputes: During the pendency of any proceeding or action involving a complaint, unless the state agency and the parents otherwise agree, the child has the right to continue to receive the early intervention services currently being provided or, if applying for initial services, the services not in dispute.[74]

6. Surrogate Parents

Part C requires the lead agency to ensure that all infants and toddlers with disabilities have the equivalent of a parent to act on their behalf. If a child's parents or guardian are not known or cannot be located after reasonable efforts, or if a child is a ward of the state, a "surrogate parent" must be appointed to fulfill the role otherwise played by parents under Part C.[75] The surrogate parent cannot be an employee of any state agency, or a person or employee of a person providing early intervention services to the child or any family member; must have no interest that conflicts with the child's interest; and must have the knowledge and skills necessary to ensure that the child will be adequately represented.[76] Once appointed a surrogate parent may — and has a responsibility to — represent the child in all matters related to Part C rights, including (but not limited to) evaluation and assessment, development and implementation of IFSPs, periodic IFSP reviews and annual evaluations, and the ongoing provision of early intervention services.[77]

I. TRANSITION FROM EARLY INTERVENTION SERVICES UNDER PART C TO A FREE APPROPRIATE PUBLIC EDUCATION UNDER PART B

1. Transition Requirements in General

As discussed above, IFSPs must include services to support the child and his or her family in making the transition from early intervention services under Part C to Part B preschool or other appropriate services. IDEA contains several additional provisions aimed at ensuring a smooth transition without any interruption in services; some of the key provisions are discussed below.

Interagency agreements If the state educational agency (which is responsible for administering IDEA part B, including preschool programs) is not the lead agency for early intervention services under Part C, the two agencies must enter into an interagency agreement to ensure coordination on transition matters.[78]

Policies and procedures under Part C States must have in effect policies and procedures to ensure a smooth transition not only to Part B but, for children who will not be eligible for IDEA as three-year-olds, to other appropriate services. These policies and procedures must:

- describe how families will be included in transition plans;

- describe how the lead agency will notify the responsible school system that the child will shortly reach the age of eligibility for preschool services under Part B;

- describe how, in the case of a child who may be eligible for pre-school services, the lead agency will, *with the approval of the family*, convene a conference among the lead agency, the family, and the local school system at least 90 days (and, at the discretion of the parties, up to six months) before the child's third birthday, to discuss any such services that the child may receive;[*]

- describe how, in the case of a child who may *not* be eligible for preschool services, the lead agency will, *with the approval of the family*, make reasonable efforts to convene a conference among the lead agency, the family, and providers of other appropriate services for children who are not eligible for preschool services under part B, to discuss the appropriate services that the child may receive;

- provide for a review of the child's program options for the period from the child's third birthday through the remainder of the school year; and

- provide for the development of a transition plan.[79]

Part B requirements Part B of IDEA provides that, in order to be eligible for funds to assist in providing a free appropriate public education to 3- through 21-year olds under Part B, states must have "in effect policies and procedures to ensure that…[c]hildren participating in early-intervention programs…under part C…who will participate in preschool programs assisted under this part, experience a smooth and effective transition to those preschool programs…."[80] and that "[b]y the third birthday of such a child, an individualized education program or, if consistent with [the pertinent provisions of parts B and C]…an individualized family service plan, has been developed and is being implemented for the child."[81] In

---

[*] Compliance with this requirement should prevent gaps in services because, for example, a school system stops conducting evaluations after a certain date in the school year, or because key personnel are not available during the summer months or other vacation periods.

addition, local school systems must participate in the transition planning conferences convened by the early intervention agency.[82]

Funding flexibility At its discretion, a state may use Part C funds to provide FAPE (in accordance with Part B of IDEA) to children with disabilities from their third birthday to the beginning of the following school year.[83] As the Department of Education has noted, this gives states the flexibility to use early intervention funds to provide FAPE to 3-year olds during the summer.[84] States may also use Part *B* preschool funds to provide FAPE to 2-year olds who will reach age three during the school year.[85]

2. Children who Turn Three During the Summer

The above-discussed statutory requirements evince Congress' intent to create a seamless system of early childhood services and education, with a smooth transition for all three- year olds with disabilities. In contrast, the U.S. Department of Education has taken the position that school systems need not provide Part B preschool services to children who turn three during the summer until the start of the school year, unless the child meets the standards for receiving extended school year services.[86] Consistent with this view, in 1999 the Department issued a regulation stating that when a child will turn three during the summer, it is up to the IEP team to decide when Part B preschool services will begin — leaving children at risk of lengthy gaps in services once their early intervention services end.[87] The Department's view and the regulation, however, are inconsistent with the statute and Congressional intent.

As discussed above, Part B of the statute requires states to ensure "a smooth and effective transition," with an IEP or, where permissible, an IFSP developed by the school system via the IEP process, "being implemented" "by the third birthday."[88] Denial of services from a child's third birthday until school begins effects neither a smooth transition nor implementation of an IEP or permissible IFSP by that birthday.

The legislative history of Part C further demonstrates that the Department's interpretation and regulation are erroneous. Congressional committee reports discussing the 1986 legislation creating what is now Part C, and the 1991 legislation amending it, reveal that a smooth, uninterrupted transition from early intervention to preschool services under Part B was a critical concern of Congress from the start, and remained so.

In first adding early intervention to IDEA in 1986, Congress made a point of explaining that while eligible infants and toddlers with disabilities were those from birth to age two, inclusive, meaning "until they reach their third birthday…this provision shall not be construed to prohibit an agency from continuing to provide services where a child turns three during the summer and services provided by a local educational agency do not commence until September."[89] It went on to point out that "[w]here the local provider of early intervention services and the local educational agency are not the same, it is essential that the agencies coordinate their efforts to transition the child to the special education system operated by the local educational agency."[90]

Congress revisited the early intervention program five years later in the Individuals with Disabilities Education Act Amendments of 1991, making changes that the report of the House of Representatives Committee responsible for the legislation explained were "designed to facilitate the development of a comprehensive 'seamless' system of services for children, aged birth to 5, inclusive, and their families which will ensure…a smooth transition for children moving from early intervention programs…to preschool programs under Part B and…the delivery of appropriate services."[91] In a section entitled "Providing A Comprehensive Delivery System For Children Birth Through Five Years OF Age And Their Families," the committee report went on to note its finding "that it is critical that there will be *no gap in services when a child turns three*, and that the services continue to be appropriate and family focused."[92] It was for this reason, the report explained, that part B of IDEA was being amended to require states to implement policies to ensure a smooth transition from early intervention to preschool programs, including a method of ensuring that an IEP or, when permissible, an IFSP "is being implemented by the child's third birthday."[93] It was at this same time that Congress added to Parts B and C the above-described requirements regarding transition conferences and transition planning, along with the above described provisions allowing funding flexibility — all likewise part of its effort "to facilitate the development of a comprehensive 'seamless' system of services for children, aged birth to 5."[94]

Until successfully challenged, the Department's erroneous interpretation and regulation leave parents and advocates in a difficult position, as many school systems are sure to rely upon them to deny services during the summer months. However, even where school systems do so, in light of the unique developmental needs of such young children, and the short windows of opportunity for effectively addressing certain areas of need, it should be possible in most cases to successfully advocate for services from the date of a child's summertime third birthday as constituting required extended school year services.[95]

NOTES

1. 20 U.S.C. §1433.

2. 20 U.S.C. §1431(a). What is now Part C of IDEA was first added to the statute in 1986, as part H of what was then called the Education of the Handicapped Act (renamed IDEA in 1990). *See* Pub. L. 99-457, 100 Stat. 1145. The IDEA Amendments of 1997 reorganized the statute, including moving the provisions governing early intervention services from Part H to Part C.

3. *See, e.g.,* 20 U.S.C. §1435(d), (e).

4. 20 U.S.C. §§1434, 1435(a)(2).

5. *See, e.g., Marie O. v. Edga*r, 131 F.3d 610 (7th Cir. 1997).

6. 20 U.S.C. §§1435(a), 1437(b)(7); 34 C.F.R. §303.128.

7. *See generally* 20 U.S.C. §1435(a)(10); 34 C.F.R. §§303.500, 303.501, 303.523 - 303.526.

8. *See Inquiry of Gould*, 26 IDELR 24 (OSEP 2/5/97).

9. 20 U.S.C. §1432(5)(A); 34 C.F.R. §303.16(a). In regard to "a diagnosed physical or mental condition that has a high probability of resulting in developmental delay," Note 1 to 34 C.F.R. §300.16 clarifies that this phrase applies to conditions that typically result in developmental delay, citing as examples chromosomal abnormalities; genetic or congenital disorders; severe sensory impairments; inborn errors of metabolism; disorders reflecting disturbance of development of the nervous system; congenital infections; disorders secondary to exposure to toxic substances, including fetal alcohol syndrome; and severe attachment disorders.

10. *See* 20 U.S.C. §1432(3); 34 C.F.R. §303.10.

11. 34 C.F.R. §303.300(a).

12. 20 U.S.C. §§1432(1), (5)(B); 34 C.F.R. §303.16(b).

13. 34 C.F.R. §303.300(c).

14. *See* Note 2 to 34 C.F.R. §303.16.

15. 20 U.S.C. §1431(b)(4). According to the U.S. Department of Education's annual report to Congress on IDEA implementation for the year 2000, only California, Guam, Hawaii, Indiana, Massachusetts, New Hampshire, New Mexico, North Carolina and West Virginia currently include at risk children in their definitions of an eligible infant or toddler with a disability. *See To Assure the Free Appropriate Public Education of All Children with Disabilities: Twenty- second Annual Report to*

Congress on the Implementation of the Individuals with Disabilities Education Act at II-3.

16. *See* 20 U.S.C. §1438(4).

17. 20 U.S.C. §1432(4)(C), (E); 34 C.F.R. §303.12. For definitions of the listed examples, see 34 C.F.R. §§303.12(b), 303.13 and 303.23.

18. 20 U.S.C. §1432(4); 34 C.F.R. §303.12(a).

19. *See generally* 20 U.S.C. §1436(a), (d); 34 C.F.R. §§303.322, 303.344; *Inquiry of Zimenoff*, 2 ECLPR ¶150 (OSEP 1995).

20. 20 U.S.C. §1436(d)(7); 34 C.F.R. §303.23.

21. 20 U.S.C. §§1432(4)(G), 1435(a)(16); 34 C.F.R. §§303.12(b), 303.167.

22. 34 C.F.R. §303.18.

23. 20 U.S.C. §1432(4)(G); 34 C.F.R. §303.12(b).

24. *Inquiry of Woolsey*, 34 IDELR 36 (OSEP 3/21/2000); *Inquiry of Heskett*, 4 ECLPR ¶221 (OSEP 5/26/99).

25. *Inquiry of Heskett, supra.*

26. 20 U.S.C. §1436(d)(5); 34 C.F.R. §303.344(d)(ii); *Inquiry of Woolsey, supra; Inquiry of Zimenoff, supra.*

27. 34 C.F.R. §303.344(d)(ii); *Inquiry of Woolsey, supra; Inquiry of Zimenoff, supra.*

28. *See* 20 U.S.C. §§1435(a)(3), 1436(a)(1).

29. 34 C.F.R. §303.322(b).

30. 34 C.F.R. §303.322(c).

31. 20 U.S.C. §1436(a)(2); 34 C.F.R. §303.322(d)(1).

32. 34 C.F.R. §303.322(d)(2).

33. 34 C.F.R. §303.322(d)(3).

34. 34 C.F.R. §303.323.

35. 34 C.F.R. §303.343(a)(1).

36. 34 C.F.R. §303.342(d)(1).

37. 34 C.F.R. §303.342(d)(2).

38. 20 U.S.C. §1436(d); 34 C.F.R. §§303.344, 303.460(a).

39. 34 C.F.R. §303.321(e).

40. 20 U.S.C. §1436(c); 34 C.F.R. §303.345.

41. 34 C.F.R. §303.345.

42. 20 U.S.C. §1436(b); 34 C.F.R. §303.342(b)(1).

43. 34 C.F.R. §§303.(b)(2), 303.343(b0.

44. 20 U.S.C. §1436(b); 34 C.F.R. §303.342(c).

45. 34 C.F.R. §303.342(c).

46. 34 C.F.R. §303.343(a).

47. 34 C.F.R. §303.342(d)(1).

48. 34 C.F.R. §303.342(d)(2).

49. 20 U.S.C. §1432(4)(B); 34 C.F.R. §303.12(a)(3)(iv).

50. 34 C.F.R. §303.521(b).

51. 34 C.F.R. §303.520(b)(3)(ii).

52. *See Inquiry of Lucas*, 3 ECLPR ¶32 (OSEP 7/22/96); *Inquiry of Thaler*, 2 ECLPR 253 (OSEP 7/12/96). Note that proposed changes to the Part C regulations published in the *Federal Register* on September 5, 2000 and pending as of this writing expressly address the use of public and private insurance and other issues regarding systems of payment and charges to parents. *See* 65 Fed. Reg. 53808 *et seq.* (September 5, 2000).

53. 20 U.S.C. §1439(a)(3); 34 C.F.R. §303.405.

54. 20 U.S.C. §1439(a)(6); 34 C.F.R. §303.403(a).

55. 34 C.F.R. §303.403(b).

56. 34 C.F.R. §303.403(c).

57. *Id.*

58. *Id.*

59. 34 C.F.R. §303.404.

60. 34 C.F.R. §303.432(e).

61. 34 C.F.R. §303.432(e).

62. 34 C.F.R. §303/401(a).

63. *Id.*

64. 20 U.S.C. §1439(a)(2); 34 C.F.R. §303.460.

65. 20 U.S.C. §1439(a)(4); 34 C.F.R. §303.402.

66. *See* 20 U.S.C. §1439(a)(1); 34 C.F.R. §§303.420 - 423.

67. 20 U.S.C. §1439(a)(1); 34 C.F.R. §303.424.

68. *See* 34 C.F.R. §303.510 - 303.512.

69. *Id.*

70. 34 C.F.R. §303.510(b).

71. 20 U.S.C. §1439(a)(8); 34 C.F.R. §303.419.

72. 34 C.F.R. §303.419(a).

73. 34 C.F.R. §303.419(b)(1)(ii).

74. 20 U.S.C. §1439(b); 34 C.F.R. §303.424.

75. 20 U.S.C. §1439(a)(5); 34 C.F.R. §303.406.

76. 20 U.S.C. §1439(a)(5); 34 C.F.R. §303.406(c), (d).

77. 34 C.F.R. §§303.406(e).

78. 34 C.F.R. §303.148(c).

79. 20 U.S.C. §1437(a)(8); 34 C.F.R. §303.148. In a Note to 34 C.F.R. §303.348, the U.S. Department of Education has explained that in developing these policies and procedures, states should consider such matters as the mechanisms to ensure the uninterrupted provision of services to the child; the responsibility for performing evaluations; the development and implementation of an IEP (or IFSP, consistent with the legal requirements regarding IFSPs for 3-5 year olds, discussed in Chapter 6, *infra*); coordination of communication between agencies and the child's family; and the financial responsibilities of all appropriate agencies. *See id.*

80. 20 U.S.C. §1412(a)(9).

81. *Id.*

82. *Id.*

83. 20 U.S.C. §1438(3).

84. *See* OSEP Memorandum 93-14, April 1, 1993, *reprinted in* 1 ECLPR ¶300 (hereinafter "OSEP Memo 93-14").

85. 20 U.S.C. §1419(a)(2).

86. *See, e.g., Inquiry of Anonymous*, 22 IDELR 980 (OSEP 3/24/95); OSEP Memo 93-14, *supra.*

87. *See* 34 C.F.R. §300.121(c)(2).

88. 20 U.S.C. §1412(a)(9).

89. H.R. Rep. No. 860, 99th Cong., 2d Sess. 6 (1986), *reprinted in* 1986 U.S.C.C.A.N. 2401, 2407.

90. *Id.*

91. H.R. Rep. 198, 102d Cong., 1st Sess. 4 (1991), *reprinted in* 1991 U.S.C.C.A.N. 310, 313.

92. *Id.* at 7 (emphasis added).

93. *Id.*

94. *Id.* at 4.

95. In regard to extended school year services, see Chapter 2, *infra*.

Appendix A

Guide To Legal Notations And References Used In This Book

Legal citations (or "cites") such as those found in the endnotes of this book contain the basic information needed to locate court decisions, statutes, regulations, decisions of administrative agencies, journal articles and other documents. These materials can generally be found in law libraries at law schools, state houses, and federal and state courthouses and, increasingly, via the internet. There is a standardized format and set of abbreviations used in citations, depending upon the source of the information.

CITATIONS TO COURT DECISIONS

The bound volumes in which court decisions are published are called "reporters." A typical case citation to a reporter looks like this:

Mavis v. Sobol, 839 F. Supp. 968 (N.D.N.Y. 1994)

In other words, the case in which Mavis sued Sobol was decided by the United States District Court for the Northern District of New York in 1994. The courts opinion can be found in volume 839 of the reporter entitled Federal Supplement, at page 968. Where more than one page number is listed — for example, "839 F. Supp. 968, 974 (N.D.N.Y. 1994)" — the first page number (968) indicates where the opinion begins, while the second page number (974) indicates where the specific point being cited can be found. The citation "839 F. Supp. at 974" refers to a point being made at page 974 of the opinion.

The decisions issued by the various levels or types of courts are each published in a separate series of volumes. The following information explains how to recognize and locate decisions in legal reporters.

U.S. Supreme Court Abbreviations — "U.S." or "S.Ct or "L.Ed."

Decisions of the United States Supreme Court can be found in any one of three published reporters: the United States Reports (U.S.), the Supreme Court Reporter (S.Ct.), or the Lawyers Edition (L.Ed.).

Example: 526 U.S. 66; 119 S. Ct. 992; 143 L. Ed. 2d 154 (1999)

In this citation, 526 is the volume number, U.S. indicates United States Reports, and 66 is the page number. The decision was reached in 1999. Supreme Court citations do not contain a court reference next to the date inside the parentheses. Instead, the court is indicated by the reporter abbreviation (U.S. or S.Ct.) alone.

Federal Court of Appeals Abbreviations — "F.2d" or "F.3d" and "Cir."

Example: 67 F.3d 484 (3rd Cir. 1995)

A decision by a federal court of appeals, in this case the United States Court of Appeals for the Third Circuit, in 1995. This decision can be found in volume 67 of the Federal Reporter, 3rd Series at page 484. "F.2d," instead of "F.3d," would indicate the Federal Reporter, 2nd Series.

The courts of appeals are the second highest level in the federal court system, and generally review the decisions of the federal district courts within a specific geographic region or "circuit." (See "Effect and Weight of Court Decisions," below.) There are eleven numbered circuits, each consisting of several states and/or territories, plus one exclusively for the District of Columbia, the D.C. Circuit.[*]

---

[*] The **First Circuit** covers Massachusetts, Maine, New Hampshire, Rhode Island and Puerto Rico; the **Second Circuit** Connecticut, New York and Vermont; the **Third Circuit** Delaware, New Jersey, Pennsylvania and the Virgin Islands; the **Fourth Circuit** Maryland, North Carolina, South Carolina, Virginia and West Virginia; the **Fifth Circuit** Louisiana, Mississippi and Texas; the **Sixth Circuit** Kentucky, Michigan, Ohio and Tennessee; the **Seventh Circuit** Illinois, Indiana and Wisconsin; the **Eighth Circuit** Arkansas, Iowa, Minnesota, Missouri, Nebraska, North Dakota, and South Dakota; the **Ninth Circuit** Alaska, Arizona, California, Guam, Hawaii, Idaho, Montana, Nevada, Oregon and Washington; the **Tenth Circuit** Colorado, Kansas, New Mexico, Oklahoma, Utah and Wyoming; and the **Eleventh Circuit** Alabama, Florida and Georgia. Prior to October 1, 1981, what is now the Eleventh Circuit was part of the Fifth Circuit. All Fifth Circuit decisions issued before that date are treated as binding precedent in the Eleventh Circuit.

Federal District Court Abbreviations — "F. Supp." or "F. Supp. 2d" and "D."

Example: 753 F. Supp. 922 (M.D. Ala. 1990)

A decision by the federal district court, in this case in the Middle District of Alabama in 1990. The decisions of these courts are reported in the Federal Supplement, in this case at page 922 of volume 753. "F. Supp.2d" would indicate the Federal Supplement, 2nd series.

Each state has at least one federal district court. In states which have only one, it is abbreviated as D., such as D. Mass. In addition to North, South, East, or West, a few states also have a Middle District (M.D. Ala.) or a Central District (C.D. Cal.). The district courts are the lowest, or trial court, level in the federal court system.

State Court Abbreviations

Example: 62 N.J. 473, 303 A.2d 273 (1973)

A state appellate court decision. These decisions can be found in either of two places, the state reporter (here page 473 of volume 62 of the New Jersey Reporter) or the regional reporter which reports the state appellate cases for several states in a region (here the Atlantic Reporter, 2nd Series). Other regions are Pacific (P.), South Western (SW.), North Western (NW), Southern (So.), South Eastern (SE), and North Eastern (NE). Each of these regional reporters also has a second series for more modern cases.

The particular court will be indicated in the parentheses or can be determined by looking at the reporter abbreviation. Where, as in the case above, no court level is indicated, the decision was issued by the States supreme court. Examples of lower state court abbreviations are "Asleep." (Illinois Court of Appeals) and "Pa.Super." (Pennsylvania Superior Court). [In New York State, however, the highest court is actually the Court of Appeals (Ct.App.), while the state Supreme Court (Sup.Ct.) is in fact a lower level court.]

Individuals with Disabilities Education Law Report —"IDELR"

Individuals with Disabilities Education Law Report is a specialized reporter publishing selected decisions in special education cases from both federal and state courts. "IDELR" also publishes selected state due process hearing decisions, decisions of the U.S. Department of

Education/Office of Civil Rights ("OCR) on §504 and ADA matters, and selected letters, policy statements and memoranda of the U.S. Department of Education/Office of Special Education Programs ("OSEP") regarding IDEA requirements. Examples:

> 25 IDELR 227 (6th Cir. 1997) — A 1997 decision by the U.S. Court of Appeals for the Sixth Circuit, beginning on page 227 of volume 25 of the IDELR.

> 21 IDELR 1152 (OSEP 1994) — A 1994 policy letter, memorandum or other document by the U.S. Department of Education/Office of Special Education Programs, beginning on page 1152 of volume 21 of the IDELR.

Education for the Handicapped Law Report — "EHLR"

Prior to April 5, 1991, the Individuals with Disabilities Education Law Report was called Education for the Handicapped Law Report. The "EHLR" reporting format changed a number of times in the years prior to the name change. EHLR materials are cited here in three ways:

> 17 EHLR 267 (M.D. Ala. 1990) — A 1990 decision by the federal district court for the Middle District of Alabama, beginning on page 267 of volume 17 of the EHLR.

> 1986-87EHLR DEC. 558:143 (2nd Cir. 1986) — A 1986 decision of the U.S. Court of Appeals for the Second Circuit, beginning on page 558:143 of the 1986-87 volume of EHLR decisions.

> EHLR 352:185 (OCR 4/18/86) — An April 18, 1986 complaint decision or other document by the U.S. Department of Educations Office of Civil Rights, published at page 352:185 of the EHLR volume containing OCR materials for that year. A citation in this format which refers to "OSEP" rather than "OCR" means a U.S. Department of Education/Office of Special Education Programs letter, policy statement or other document.

Early Childhood Law and Policy Reporter — "ECLPR"

The ECLPR publishes selected judicial decisions, U.S. Department of

Education documents, and state administrative decisions relevant to preschool and early intervention services for children with disabilities. Example:

> 4 ECLPR ¶221 (OSEP 1999) — A 1999 document by the U.S. Department of Education/Office of Special Education Programs, appearing at paragraph 221 of volume 4 of the ECLPR.

CITATIONS TO STATUTES AND REGULATIONS

Federal Statutes — "U.S.C."

Example 20 U.S.C. §1400

A statute is a law passed by Congress or a state legislature. The statute here is Section 1400 of Title 20 of the United States Code. The United States Code is the permanent system for maintaining federal statutes. It can be found in bound volumes in law libraries, and via the internet at <www.access.gpo.gov>.

Federal Regulations — "C.F.R." or "Fed. Reg."

Example: 34 C.F.R. §300.2

Title 34, Section 300.2 of the Code of Federal Regulations, which is the permanent system for maintaining the regulations issued by various federal agencies and departments to implement the statutes passed by Congress. The regulations are legally binding unless and until someone demonstrates to a court that the regulations go beyond what the statute authorizes. The Code of Federal Regulations can be found in bound volumes in law libraries, and via the internet at <www.access.gpo.gov/nara/cfr>.

Example:40 Fed. Reg. 18998 (June 20, 1975)

Page 18998 of volume 40 of the Federal Register. The Federal Register is issued daily and contains regulations when they are proposed, changed or finally adopted (along with other material issued by federal agencies and departments). Those that are finally adopted are later entered in the Code of Federal Regulations as well (see above). The Federal Register can be found at law libraries and public (and other) libraries that are Federal

Depository libraries. For the years 1994 onward, it can also be accessed via the internet at <www.access.gpo.gov>.

EFFECT AND WEIGHT OF COURT DECISIONS

Only the decisions of courts which have jurisdiction in a particular geographical area represent the clear judicial interpretation of the law for that area. Thus, for example, schools in Boston are obligated to follow the law as interpreted by the United States Supreme Court, the United States Court of Appeals for the First Circuit, the United States District Court of the District of Massachusetts, and the relevant Massachusetts state courts. Nevertheless, the decisions of courts in other jurisdictions are relevant in that they will generally be given some weight by courts in your jurisdiction, and they serve as indications of judicial reasoning.

EFFECT AND WEIGHT OF OCR AND OSEP INTERPRETATIONS

OCR's regional offices investigate and issue decisions on §504 complaints. OCR has stated that the decisions of one regional office are binding on other regions. Neither OCR's interpretations of §504 nor OSEP's interpretations of IDEA are binding on courts, although they may be influential.

OTHER NOTATIONS

§	Section
supra	Above
infra	Below
affd	Affirmed. The higher court, cited after the abbreviation, has reviewed and upheld the decision of the lower court, cited before the abbreviation.
affg	Affirming. The first citation is the higher, reviewing court, and the second is to the lower court decision.
rev 'd, rev'g	Reversed, Reversing. On appeal, the higher court has reviewed and reversed the deci-

sion of the lower court.

vacated as moot

The order of the lower court has been lifted because by the time the case was appealed, there was no longer a "live" controversy. This might occur, for instance, when a court refuses to order a school to readmit a suspended student, but the student has graduated before the appeal of the courts decision is heard. An order which has been vacated is no longer legally binding, but the opinion may still be cited as evidence of the courts legal reasoning.

vacated on other grounds,

reversed on other grounds

The lower court's order is no longer legally binding, but the decision on appeal does not affect the legal reasoning in the portion of the decision which has been cited.

cert. denied

The Supreme Court "denied certiorari" — i.e., it has declined to review the case, and it is expressing no opinion concerning the lower court decision, which remains standing.

Cf

The case supports a statement, opinion, or conclusion of law different from that in the text but sufficiently analogous to lend some support to the statement in the text.

But see

The case strongly suggests a contrary proposition from the preceding statement in the text.

But cf

The case supports a proposition which, while not directly contradictory to the preceding statement in the text, is sufficiently analogous to suggest a contrary conclusion.

APPENDIX B

TABLE OF CASES

JUDICIAL DECISIONS

A.P. v. McGrew, 28 IDELR 19 (N.D. Ill. 1998)

A.W. v. Northwest R-1 School. Dist., 813 F.2d 158 (8th Cir.), *cert. denied,* 484 U.S. 847, 108 S.Ct. 144 (1987)

Adler v. New York Department of Education, 760 F.2d 454 (2nd Cir. 1985)

Alamo Heights Independent School District v. State Board of Education, 790 F.2d 1153 (5th Cir. 1986)

Alexander v. Choate, 469 U.S. 287, 105 S. Ct. 712 (1985)

Alexopulos v. Riles, 784 F.2d 1408 (9th Cir. 1986)

Alexopulos v. San Francisco Unified School District, 817 F.2d 551 (9th Cir. 1987)

Amann v. Town of Stow, 991 F.2d 929 (1st Cir. 1993)

Anderson v. District of Columbia, 877 F.2d 1018 (D.C. Cir. 1989)

Andrews v. Consolidated Rail Corporation, 831 F.2d 678 (7th Cir. 1987)

Asbury v. Missouri Dept. of Elementary and Secondary Education, 29 IDELR 877 (E.D. Mo. 1999)

Babb v. Knox County School System, 965 F.2d 104 (6th Cir. 1992), *cert. denied,* 506 U.S. 941, 113 S.Ct. 380

Barlow-Gresham Union High School District No.2 v. Mitchell, 940 F.2d 1280 (9th Cir. 1991)

Barnett v. Fairfax Co. Schl. Bd., 927 F.2d 146 (4th Cir.), *cert. denied,* 502 U.S. 859, 112 S.Ct. 175 (1991)

Barwacz v. Michigan Department of Education, 674 F. Supp. 1296 (W.D. Mich. 1987)

Battle v. Commonwealth of Pennsylvania, 629 F.2d 269 (3rd Cir. 1980), *cert. denied,* 452 U.S. 968, 101 S.Ct. 3123 (1981)

Blazejewski v. Board of Education of Allegany Central School District, 560 F. Supp. 701 (W.D.N.Y. 1983)

Bd. of Ed. of Co. of Cabell v. Dienelt, 1986-87 EHLR DEC. 558:305 (S.D. W.Va. 1987), *aff'd. per curiam,* 843 F.2d 813 (4th Cir. 1988)

Corey H. v. Bd. of Ed. of the City of Chicago, 995 F. Supp. 900 (N.D. Ill. 1998)

Co. of San Diego v. California Special Education Hearing Office, 93 F.3d 1458 (9th Cir. 1996)

Cronin v. Board of East Ramapo Central Sch. Dist. 689 F. Supp. 197 (S.D.N.Y. 1988)

Crump v. Gilmer Independent Sch. Dist., 797 F. Supp. 552 (E.D. Texas 1992)

Daniel R.R. v. State Bd. of Ed., 874 F.2d 1036 (5th Cir. 1989)

Daniel S. v. Scranton Sch. Dist., 230 F.3d 90 (3rd Cir. 2000)

David D. v. Dartmouth Sch. Committee, 775 F.2d 411 (1st Cir. 1985), *cert. denied*, 475 U.S. 1140, 106 S.Ct. 1790 (1986).

Davis v. District of Columbia Board of Education, 530 F. Supp. 1209 (D.D.C. 1982)

Debra P. v. Turlington, 644 F.2d 397 (5th Cir. 1981)

Dept. of Ed. of Hawaii v. Mr. and Mrs. S., 632 F. Supp. 1268 (D. Hawaii 1986)

Doe v. District of Columbia, 796 F. Supp. 559 (D.D.C. 1992)

Doe v. New York University, 666 F.2d 761 (2nd Cir. 1981)

Doe v. Smith, 16 EHLR 65 (M.D. Tenn. 1988)

Doe v. Smith, 879 F.2d 1340 (6th Cir. 1989), *cert. denied*, 493 U.S. 1025, 110 S. Ct. 730 (1990)

Doe v. Southeastern University, 732 F. Supp 7 (D. D.C. 1990)

Duane M. v. Orleans Parish Sch. Bd., 861 F.2d 115 (5th Cir. 1988)

E.H. v. Tirozzi, 735 F. Supp. 53 (D. Conn. 1990)

Eggers v. Bullitt Co. Sch. Dist., 854 F.2d 892 (6th Cir. 1988)

Emma C. v. Eastin, 985 F. Supp. 940 (N.D. Cal. 1997)

Flint Bd. of Ed. v. Williams, 276 N.W.2d 499 (Mich. App. 1979)

Florence Co. Sch. Dist. No. 4 v. Carter, 510 U.S. 7, 114 S.Ct. 361 (1993).

Flour Bluff Independent School District v. Katherine M., 91 F.3d 689 (5th Cir. 1996)

Franklin v. Gwinnett, 503 U.S. 60, 112 S.Ct. 1028 (1992)

Frederick L. v. Thomas, 408 F. Supp. 832 (E.D. Penn. 1976)

G.I. Forum v. Texas Education Agency, 87 F. Supp.2d 267 (W.D. Tex. 2000)

Garland Independent Sch. Dist. v. Wilks, 657 F. Supp. 1163 (N.D. Tex. 1987)

Geis v. Bd. of Ed. of Persippany-Troy Hills, 774 F.2d 575 (3rd Cir. 1985)

Goss v. Lopez, 419 U.S. 565, 95 S.Ct. 729 (1975)

Mitten v. Muscogee Co. Sch. Dist., 877 F.2d 932 (11th Cir. 1989), *cert. denied*, 493 U.S. 1072, 110 S. Ct. 1117 (1990)

Mohawk Trail Regional Sch. Dist. v. Shaun D., 35 F. Supp. 2d 34 (D. Mass. 1999)

Monticello Sch. Dist. No. 25 v. George L., 102 F.3d 895 (7th Cir. 1996)

Moore v. D.C. Bd. of Ed., 907 F.2d 165 (D.C. Cir.), *vacating* 886 F.2d 335, *cert. denied*, 498 U.S. 998, 111 S. Ct. 556 (1990)

Morgan v. Chris L., 927 F. Supp. 267 (E.D. Tenn. 1994), *aff'd without published opinion*, 106 F.3d 401 (6th Cir.), *cert. denied*, 520 U.S. 1271, 117 S.Ct. 2448 (1997)

Morgan v. Chris L., 25 IDELR 227 (6th Cir.), *cert. denied*, 520 U.S. 1271, 117 S.Ct. 2448 (1997)

Mullen v. District of Columbia, 16 EHLR 792 (D.D.C. 1990)

Murphy v. Arlington Central Sch. Dist., 86 F. Supp. 2d 354 (S.D.N.Y. 2000)

Murphy v. Timberlane Regional Sch. Dist., 22 F.3d 1186 (1st Cir. 1994)

Murray v. Montrose Co. Sch. Dist., 51 F.3d 921 (10th Cir.), *cert. denied*, 516 U.S. 909, 116 S. Ct. 278 (1995)

New Mexico Association for Retarded Citizens v. State of New Mexico, 678 F.2d 847 (10th Cir. 1982)

Newsome v. Batavia Local Sch. Dist., 842 F.2d 920 (6th Cir. 1988)

North v. District of Columbia Bd. of Ed., 471 F. Supp. 136 (D.D.C. 1979)

Oberti v. Bd. of Ed. of Borough of Clementon Sch. Dist., 995 F.2d 1204 (3rd Cir. 1993)

Ojai Unified School District v. Jackson, 4 F.3d 1467 (9th Cir. 1993)

Padilla v. Sch. Dist. No. 1, 35 F. Supp.2d 1260 (D. Colo. 1999), *rev'd. in part*, 233 F.3d 1268 (10th Cir. 2000)

Pasatiempo v. Aizawa, 103 F.3d 796 (9th Cir. 1996)

Pennsylvania Association for Retarded Citizens v. Pennsylvania, 334 F. Supp. 279 (1972)

Perez v. Philadelphia Housing Authority, 677 F. Supp. 357 (E.D. Penn. 1987), *aff'd.*, 841 F.2d 1120 (3rd Cir. 1988)

Pihl v. Massachusetts Dept. of Ed., 9 F.3d 184 (1st Cir. 1993)

Pink v. Mt. Diablo Unified Sch. Dist., 738 F. Supp. 345 (N.D. Cal. 1990)

Plyler v. Doe, 457 U.S. 202, 102 S.Ct. 2382 (1982)

Polk v. Susquehanna Intermediate Unit 16, 853 F.2d 171 (3rd Cir.), *cert. denied*, 488 U.S. 1030, 109 S.Ct. 838 (1988)

Rapid City Sch. Dist. 51-4 v. Vahle, 733 F. Supp. 1364 (D.S.D. 1990), *aff'd.* 922 F.2d 476 (8th Cir. 1990).

Reusch v. Fountain, 872 F. Supp. 1421 (D. Md. 1994)

U.S. DEPARTMENT OF EDUCATION/OFFICE FOR CIVIL RIGHTS COMPLAINT DECISIONS AND COMPLIANCE REVIEWS

Akron (OH) City School District, 19 IDELR 542 (OCR 11/18/92)

Anderson CO. (TN) School District, 16 IDELR 760 (2/26/90)

Auburn (AL) City School District, EHLR 353:374 (OCR 8/7/89)

Augusta County (VA) School Division, EHLR 352:233 (OCR 8/21/86)

Bethpage (NY) Union Free School District, EHLR 353:147 (OCR 1988)

Boston (MA) Renaissance Charter School, 26 IDELR 889 (OCR 9/5/97)

Bristol-Plymouth Regional Vocational-Technical School District, EHLR 353:241 (OCR 6/27/89)

Burlington (MA) Public Schools, 29 IDELR 848 (OCR 7/8/97)

Calcasieu Parish Public School System, 20 IDELR 762 (8/3/93)

Carbon-Lehigh (PA) Intermediate School District #21, EHLR 352:108 (OCR 9/20/85)

Chatham Co. (GA) School District, 26 IDELR 29 (OCR 11/6/96)

Chicago (IL) Board of Education, EHLR 257:453 (OCR 3/11/83)

Chicago (IL) Board of Education, EHLR 257:568 (OCR 7/9/84)

Clark County (NV) School District, EHLR 257:245 (OCR 1/16/81)

Clermont (OH) Northeastern Schools, EHLR 257:577 (OCR 7/23/84)

Community Unit School District #300 (IL), EHLR 353:296 (OCR 1989)

Compliance Review of Riverview (WA) School District, EHLR 311:103 (OCR 6/30/87)

Dade County (FL) School District, 20 IDELR 267 (OCR 5/11/93)

Duchesne County (UT) School District, 17 EHLR 240 (OCR 9/13/90)

East Baton Rouge (LA) Parish School System, EHLR 353:252 (OCR 6/14/89)

Fayette County (KY) School District, EHLR 353:279 (OCR 3/1/89)

Frederick County (MD) School District, EHLR 352:407 (OCR 3/25/87)

Fremont (CO) School District RE-3, EHLR 257:273 (OCR 10/27/80)

Garaway (OH) Local School District, 17 EHLR 237 (OCR 9/13/90)

Georgia Department of Education, EHLR 352:05 (OCR 5/20/85).

Harrison County (WV) School District, EHLR 353:120 (OCR 6/29/88)

Hawaii State Department of Education, 17 EHLR 360 (OCR 10/11/90)

Illinois State Bd. of Ed., 20 IDELR 687 (OCR 12/3/93).

Inquiry of Rhys, EHLR 305:26 (OCR 4/14/85)

Jefferson County (KY) School District, EHLR 353:176 (OCR 9/19/88)

Kanawha County (WV) School District, EHLR 257:439 (OCR 9/28/83)

Lumberton (MS) Public School District, 18 IDELR 33 (OCR 6/24/91)

Mt. Gilead (OH) Exempted Village School District, 20 IDELR 765 (OCR 8/13/93)

Mineral County (NV) School District, 16 EHLR 668 (OCR 3/16/90)

Mobile County (AL) School District, 19 IDELR 519 (OCR 11/6/92)

Modoc County (CA) Office of Education, 24 IDELR 580 (OCR 1/28/96)

Muscogee (GA) County School District, EHLR 257:540 (OCR 6/30/84)

Napa Valley (CA) Unified Sch. Dist., 27 IDELR 505 (OCR 6/5/97)

Nash County (NC) School District, EHLR 352:37 (8/12/85)

Nashville-Davidson County (TN) Schools, 16 EHLR 379 (OCR 12/21/89)

New Carlisle-Bethel Local School District, EHLR 257:477 (OCR 1/30/84)

Niagra Falls City (NY) School District, EHLR 352:472 (OCR 2/6/87)

Northwest Jefferson County (MO) R-I School District, EHLR 257:354 (OCR 3/31/82)

Oakland (CA) Unified School District, 20 IDELR 1338 (OCR 11/3/93)

Ogden (UT) City School District, 21 IDELR 387 (OCR 3/23/94)

Orange County (FL) School District, 28 IDELR 492 (OCR 11/18/97)

Pocantico Hills (NY) Central School District, 20 IDELR 265 (OCR 5/3/93)

Prescott (AZ) Unified School District No. 1, EHLR 352:540 (OCR 5/22/87)

Prince George's County (MD) Public Schools, 17 EHLR 875 (OCR 3/22/91)

Pueblo (CO) School Dist. No. 60, 20 IDELR 1066 (OCR 9/1/93)

Roane Co. (TN) School District, 27 IDELR 853 (OCR 8/8/97)

San Juan (CA) Unified School District, 20 IDELR 549 (OCR 7/6/93)

San Luis Valley (CO) Board of Cooperative Services, 21 IDELR 304 (OCR 3/4/94)

School Administrative Unit 19 (NH), 16 EHLR 86 (OCR 1/4/89)

School Administrative Unit #38 (NH), 19 IDELR 186 (OCR 7/23/92)

School District #220 (IL), EHLR 257:200 (OCR 2/12/81)

South Carolina Department of Education, EHLR 352:475 (OCR 6/23/87).

South Central (IN) Area Special Education Cooperative, 17 EHLR 248 (OCR 9/25/90)

Sumter County (SC) School District #17, 17 EHLR 193 (OCR 9/28/90)

Templeton (CA) Unified School District, 17 EHLR 859 (OCR 3/19/91)

Tift Co. (GA) School District, 31 IDELR 59 (OCR 1998)

Tippecanoe (IN) School Corporation, EHLR 353:217 (OCR 6/14/88)

Trans Allied-Medical Services, Inc., 16 EHLR 963(OCR 5/30/90)

Tucson (AZ) Unified School District No. 1, EHLR 352:47 (OCR 2/16/84)

William S. Hart (CA) Union School District, 26 IDELR 181 (OCR 12/13/96)

York (SC) School District, 17 EHLR 475 (OCR 11/13/90)

U.S. DEPARTMENT OF EDUCATION/OFFICE OF SPECIAL EDUCATION POLICY LETTERS

Inquiry of Anonymous, 20 IDELR 1219 (OSEP 12/13/93)

I*nquiry of Anonymous*, 22 IDELR 637 (OSEP 2/2/95)

Inquiry of Anonymous, 22 IDELR 980 (OSEP 3/24/95)

Inquiry of Armstrong, 28 IDELR 303 (OSEP 6/11/97)

Imquiry of Breecher, 18 IDELR 261 (OSEP 6/29/91)

Inquiry of Fields, EHLR 211:437 (OSEP 2/26/87)

Inquiry of Fisher, 23 IDELR 565 (OSEP 12/4/95)

Inquiry of Goodman, 16 EHLR 1317 (OSEP 8/10/90)

Inquiry of Gould , 26 IDELR 24 (OSEP 2/5/97)

Inquiry of Hellmuth, 16 EHLR 503 (OSEP 1/30/90)

Inquiry of Heskett, 4 ECLPR 221 (OSEP 5/26/99)

Inquiry of Imber, 19 IDELR 352 (OSEP 8/18/92).

Inquiry of Kohn, 17 EHLR 522 (OSEP 2/13/91).

Inquiry of Latshaw, EHLR 213:124 (OSEP 3/1/88)

Inquiry of Lucas, 3 ECLPR 32 (OSEP 7/22/96)

Inquiry of Rainforth, 17 EHLR 222 (OSEP 10/24/90)

Inquiry of Rambo, 16 EHLR 1078 (OSEP 6/22/90)

Inquiry of Richards, 17 EHLR 288 (OSEP 1991)

Inquiry of Scovill, EHLR 211:14 (3/3/78)

Inquiry of Siegel, 16 EHLR 797 (OSEP 4/22/90)

Inquiry of Thaler, 2 ECLPR 253 (OSEP 7/12/96)

Inquiry of Thorne, 16 EHLR 606 (OSEP 2/15/90)

Inquiry of Van Buiten, EHLR 211:429 (OSEP 6/17/87)

Inquiry of Wilson, 16 EHLR 83 (OSEP 10/17/90)

Inquiry of Woolsey, 34 IDELR 36 (OSEP 3/21/2000)

Inquiry of Zimenoff, 2 ECLPR 150 (OSEP 6/6/95)

U.S. DEPARTMENT OF EDUCATION/FAMILY POLICY COMPLIANCE OFFICE POLICY LETTERS

Inquiry of Wisconsin Department of Public Instruction, 28 IDELR 497 (FPCO 1997)

INDEX

A

Adoptive parents 101

Age of majority 76, 102-103, 108

Assistive technology 20, 21-23, 27, 75

Attorney fees 106, 121-122

B

Base schools 29-30

Behavioral needs
and FAPE 47-51
behavioral intervention plan 138
functional behavior assessment 138, 144
positive supports and interventions 49, 74, 144, 146
relevance to LRE 28-29, 49-50

Board of Education of the Hendrick Hudson Central School District v. Rowley, *Rowley* 15, 147

Braille 74

Brookhart v. Illinois State Board of Education 96

Burlington See *School Committee of Town of Burlington v. Department of Education*

C

Carl D. Perkins Vocational and Technical Education Act 9-10, 84

Carter See *Florence County School District No. 4 v. Carter*

Cedar Rapids Community School District v. Garret F., *Garret F.* 21

Child find 54-55, 149, 162, 169

Chris L. See *Morgan v. Chris L.*

Civil actions 115-116, 148, 171
additional evidence 117
exhaustion of administrative remedies 116-117
statute of limitations 116

Communication needs 63, 74

Comparable benefits and services 17-18, 89, 91, 94-95

Compensatory education 109, 118, 120-121

Complaints 108
for due process hearing 67, 82, 111, 112, 137
regarding early intervention services 171
to Office for Civil Rights 110
to state educational agency 82-83, 109-110, 116

Confidentiality *See* Family Educational Rights and Privacy Act, Early intervention services

Consent 77, 106-107
for early intervention services 170, 177
for evaluations and reevaluations 56-57, 106-107
for release of records 152-153, 168
for use of insurance 24-25, 169

D

Damages 118, 121

Debra P. v. Turlington 96

Developmental delay 2, 162, 163

Discipline *See also* Behavioral needs 44, 134-153
alcohol and 142, 147

ABOUT THE AUTHOR

Eileen L. Ordover is a Senior Attorney at the Center for Law and Education, where she has represented the rights of children and youth with disabilities in the courts and before state and federal legislative and administrative bodies since 1990. She has participated in major litigation, assisted in drafting critical legislation and regulations, provided technical assistance and training to attorneys, parents and other advocates, and advised attorneys nationwide on education issues affecting students with disabilities.

Her work over the years has included preparing, with her colleague Kathleen B. Boundy, the student's brief to the U.S. Supreme Court in *Florence Co. School District No. 4 v. Carter*, co-authoring a legal background paper on standards-based education reform and students with disabilities for the National Academy of Sciences in connection with its 1997 book, *Educating One and All*, representing *amici curiae* supporting the student and preparing their brief to the U.S. Court of Appeals for the Sixth Circuit in *Morgan v. Chris L.*, and authoring or co-authoring publications on a range of legal topics of interest to students with disabilities and their advocates, including discipline, rights to participate in high quality vocational education and school-to-work systems, inclusion rights of children whose behavior challenges schools, and the education rights of court-involved youth.